GROWING INTO GOD

PATRISTIC THEOLOGY

SERIES EDITORS

John C. Cavadini
University of Notre Dame

Thomas Clemmons
The Catholic University of America

EDITORIAL BOARD

Paul M. Blowers
Milligan University

Ellen Scully
Seton Hall University

Brian Dunkle, SJ
Boston College

J. Warren Smith
Duke University

Andrew Hofer, OP
Dominican House of Studies

Susan Wessel
The Catholic University of America

Joseph T. Lienhard, SJ
Fordham University

Jeffrey Wickes
University of Notre Dame

Growing into God

The Fathers of the Church on Christian Maturity

John Gavin, SJ

Foreword by Angela Franks

THE CATHOLIC UNIVERSITY OF AMERICA PRESS
WASHINGTON, D.C.

Copyright © 2025
The Catholic University of America Press

All rights reserved

Cataloging-in-Publication Data is available from the Library of Congress

ISBN (paper): 978-0-8132-3954-5
ISBN (ebook): 978-0-8132-3955-2

Interior design by Burt&Burt
The text is set in Minion Pro and Adriane Text.

*To all past and present members
of the Society of Saints Peter and Paul
and to the Sisters of Life—
in thanksgiving
for their mature Christian witness
and friendship in the Lord.*

CONTENTS

List of Tables // viii
Foreword // ix
Acknowledgments // xi
Abbreviations // xiii
Introduction // 1

Part 1: The Pillars of Maturation

1. Form and Finality // 9
2. Virtue and Character // 23
3. Vocation and Commitment // 37
4. Satan's Tantrum // 55

Part 2: The Means of Maturation

5. Maturation and the Scriptures // 71
6. Maturation and the Mysteries // 85
7. Maturation and Asceticism // 101

Part 3: Expressions of Maturity

8. Witness // 117
9. Teacher // 131
10. Servant // 147
11. Fool // 159

Conclusion // 169
Appendix // 175
Bibliography // 181
General Index // 199
Scripture Index // 205

LIST OF TABLES

Table 2.1: Appendix to chapter 2 // 34

Table 4.1: Day, evening, and morning knowledge // 59

Table 5.1: Maturation in salvation history // 80

Table 5.2: From infancy to rest // 83

FOREWORD
by Angela Franks

Steeped as we are in a culture that prizes flexibility more than almost anything else, we are confronted with a dilemma. Having as many options as possible is not yet a strategy for life, much less a guide to decision-making. It is, in fact, the exact opposite, for every decision reduces one's options, for better or for worse. The command to maximize options is actually a demand to choose nothing, ever. But that is no rule at all, simply the lack of one.

To make any decision, much less a good one, the decision-maker needs to know what good should guide her decisions. She needs to know, in other words, where she is going. She also needs to know where she is now—who and what she is. Only then can she move toward the good she desires.

These basic operating instructions are missing for most people, and Fr. John Gavin, SJ, has written a lucid and insightful book to reintroduce necessary principles for human maturity. Such principles are not only about human flourishing; they are also about the greatest good that human persons can desire, namely, the triune God revealed in Christ. We are made for a life of virtue, as the pagan ancients saw as well, but in participation with our divine origin and end, the Alpha and Omega that is God himself. The Church Fathers whom he exegetes had a profound understanding of this supreme good, as well as the ways to proceed toward it.

One of them, St. Irenaeus, writes, "God, therefore, is one and the same, who rolls up the heaven as a book, and renews the face of the earth; who made the things of time for man, so that coming to maturity in them, he may produce the fruit of immortality; and who, through His kindness, also bestows [upon him] eternal things, that in the ages to come 'He may show the exceeding riches of His grace' (Eph 2:7)."[1] Here we see the distinctiveness of the Christian path to maturity. It is a path that was laid out by God the Creator, and it can only be followed by the strength and grace provided by God the redeemer. It is a path from the Trinity and back to it.

---

1 Irenaeus, *Against the Heresies* IV, 5, 1 (SC 100.1, 424, lines 1-5; ANF 1, 466).

Indeed, it is nothing less than the way that the incarnate divine Son himself walked for us—the way he walked as well as the Way that he himself is. The path itself is the triune God, the deification gradually wrought by the Holy Spirit of the Father and the Son. But rather than promoting a quietism, this knowledge must stir up a desire to respond to this grace, through the reception of the sacraments, the moral life, and the ascesis of prayer, fasting, and almsgiving.

In an age of self-help books, Fr. Gavin has written a God-help book, and this is exactly what we need. Worn out by endless self-construction, we seek rest in a secure identity. We each ask, "Who am I? What was I made for?"

The riches of Christian wisdom remind us what we have forgotten today: such self-knowledge cannot be created but only received. "Oh Lord, combing his long white hair, saying my name / How could he know when I did not even know my name?"[2] The Fathers trace out how to gain maturity we need to grow into our God-given name.

---

2 Nick Cave and the Bad Seeds, "Long Dark Night," from *Wild God*.

ACKNOWLEDGMENTS

I began this book during the long summer of 2020, when the forced isolation at least allowed for reading and reflection, and I continued to work on it as the world gradually unmasked itself and returned to community living. During these years I was especially grateful to those who read early drafts of this work and provided me with invaluable feedback: Patrick Gavin, Nina-Sophie Heereman, Paul McNellis, SJ, Henry Shea, SJ, and Fr. Andrew Summerson. These exceptional scholars and teachers saved me from many embarrassments and shared their important insights. Needless to say, I accept responsibility for any remaining errors and inadequacies.

Several chapters are based on papers that I gave for Ave Maria University (2021), the Academy of Catholic Theology (2021), and the Fellowship of Catholic Scholars (2020 and 2021). The responses I received from participants helped me to clarify many ideas presented in this volume.

I must express my gratitude to members of the College of the Holy Cross community who contributed in many ways to this book. In 2023, I had the pleasure of directing Liam Murphy in a Weiss Summer Research in the Humanities project on Christian confessors, and our conversations helped my own thinking on the power of witness. During the 2023–24 academic year, I collaborated with Professor Lee Oser and Professor M. Estella Cibreiro-Couce in directing Anna Moran's remarkable Fenwick Scholar Project, "From Witty Fools to Foolish Wits: Folly in Shakespeare and Cervantes." Our conversations, along with Anna's enlightening research and writing, gave me a greater sense of the fool's authority in a mad world. The librarians at the College, with their usual speed and good cheer, provided me with access to books and articles even during the restrictions of the pandemic. And my department chair, Caroline Johnson Hodge, helped me to remain focused and (moderately) sane amid many challenges and disruptions.

This is my second book with the Catholic University of America Press, and I remain indebted to the CUAP team's guidance and support. I would like to thank the anonymous reviewers for their corrections, helpful suggestions, and encouragement. And I am truly grateful to John Martino for accepting this project and shepherding it across the finish line, and to Gabriel Bartlett for his attentive copyediting.

Finally, I express my gratitude for the support of my Jesuit community. I thank especially my superior, Andrew Garavel, SJ, for his leadership, and William Reiser, SJ, for his suggestions and encouragement. Our community may have changed location, but our spiritual brotherhood remains a constant.

A.M.D.G.

ABBREVIATIONS

ACW	Ancient Christian Writers
ANF	Ante-Nicene Fathers
CCSG	Corpus Christianorum Series Graeca
CCSL	Corpus Christianorum Series Latina
CSEL	Corpus Scriptorum Ecclesiasticorum Latinorum
FC	Fathers of the Church: A New Translation
GNO	Gregorii Nysseni Opera
LCL	Loeb Classical Library
NPNF	Nicene and Post Nicene Fathers
PG	Patrologia Graeca
PL	Patrologia Latina
PPS	Popular Patristics Series
PTS	Patristische Texte und Studien
SC	Sources Chrétiennes
WSA	Works of Saint Augustine. A Translation for the 21st Century

A note on Scripture quotations: All Scripture quotations come from the Revised Standard Version (*Revised Standard Version Bible, Catholic Edition*, 1966), unless otherwise noted.

GROWING INTO GOD

INTRODUCTION

The Christian who is prayerfully united with the ever present, ever guiding, ever commanding Holy Spirit of Jesus and is able to understand that he must give up all that he has planned himself —for the sake of God's plan—is a mature Christian.

Hans Urs von Balthasar[1]

The Church and the world must confront a crisis of immaturity. We see the signs everywhere. Politicians engage in childish histrionics and avoid their true responsibility toward the common good. Church leaders often refuse to teach truths and instead pander to popular culture. Adolescents lack genuine role models and fill the gap by imitating the antics of superficial celebrities. Many now renounce marriage and family; priesthood and religious life fade evermore from the ecclesial landscape. One may reasonably ask: where have all the adults gone?

The reasons for the crisis are many, including the corruption wrought by social media and the corporate exploitation of "youth culture."[2] Yet, the primary explanation lies with the rejection of God and, in turn, human nature—that is, the very idea that certain norms define what we are as a species. Once our age turned from God and replaced nature with self-definition, maturity ceased to exist, since maturity requires an end or form to

---

1 Hans Urs von Balthasar, *Who is a Christian?*, trans. John Cumming (New York: Newman Press, 1968), 86.

2 Many cultural commentators in recent decades have noted this maturity crisis. See, for instance, Robert Bly, *Iron John: A Book about Men* (Boston: Da Capo Press, 2015); Gary Cross, *Men to Boys. The Making of Modern Immaturity* (New York: Columbia University Press, 2008); Jordan Peterson, *12 Rules for Life. An Antidote to Chaos* (New York: Penguin, 2019); Andreas Georg Scherer et al., "New Challenges to the Enlightenment: How Twenty-First Century Sociotechnological Systems Facilitate Organized Immaturity and How to Counteract It," *Business Ethics Quarterly* 33, no. 3 (July 2023): 409–39. Peterson calls for a responsible, productive, and mature life: "To stand up straight with your shoulders back is to accept the terrible responsibility of life, with eyes wide open. It means deciding to voluntarily transform the chaos of potential into the realities of habitable order. It means adopting the burden of self-conscious vulnerability, and accepting the end of the unconscious paradise of childhood, where finitude and mortality are only dimly comprehended" (Peterson, *12 Rules,* 27).

give it shape. As many believe that neither moral nor physical norms govern what we are, there is no longer anything for us to grow into. As Walker Percy noted almost fifty years ago, "You live in a deranged age—more deranged than usual, because despite great scientific and technological advances, man has not the faintest idea of who he is or what he is doing."[3]

Science has not saved us from this predicament. While stage theories of psychic and moral development from such thinkers as Erik Erikson, Jean Piaget, and others provide frameworks for understanding human cognitive development, they do not answer essential questions about what it is to be human. Furthermore, humans do indeed progress and regress in their abilities to cope in relationships with the world and other persons, but the obstacles and frustrations with such an enterprise can often lead to despair. Do only the elites have the hope of finding fulfillment? Can only the gifted become adults? What about those who struggle with trauma or mental illness? Is the endless recourse to drugs and therapy the only solution?

PERFECTION OR MATURITY?

Traditionally, spiritual authors have preferred the word "perfection" to designate Christian fulfillment, the joy in God that all human beings long for. The term finds its origin in Jesus's own words: "You, therefore, must be perfect [*teleios*] as your heavenly Father is perfect" (Matt 5:48). The Jesuit scholar of Christian spirituality Joseph de Guibert describes this Christian perfection as follows: "They [humans] are perfect when they have everything required for their nature and the fullness thereof, when they have everything that is fitting for them in the state in which the Creator places them, and when they so attain the end set out for them that there can be no more progress possible for them in attaining this end. Therefore, in the supernatural order man will enjoy this absolute perfection after the resurrection of the body, when he possesses the intuitive vision of God in Heaven."[4] De Guibert goes on to note that, in one sense, a man in the state of grace has, in his supernaturally elevated nature, come to perfection; yet, in an absolute sense, no man has true perfection while living in the world, since perfection belongs to the

---

3 Walker Percy, *Lost in the Cosmos. The Last Self-Help Book* (New York: Farrar, Straus & Giroux, 1983), 76.

4 Joseph de Guibert, SJ, *The Theology of the Spiritual Life*, trans. William Young (New York: Sheed and Ward, 1953), 41.

resurrected state. Thus, one can, like Saint Catherine of Siena or Saint Francis of Assisi, acquire a form of perfection in the world, while not yet reaching this end in its absolute sense.[5]

In this short volume, however, I propose to substitute the term "maturation" for "perfection," a move that finds support in the Scriptures.[6] The Scriptures can at times present contrasting images of maturation. On the one hand, Jesus holds up the child as the model for a humble, trusting relationship with God: "Truly, I say to you unless you turn and become like children [*ta paidia*], you will never enter the kingdom of heaven. Whoever humbles himself like this child [*paidion*], he is the greatest in the kingdom of heaven" (Matt 18:2–3). He celebrates the receptivity of the childlike toward the Gospel message: "I thank you, Father, Lord of Heaven and earth, that you have hidden these things from the wise and understanding and revealed them to infants [*nēpiois*]; yes, Father, for such was your gracious will" (Luke 10:21). An adult must therefore become childlike before God the Father, *receiving* the gift of fulfillment and becoming transformed by it.

On the other hand, Saint Paul tells Christians to grow from spiritual infancy to adulthood in the Church: "When I was a child, I spoke like a child [*nēpios*],[7] I thought like a child, I reasoned like a child; when I became a man, I gave up childish ways" (1 Cor 13:11). As spiritual infants, Paul notes, we remain subject to the whims of the world, but in Christ we acquire a new status: "I mean that the heir, as long as he is a child [*nēpios*], is no better than a slave, though he is the owner of all the estate; but he is under guardians and trustees until the date set by the father. So with us; when we were children [*nēpioi*], we were slaves to the elemental spirits of the universe. But when the time had fully come, God sent forth his son, born of woman, born under the law, to redeem those who were under the law, so that we might receive adoption as sons" (Gal 4:1–5). As the baptized, Christians of all ages and times receive a new trajectory for their maturation that includes the proper use of their freedom and responsibility: they grow to become full sharers in the divine life.

---

5 de Guibert, *Theology of the Spiritual Life*, 41.

6 In making this substitution, I in no way mean to imply that we should reject the idea of "perfection." I hope, rather, to provide another perspective on our finality in God that is grounded in both the Scriptures and the Fathers of the Church. "Maturity" complements the idea of "perfection."

7 The Greek *nēpios*, like the Latin *infans*, means "nonspeaker"—an infant.

What are we to make of the paradoxical "childlike adult" that is the Christian? First, the fact that the Christian must humble himself as a child, while also growing up in the Spirit, indicates that Christian maturity is a divine *gift*. One receives it in the manner of child, no matter what stage of life one may be in and no matter what weaknesses one may have. Since one does not accomplish it through the wisdom of the world, a five-year-old suffused with grace can be more mature than a college student! Christian maturation, as we shall see, embraces all that is human, but finds its graced end in the very participation in the life of the Trinity—a fulfillment that only God may give.

Second, Christian maturity incorporates human freedom and responsibility. Paul admonishes the Corinthians as follows: "Brethren, do not be children [*paidia*] in your thinking; be infants [*nēpiazete*] in evil, but in thinking be mature [*teleioi*]" (1 Cor 14:20). Thinking and living as a Christian means the free application of the Gospel to one's way of being. To the Ephesians, Paul warns that "we may no longer be children [*nēpioi*], tossed back and forth and carried about with every wind of doctrine, by the cunning of men, by their craftiness in deceitful wiles. Rather, speaking the truth in love, we are to grow up [*auxēsōmen*] in every way into him who is the head, into Christ" (Eph 4:14-15). Furthermore, Christ himself calls for his disciples to bear fruit in their lives through their unity with him and their practice of his teachings: "I am the vine, you are the branches. He who abides in me, and I in him, he it is that bears much fruit, for apart from me you can do nothing" (John 15:5). Not to mature and bear fruit represents a failure to abide in Christ and manifest the Kingdom in the world (Luke 13:6-9; Matt 3:8-10; Matt 13:1-23). Thus, the Christian adult must freely grow into Christ, who reveals and establishes the fullness of humanity.

In choosing to work with the term "maturation," I do not mean to imply that the term "perfection" is lacking or deceptive. And yet, other words have been used to designate the goal of the spiritual life, such as holiness, sanctity, beatitude, and deification. Each term provides a helpful perspective on a reality that Mary alone, in her Assumption, truly knows. I believe, however, that Christian maturation offers an approach that, as we shall see, speaks well to our own time. It recovers the teleological and relational elements of human development while also emphasizing both the giftedness and responsibility involved in becoming both fully human and deified.

MATURITY AND THE FATHERS OF THE CHURCH

I turn to the greatest expositors of God's Word, the Fathers of the Church, for wisdom regarding Christian maturation. These pastors, preachers, teachers, catechists, and theologians from the first seven centuries of Christianity have provided the Church with a treasure trove of insights. In fact, one might say that the Church of today rests on the intellectual and spiritual edifice of these holy men. Though they spoke different languages, inhabited different lands, and lived in different times, they demonstrated a remarkable unity in their desire to share the mysteries of their Trinitarian faith. Though each one certainly had his flaws and struggled to grow ever more in the divine likeness, they all nonetheless exhibited Christian maturity in their lives: they were models of Christian adulthood.

This book constructs a mosaic of maturity from their writings. I do not claim to capture all the perspectives that the Fathers offer on this theme; rather, I hope to recover a selection of voices that, together, express much needed teachings from the tradition. These pieces from such figures as Augustine of Hippo, Maximus the Confessor, Mark the Monk, and many others will together form an image of Christ, the one who reveals to us the fullness of humanity in the life of the Trinity.

This mosaic of maturity has three parts. Part 1 establishes the three pillars of Christian maturity: form and finality; virtue and character; vocation and commitment. It concludes by exploring the opposition to maturation in the form of demonic infantilism. Part 2 examines the means of maturity given to us in the life of the Church: the Scriptures, the Mysteries (Sacraments), and asceticism. Finally, Part 3 reviews four essential expressions of Christian adulthood: the witness, the teacher, the servant, and the fool. A concluding chapter will hold the mosaic up to our modern world to see in what ways our times need to "grow up." Along the way we shall meet many Fathers of the Church, both well-known and obscure: Irenaeus of Lyons, Origen of Alexandria, Gregory of Nazianzus, Gregory of Nyssa, Basil of Caesarea, Augustine of Hippo, Ambrose of Milan, John Cassian, Mark the Monk, Maximus the Confessor, Symeon the Holy Fool, and others. Their collective insights, all the fruits of vast learning and the contemplation of God's word, will give us a dazzling picture of a wonderous figure: the saint, the mature Christian, transformed by union with the Father, the Son, and the Holy Spirit.

This book will hardly exhaust the theme of Christian maturity, which has a long history in the life of the Church. Yet, I hope that even a brief introduction will inspire Christians to go to the sources—the Scriptures and the Fathers—and to recover the desire "to grow into God."

❋ ❋ ❋ ❋ ❋

PART 1

❋ ❋ ❋ ❋ ❋

The Pillars of Maturity

CHAPTER 1

Form and Finality

I am wise because I follow Nature as the best of guides and obey her as a god; and since she has fully planned the other acts of life's drama, it is not likely that she has neglected the final act as if she were a careless playwright. And yet there had to be something final, and—as in the case of orchard fruits and crops of grain in the process of ripening which comes with time—something shriveled, as it were, and prone to fall. But this state the wise man should endure with resignation. For what is warring against the gods, as the giants did, other than fighting against Nature?

Marcus Tullius Cicero[1]

Whoever belongs to Christ, must go the whole way with him. He must mature to manhood; he must one day or other walk the way of the cross to Gethsemane and Golgotha.

Saint Teresa Benedicta of the Cross[2]

You, therefore, must be perfect, as your heavenly Father is perfect.

Matthew 5:48

---

[1] Marcus Tullius Cicero, *On Old Age* 2 (LCL 154, 13–15).
[2] Teresa Benedicta of the Cross, *The Mystery of Christmas. Incarnation and Humanity,* trans. Josephine Rucker, SSJ. (Darlington: Darlington Carmel, 1985), 15.

Cato the Elder, the principal locutor in Cicero's dialogue *De senectute* ("On Old Age"), likens the final days of life to a *tempestiva maturitas*, a "seasonable ripening." Just as fruit on a tree, having achieved its completeness, must fall to the ground, so even a renowned statesman must "with resignation" conclude his life in an earthen tomb. One may, of course, embrace senescence with the alacrity of Cato, rejoicing in the hard-won virtues and wisdom of a well-formed life, but the end is the same for all—one cannot elude the laws of nature.

The Latin *maturitas* suggests ripeness, perfection, and fulfillment. Yet, all these ideas apply to a process of growth into a defined *form*. The mature apple unfolds over time and assumes a proper shape for its kind. The fertilized blossom grows to become an apple, not a peach or a banana. Thus, maturation seeks an end, a perfection grounded in a thing's very nature. Failure to achieve that end owing to disease or drought cuts short the potential for beauty and perfection.

Humans are not apples, and therefore mere "ripening" does not suffice for the formation of the *homo integer*, the complete man. Biological growth, with all its complications and challenges, does not guarantee human maturation. Embodiment does indeed shape the psychological and even spiritual sides of the person, but the mystery of human freedom and interiority defy the parameters of corporeal extension, girth, and hormones. The precocity of a youth, the vigor of an elder, and the childish behavior of some adults demonstrate that humans ripen or rot at any time of life.

Most significantly, *Christian maturation* incorporates the various elements of human maturation—the biological, the intellectual, the psychological—in a movement toward a supernatural end. This finality, in fact, defines what it is to be human. Furthermore, this "end" both fulfills human nature *and* elevates it beyond its own innate capacities. For the Fathers of the Church, this end is *theōsis*, "deification," a union so intimate with God that one may only glimpse its depths in the revelation of the risen one, Jesus Christ. Christian maturity unfolds in this "mystery hidden for the ages in God," the defining form of each person and all humanity.

MATURITY AS *TELOS*

Several Greek words commonly designate the various aspects of human maturation: *hēlikia*, "stature"; *horaios*, "ripe, mature, seasoned"; and *teleios*, "perfect, complete, mature." *Teleios*, in particular, reveals both the dynamic and the formal elements of maturation. The word is derived from *telos*, meaning "a thing that has come to pass" or "a conclusion derived from a preconceived purpose or state."[3] Thus, *telos andros*, "the completeness or perfection of man," indicates the fulfillment of human nature in all its potential.

Aristotle provides two definitions of the term in his *Metaphysics*: "We call complete [*teleion*] [1] that outside which it is not possible to find even one of the parts proper to it" and [2] "that which in respect of excellence and goodness cannot be excluded in its kind." The complete or mature thing *achieves* a goal: its full acquisition of essential qualities necessary for flourishing. Aristotle continues: "An excellence is a completion [*teleiōsis*]; for each thing is complete [*teleion*] and every substance is complete [*teleia*] when in respect of its proper kind of excellence it lacks no part of natural [*kata physin*] magnitude. The things which have attained a good end [*telos spoudaion*] are called complete [*teleia*]; for things are complete in virtue of having attained their end [*telos*]."[4] Thus, for Aristotle, a thing contains its "completion" in potency, in the very definition of its nature (*physis*), and its maturation unfolds in a dynamic movement toward a goal of excellence in its kind.

In the Neoplatonic tradition, the term came to designate a participation in and assimilation to the Good or the One. The late Neoplatonist Proclus (41–85), for example, taught that "the participant was incomplete [*ateles*] before the participation [in a higher perfection] and by the participation has been made complete [*teleion*]."[5] This means that the closer one approaches the Good, the more perfect or mature one becomes: "For completeness [*teleiotēs*] is a part of the Good, and the complete [*teleion*], *qua* complete, imitates the Good."[6] Thus, perfection or maturation emerges from a relationship with and reception of the Good in ever greater degrees.

The gnostics also made use of this concept. Recent decades have witnessed major reassessments of what has been traditionally called Gnosticism,

---

3 Paul Johannes Du Plessis, *Teleios: The Idea of Perfection in the New Testament* (Kampen: J. H. Kok, 1959), 39–40.

4 Aristotle, *Metaphysics* 1021b, in *The Complete Works of Aristotle*, ed. Jonathan Barnes, trans. W. D. Ross (Princeton, NJ: Princeton University Press, 1995), 1613.

5 Proclus, *The Elements of Theology*, Prop. 24, ed. and trans. E. R. Dodds (Oxford: Clarendon Press, 1963), 28, lines 10–13.

6 Proclus, *Elements*, Prop. 25, 28, lines 27–29. On sharing in the perfection of the One, see Radek Chlup, *Proclus: An Introduction* (Cambridge: Cambridge University Press, 2016), 242–46.

with some scholars rejecting the category all together.[7] In general, however, we can say that *gnōsis* was not so much esoteric knowledge as an "acquaintance" or transformative contact with the divine. Thus, in the second-century *Gospel of Truth*, the "perfect" or "mature" are those who receive saving knowledge through acquaintance: "It is to the perfect [mature] that this, the proclamation of the one they search for, has made itself known, through the mercies of the father."[8] As they grow in relationship with the divine, they return to the perfection of their prelapsarian state: "So that whoever has acquaintance [*gnōsis*] is from above: and if called, hears, replies, and turns to the one who is calling; and goes to him."[9]

The first-century Jewish philosopher and biblical exegete, Philo of Alexandria, made use of the term in scriptural exegesis. For example, he shows how God guided the patriarch Abraham in his journey, teaching him the virtues that perfect or complete nature. "And the words, 'He [God] finished speaking to him [Abraham],' are equivalent to saying, 'He made his hearer perfect [mature] [*teleios*],' though he was devoid of wisdom before, and he filled him with immortal lessons."[10] Thus, maturity or perfection did not always remain confined to the cultivation of natural virtues, but especially took place through an encounter with the loving Creator.

To understand the Christian use of *teleios*, one must turn to the Christian *telos*, the Christian end: Jesus Christ. Christians discover the truth of humanity in the God-man, the *Alpha* and the *Omega*, and are defined by their relationship with him. The council fathers of Vatican II wrote: "The truth is that only in the mystery of the Incarnate Word does the mystery of man take on light. For Adam, the first man, was a type of him who was to come (Rom 5:14), Christ the Lord. Christ the new Adam, in the very revelation of the mystery of the Father and of his love, fully reveals man to himself

---

7 See David Brakke, *The Gnostics: Myth, Ritual, and Diversity in Early Christianity* (Cambridge, MA: Harvard University Press, 2010), 1–29; Bentley Layton, "Prolegomena to the Study of Ancient Gnosticism," in *The Social World of the First Christians. Essays in Honor of Wayne Meeks*, ed. L. Michael White and O. Larry Yarborough (Minneapolis: Fortress Press, 1995), 334–50.

8 *The Gospel of Truth* 18, in *The Gnostic Scriptures*, trans Bentley Layton (Garden City, NY: Doubleday, 1987), 254, lines 11–15.

9 *The Gospel of Truth* 22, 256, lines 2–8.

10 Philo of Alexandria, *De mutatione nominum* 48, 270, in *The Works of Philo*, trans C. D. Yonge (Peabody, MA: Hendrickson, 1993), 364.

and brings to light his most high calling."[11] Christ shows us not only the *homo integer* or mature human but, more importantly, he realizes the deified man.

CHRIST AS ALPHA–OMEGA

The modern scientific viewpoint has robbed the cosmos of its end and its personality—the sense of a universe alive with the music of the spheres and a purposeful harmony. Even the varieties of New Age pantheisms reduce the cosmos to a commercialized idol, worshipped through dead crystals and hemp products. C. S. Lewis, in his *Space Trilogy*, sought to restore the vision of an ensouled cosmos with his angelic *oyarses* and celestial paradises, all subject to the Christian God, but not even his genius could overcome the contemporary desire for dominance. As Joseph Ratzinger has taught us, we have rejected the philosophy of "being," the view of things as given and gifted, for a philosophy of "making"—that is, the human manipulation of all things.[12] We now live in a world of tools for man's exploitation of nature.

The book of Revelation, however, gives us a very different view of the cosmos and history. The beginning (*archē*) and the end (*telos*) of all things are not matter and energy subject to natural laws, but a loving God, who is subject to nothing. We hear twice in the mysterious vision of John that God gives origin and completion to all that is: "'I am the Alpha and the Omega,' says the Lord God, 'who is and who was and who is to come, the Almighty'" (Rev 1:8); "And he who sat upon the throne said, 'Behold, I make all things new'... 'It is done! I am the Alpha and the Omega, the beginning and the end [*telos*]'" (Rev 21:5–6). The Creator God—the *Alpha*—promises not to destroy all things at the end but rather "to make them new," to restore and transform the cosmos.[13] *I AM*—the divine name revealed to Moses—gives meaning to the world and its history. God did not just make a world but *created* a world in love that unfolds toward a providential denouement.

---

11 Vatican Council II, *Gaudium et spes* (December 7, 1965), 22.

12 Joseph Ratzinger, *Introduction to Christianity*, trans. J. R. Foster (San Francisco: Ignatius Press, 2004), 66–69.

13 See Wilfrid Harrington, OP, *Revelation* (Collegeville, MN: Liturgical Press, 2008), 207–8.; Craig Koester, *Revelation: A New Translation with Introduction and Commentary* (New Haven, CT: Yale University Press, 2015), 799. God as "the first and last" of all things may also be found in the book of the prophet Isaiah: "Who has performed and done this, calling the generations from the beginning? I, the Lord, the first, and with the last; I am he" (Isa. 41:4). See also 44:6–7; 48:12.

Two more verses in the book of Revelation specify Christ as the *Alpha and Omega*: "When I saw him [Christ], I fell at his feet as though I were dead. But he laid his right hand on me, and said, 'Do not be afraid. I am the first [*prōtos*] and the last [*eschatos*], the living one who was dead, and I hold the keys of Death and Hades'" (Rev 1:17–18); "Behold, I am coming soon, bringing my reward with me, to repay everyone according to what one has done. I am the Alpha and the Omega, the first [*prōtos*] and the last [*eschatos*], the beginning [*archē*] and the end [*telos*]. Blessed are those who wash their robes so as to have the right to the tree of life, and may enter the city by the gates" (Rev 22:12–14). These expressions indicate the absolute authority of Christ—not even death can subdue him. Yet, they also designate Christ as the origin (the *Alpha*, the first, the beginning) and the fulfillment (the *Omega*, the last, the end) of creation.[14] In fact, the *incarnate* Word completes creation in himself (1) "before" creation, (2) in his history as man, and (3) in his union with the Father and Spirit. He reveals and effects in his *person* the truth and the graced potential of humanity and all creation. Hans Urs von Balthasar summarizes this fullness of Christ as follows:

> On the one hand, Christ is God's image, word and expression (Heb 1:3) who impresses his stamp on the world from beginning to end. He is therefore the archetype of every creature, which must have a corresponding image —and word—character. On the other hand, the process stretching from the origin of the world to its end takes the form of a bloody drama, of a battle into which we see the *Logos* himself marching with blood-drenched garments and a sharp sword in his hand (Rev 19:11–13; Eph 1:7; 2:23–28; Col 1:20). Indeed, we are expressly told that in this battle he dies (Rev 1:18, etc.). Christ dies in an utterly realistic death in darkness and Godforsakenness, a death that makes him, who from the origin was "light" and "life of men" (John 1:4), possessor of the key to every death and all the darkness death contains.[15]

The Mystery of the Incarnation and the Paschal Mystery therefore form Christian maturity while also responding to the groanings of all creation. To know Christ, the *Alpha* and the *Omega,* is to know the alphabet and language through which the meaning of humanity is articulated. When

---

14 Koester, 841.

15 Hans Urs Von Balthasar, "Christ: Alpha and Omega," *Communio* 23, no. 3 (Fall, 1996): 455–56.

Christ proclaims from the Cross, "It is finished!" (John 19:30: *tetelestai*), he affirms that his mission to renew and elevate humanity to new life—to a maturity—has come to completion. Now every human person may reach "mature manhood [*eis andra teleion*], the measure of the stature [*hēlikias*] of the fullness of Christ" (Eph 4:13).

MATURITY IN THE INCARNATE WORD: MAXIMUS THE CONFESSOR

Among the Fathers of the Church, Maximus the Confessor (580–662) offers the most profound theological reflections on the finality of man in Christ. From the very beginning, God desired that all persons achieve "the full stature [*hēlikia*] in Christ," such that "God shines forth through body and soul when their natural features are transcended in overwhelming glory."[16] This was the "mystery hidden for the ages in God" (Eph 3:9), the order and wonder of God's loving providence: "The plan was for him [Christ] to mingle, without change on his part, with human nature by a true hypostatic union, to unite human nature to himself while remaining immutable, so that he might become a man, as he alone knew how, and so that he might deify humanity in union with himself."[17] In short, God's intention to become enfleshed gives form and finality to humanity: God's plan is to deify humanity in the incarnate Son.

Maximus uses the image of "three births" to explain how the incarnate Son restores human nature, redirects its wayward path after the fall, and fulfills its end.[18] In the *first birth*, the natural birth, Christ assumed both the original, unblemished divine image of Adam's unfallen nature *and* the fallen conditions of that nature, but without the stain of sin.[19] Maximus therefore emphasizes that Christ's birth from the Virgin is both *ours* and *not ours*: it is

---

16 Maximus the Confessor, *Chapters on Knowledge* II, 88 (PG 90, 1168A; Berthold, 167).

17 Maximus the Confessor, *Responses to Thalassius* 22 (SC 529, 262, lines 8–13).

18 Maximus assumes the image of the "three births" from Saint Gregory of Nazianzus. See Gregory of Nazianzus, *Oration 40*, 2 (NPNF II-7, 360).

19 Maximus develops this distinction between the unfallen divine image and the fallen conditions of our nature in his response to Gregory's own distinction between Christ's "vital inspiration" (*emphthusēma* or "the divine image") and his body-flesh (the consequences of the fall). See *On the Difficulties* 42 (PG 91, 1316 D; Constas, 124–25). See also *Responses to Thalassius* 21 (SC 529, 254, 34–49) and the distinction between *genesis* (creation in the image) and *gennēsis* (birth into the state of sin).

a true human birth, but, unlike ours, it is a *voluntary* assumption of both our human nature and our fallen state. By entering our state of existence, Christ "establishes a new origin of creation and a new mode of birth."[20] Christ not only freely restores the original image of our nature through his birth from the Virgin; he also restores our potential to move toward union with God.

Christ further established the pattern of our creation and regeneration by freely submitting to the *second birth*, the Baptism in the Jordan.[21] Though Christ did not need Baptism, his free submission to the ritual of John the Baptist demonstrated the necessity of rebirth in the Spirit. Maximus states that Baptism "ushers in this grace as entirely present in actuality (*kat'energeian*), transforming voluntarily the entire free choice of the one being born so that it conforms to God who gives birth."[22] Thus, Baptism, rendered effective by Christ, restores fallen man's freedom to unite himself to God.[23] Christ demonstrates this power of Baptism by then initiating his public life, a life of *activity*, in response to the will of his Father. Thus, for Maximus, the Baptism of Christ, the second birth, is not only the moment of his submersion in the Jordan but also *the whole of his activity (kat'energeian)*—that is, all that Christ does, in both his hidden and public life, manifests the virtues and the way to the Father.

Finally, Christ fulfills the *third birth* of the Resurrection. Jesus's Resurrection deifies human nature and opens all humanity to transformation

---

20 "Thus, 'though he was beyond being, he came into being,' fashioning within nature a new origin of creation and a different mode of birth, for He was conceived having become the seed of His own flesh, and He was born having become the seal of the virginity for the one who bore Him, showing that in her case mutually contradictory things can truly come together. For she herself is both virgin and mother, innovating nature by a coincidence of opposites, since virginity and child bearing are opposites, and no one would have been able to imagine their natural combination." See *Ambiguua ad Thomam* 5 (PG 91, 1052D; Constas, 42–46).

21 Maximus, *On the Difficulties* 42 (PG 91, 1348B; Constas, 182–83).

22 Maximus, *Responses to Thalassius* 6 (SC 529, 178, lines 1–15; Constas, 108).

23 "Though we may still deviate into sin during this life, Baptism nonetheless reestablishes and elevates our freedom such that what was previously impossible—the free reorientation toward God, or well-being—now becomes possible. The Holy Spirit "takes the whole of their free choice and transposes it completely from earth to heaven, and, through true knowledge realized in actual deed, refashions the intellect with the blessed beams of [the] light of God the Father, so that it is deemed another God . . ." (Maximus, *Responses to Thalassius* 6 [SC 529, 190, lines 26–35; Constas, 109]). On the twofold nature of Baptism as (a) grace in potency and (b) grace in act, see Marcus Plested, "The Ascetic Tradition," in *The Oxford Handbook of Maximus the Confessor,* ed. Pauline Allen and Bronwen Neil (Oxford: Oxford University Press, 2015), 169–71.

in divine grace. Christ's rising reveals and effects our end: "The whole man, divinely acted upon by the grace of God incarnate, may be divinized, remaining entirely man in body and soul according to nature."[24] The rebirth of humanity becomes possible when Christ emerges from the womb of the tomb.

Jesus Christ, as the definition and fulfillment of man, is therefore not a static principle but a dynamic *person* whose entire life gives shape to what and who each person is. The Maximus scholar Paul Blowers notes that "Maximus did not make salvation (and deification) contingent on the cross alone but on the whole of Christ's incarnational ministry as purposed before the beginning of the ages."[25] On the one hand, Jesus is the *Logos*, the Word or Principle that defines man's nature and reveals the end of that nature by becoming visible in the flesh. On the other hand, his divine-human existence, encompassing all aspects of human life and freedom, gives human maturation its true meaning. The Word made flesh therefore allows persons to become *what* they are to be—human—and *who* they are to be: deified persons.

THE IMAGE AND LIKENESS OF GOD: IRENAEUS OF LYONS

The Fathers of the Church discovered the foundation of their Christian anthropology in *Genesis* 1:26. On the final day of the Hexaemeron, the six days of creation, God said: "Let us make man in our image, after our likeness. Let them have dominion over the fish of the sea, and over the birds of the air, and over the cattle, and over all the earth, and over every creeping thing that creeps upon the earth." Ever attentive to the nuances of the text, the earliest interpreters pondered the use of two words to describe man's relationship to the Creator: image (Hebrew: *tselem*; Greek: *eikōn*) and likeness (Hebrew: *demût*; Greek: *homoiōsis*). What was the difference between these two words?

The Old Testament scholar J. Gordon McConville offers several interpretations of "image" in the context of Genesis: man's capacity for just rule or dominion in the world; man's mission to procreate, to share in God's very creation of the divine image by "multiplying and filling the earth"; and the

---

24 Maximus, *On the Difficulties* 7 (PG 91, 1088C; Constas, 112–13).
25 Paul Blowers, *Maximus the Confessor: Jesus Christ and the Transfiguration of the World* (Oxford: Oxford University Press, 2016), 240.

unique relationship between man and God, demonstrated in man's worship and "presencing of God in the world."[26] In turn, "likeness" implies that the intrinsic image that is man may, even in the exile from Paradise, fully live out the moral responsibilities entailed in the image: "likeness" is the fullness of the human presencing of God in the goodness of God's creation.[27]

Modern scholars recognize that the trajectory of the Christian interpreters, who were dependent primarily on Greek and Latin translations of the Hebrew, imported some philosophical ideas that were foreign to the Hebrew context. Yet, the Fathers' basic understanding of the image-likeness relationship did not stray entirely from the suggestions given above. For some Fathers, such as Irenaeus of Lyons and Origen of Alexandria, *image* designates an intrinsic and dynamic reflection of the relationship with God in man that moves toward the fuller realization of the divine *likeness*. Furthermore, the divine image remains even after man's fall and, through the incarnate Word, recovers its potential for the likeness. God, therefore, created man for a positive movement (*kinēsis*) and growth toward a divinely gifted end (*telos*), a movement from divine image to divine likeness.

The approaches to this image-likeness dynamic vary among the Fathers, but Irenaeus of Lyons (130–202) offers one of the most compelling visions of the image's maturation. In a passage from his *On the Apostolic Preaching*, he discusses the state of Adam and Eve before the expulsion from the garden:

> Now having made the man lord of the earth, and of everything that is in it, He secretly appointed him as lord over those who were servants in it. But they, however, were in their [full-development], while the lord, that is, the man, was very little, since he was an infant, and it was necessary for him to reach full-development by growing in this way: and that his nourishment and growth might take place in luxury, a place was prepared for him, better than this earth—excelling in air, beauty, light, food, plants,

---

26 For these suggestions and others, see J. Gordon McConville, *Being Human in God's World: An Old Testament Theology of Humanity* (Grand Rapids, MI: Baker Academic, 2016), 11–29. See also Christof Betschart, *L'Humain Image Filiale de Dieu. Une anthropologie théologique en dialogue avec l'exégèse* (Paris: Les Éditions du Cerf, 2021), 35–102. Betschart reviews the various interpretations of the image-likeness dynamic: (1) spiritual—the image as gift of the spirit to man; (2) functional—the image designates the human capacities of governance and fecundity, as well as the finality of the image in the likeness; and (3) relational—the relationship with God that comes to be understood as sonship. He also notes the image-prototype (likeness) relationship suggested in Wisdom 2:23—"God made man in the image of his own eternity"—and certain Pauline texts that understand Jesus as the image (e.g., 2 Cor 4:4; Col 1:15).

27 See McConville, *Being Human in God's World*, 43–45.

fruit, waters, and every other thing needful [for life] —and its name was Paradise. And so beautiful and good was the Paradise [that] the Word of God was always walking in it: He would walk and talk with the man prefiguring the future, which would come to pass, that He would dwell with him and speak with him, and would be with mankind, teaching them righteousness. But the man was a young child, not yet having a perfect deliberation, and because of this he was easily deceived by the seducer.[28]

Several points come to the fore in this passage. First, Adam and Eve had not yet achieved full development in Paradise. They are "children" who require maturation through growth in righteousness and right deliberation. Second, although they required physical elements for their growth—food, water, light, and so on—their true maturation would take place through their relationship with the Word (*Logos*) or Son. In fact, their familiarity with the Word, even before the Incarnation, established the direction of their movement and adumbrated their future fulfillment. Finally, the roots of their fall stem from their lack of maturity and their openness to deception. This further implies that, if they had achieved their end through moral growth and their relationship with the Word, they would no longer have been susceptible to temptation—that is, their *end* would have been a true *maturation.*

Yet, what exactly does Irenaeus mean when he calls Adam and Eve children? Were they literally small children, or were they simply childish in their innocence and naïveté? Matthew Steenberg places the maturation of man within the wider context of Irenaeus's teachings on creation: any newly created thing must logically exist in a state of "imperfection" owing to its very distinction from God. Thus, everything in the cosmos requires growth and movement, and nothing emerges in full maturity.[29] The infancy and maturation of Adam and Eve encompass this very dynamic of God's creation. "The *telos* towards which humanity is moving, the adulthood for which the child strives, is nothing other than the completion of the one creative movement of God which commenced 'in the beginning,' which was revealed in its fullness in the incarnate Christ, and which will find fulfillment in the eternal kingdom."[30] Maturation, therefore, gives shape to man "from the beginning"—as

---

28 Irenaeus of Lyons, *On the Apostolic Preaching* 12 (Behr, 47).
29 See Matthew Steenberg, "Children in Paradise: Adam and Eve as 'Infants' in Irenaeus of Lyons," *Journal of Early Christian Studies* 12, no. 1 (2004): 7.
30 Matthew Steenberg, *Irenaeus on Creation: The Cosmic Christ and the Saga of Redemption* (Leiden: Brill, 2008), 7–8.

a creature, man is a maturing being—and finds its fulfillment in the unique relationship man has with the Word.

This need for maturation—that is, a growth toward the *telos* who is Christ—appears also in Irenaeus's understanding of the image-likeness dynamic. One passage in his *Against the Heresies* discusses the distinction between these two concepts:

> Now God shall be glorified in His handiwork, fitting it so as to be conformable to, and modeled after, His own Son. For by the hands of the Father, that is, by the Son and the Holy Spirit, man, and not merely a part of man, was made in the likeness of God. Now the soul and the spirit are certainly a part of man, but certainly not the man; for the perfect man consists in the commingling and the union of the soul receiving the spirit of the Father and the admixture of that fleshly nature which was molded after the image of God ... For if anyone take away the substance of flesh, that is, of the handiwork [of God], and understand that which is purely spiritual, such then would not be a spiritual man but would be the spirit of a man, or the Spirit of God. But when the spirit here blended with the soul is united to [God's] handiwork, the man is rendered spiritual and perfect because of the outpouring of the Spirit, and this is he who was made in the image and likeness of God.[31]

This passage contributes further elements to the understanding of man's maturation. First, as can already be seen in Maximus, man's *telos* finds not only its model but also its source in the Son who "accustoms" creation to himself—that is, draws it closer to his likeness and way of being. Second, Irenaeus affirms the intrinsic divine image not simply in the soul but also in the soul's union with the material body. Contrary to the gnostics, the composite nature of man—body and soul—forms an image of God. Finally, the image also becomes the likeness of God through the gift of the Spirit; that is, the deification of the image requires the supernatural gift of God's life.

Given these insights, one may now better understand the full significance of Christ as the *telos* of man. On the one hand, creation—and particularly man, the divine image—has been created for conformity to Christ, for the assumption of his form. Man, in his nature as both body and soul, moves toward this likeness through both imitation of Jesus and, more importantly,

---

31 Irenaeus, *Against the Heresies* V, 6, 1 (SC 153.2, 72–80, lines 1–56; ANF I, 531–32).

the gift of the Spirit.[32] On the other hand, Christ also restores the *telos* of man by becoming human, by joining human nature and "accustoming" it to himself:

> For He [Christ] was made in the likeness of sinful flesh that He might condemn sin, and then cast it out of the flesh as condemned; and also, *that He might invite humankind to His own likeness,* inasmuch as He designated humans as imitators of God, led them to the Father's law that they might see God, and granted them the power of receiving the Father. He was the Word of God who dwelt in humanity, and was made the Son of Man in order that He might accustom [*adsuescere*] humankind to receive God, and accustom God to dwell in humanity according to the Father's good pleasure.[33]

As the following chapters will show, Christ "recapitulates" or "sums up" the growth of humanity in himself so that man might recover the true end of his nature. "He [Christ] recapitulated in Himself the long unfolding of humankind, granting salvation by way of compendium, that in Christ Jesus we might receive what we had lost in Adam, namely, to be according to the image and likeness of God."[34]

CONCLUSION

God created human beings as a work in progress. From the moment of conception, they begin a journey of physical, psychological, and spiritual growth within the parameters of their nature and subject to a defined end. One may certainly speak of a *natural* end (*telos*) for this process of maturation—that is, the assumption of essential capacities and virtues for genuine human flourishing. Yet, the authentic end of every human person

---

32 See Irenaeus, *Against the Heresies* V, 16, 2 (SC 153.2, 216, lines 21–33; ANF I, 544). Thomas Weinandy emphasizes the Trinitarian form of the dynamic: "First, to be in the imago Dei is to live our lives within the very life of the Trinity itself. It is within the Trinity that we assume our own divine likeness, that we become, through the transforming work of the Holy Spirit, children of the Father after the image of his eternal Son. Here we perceive the depth of our dignity as human persons." See Thomas Weinandy, "St. Irenaeus and the Imago Dei: The Importance of Being Human," *Logos: A Journal of Catholic Thought and Culture* 6, no. 4 (2003): 31.

33 Irenaeus, *Against the Heresies*, III, 20, 2 (SC 211.2, 390, lines 67–71 and 392, lines 2–75; ACW 64, 96).

34 Irenaeus, *Against the Heresies*, III, 18, 1 (SC 211.2, 342, lines 9–12 and 344, line 13; ACW 64, 87).

exceeds the bounds of human nature and finds its form and fulfillment in Christ, in the flourishing of his life. Deification, or *theōsis,* is, in the words of C. S. Lewis, the next stage in evolution—a stage that requires a divine gift for its achievement.[35] Furthermore, this end becomes visible and possible only through the Incarnation and the Paschal Mystery. In short, Christian maturity moves toward a *supernatural* end (*telos*) in union with God who is Father, Son, and Spirit.

I would highlight three points stemming from the Christ-form as the *telos* of humanity. First, *human maturation is principally a gift.* We cannot "make" maturity or design it on our own. The Son of God became man to redeem us and to mature us, to gift us with his life through the Spirit. Maturity, therefore, can never be reduced to biological growth or the product of human discipline. God loves us into his life through a relationship in the Spirit.

Second, given that maturity is gift, *every person, of every age and condition, can be mature.* The newly baptized infant possesses the Christ-form in a greater way than many physical adults. The man struggling with alcoholism or the woman debilitated by trauma may, through divine grace, shine with the Christ-form more brightly than the celebrated therapist or the respected bishop. God matures persons not according to the rules of temporal growth but according to the scandalous love of eternity. It does not matter what time one arrives in the vineyard, since God gives bounteously at every hour (Matt 20:1–16).

Finally, though maturity is fundamentally a gift, *this does not exonerate people from responsible growth in time.* The human person does not mature like an apple or even like a dog. The person possesses the innate gifts of intellect, memory, and freedom that distinguish him from all other beings in the cosmos. Thus, his Christian maturation must embrace these personal endowments in a way appropriate for his age and condition. The next two chapters will consider the significance of character and vocation in this growth.

---

35 C. S. Lewis, *Mere Christianity* (New York: Macmillan, 1996), 185–86.

CHAPTER 2

VIRTUE AND CHARACTER

The previous chapter argued that Christian maturity aims toward a *telos* that integrates the composite nature of man, body and soul, and establishes a radical intimacy with God—that is, *theōsis*. This movement is the fruit of a divine gift, revealed and realized in the person of Jesus Christ, which brings the divine image of man to its fulfillment as the divine likeness.

Though the crossing of the threshold between created and uncreated, between human and divine, demands grace, this does not mean that man's freedom has no place in Christian maturation. On the contrary, God's action does not transgress personhood and freedom. Humans are not plants, mindlessly growing and producing fruit in due order; rather, God creates them with the capacity for coworking—*synergia,* synergy—with the Creator. This and the following chapter explore how the human person freely matures in union with divine grace.

THE MATURATION AND FREEDOM OF JESUS

When the Word became flesh, he assumed all aspects of human embodied existence, except for sin. He passed through conception, birth, infancy, childhood, adulthood, and even death. Yet, how could the person of the incarnate Son, preserving all the qualities of both natures, also "mature" in time? Unless we wish to fall into the heresy of docetism—the belief that Christ's humanity was a mere appearance or illusion—we must affirm the testimony of the Scriptures as an affirmation that Jesus grew "in stature and wisdom" (Luke 2:52). But, again, how can we understand the maturation of the One who is both God and man?

Jesus Recapitulates Human Maturation: Irenaeus of Lyons

How old was Jesus when he died? On the one hand, one may affirm with the vast majority of interpreters that Jesus died at the age of thirty-three. We arrive at this age by first taking Luke's statement that Jesus began his ministry at age thirty (Luke 3:23) and then calculating a three-year period by the three celebrations of the Pasch recorded in the Gospel of John (John 2:23; John 6:4; John 11:55; 12:21).

On the other hand, not everyone has adhered to this position. For instance, the second-century bishop and theologian, Irenaeus of Lyons, in his *Against the Heresies*, first states that Jesus indeed died at thirty-three.[36] However, he then moves to the startling but not unprecedented claim that Jesus did not begin his public ministry until his forties and died at fifty.[37] He makes his case as follows:

> Surely, he came to save all people through himself: I say all who would again be born to God—infants [*infantes* = zero to ten years], children [*parvuli* = ten to twenty years], youth [*pueri* = twenty to thirty], young adults [*iuvenes* = thirty to forty], and the elderly [*seniors* = forty to fifty]. Therefore, he passed through every age. Becoming an infant among infants, he sanctified infants; becoming a child among children, he sanctified those having this age and at the same time became for them an example of piety and righteousness and obedience [*subiectio*]; becoming a young adult among young adults, he was an example for young adults and sanctified them to the Lord. In the same way, he became also an elderly person among the elderly, so that he might be a mature teacher for all, not merely by explaining the truth but also by his age, that is, by the same time sanctifying the elderly and being an example for them.

---

36 See Irenaeus, *Against the Heresies* II, 22, 3 (SC 294.2, 216–20, lines 57–92).

37 For a history and interpretation of these views, see John Chapman, "Papias on the Age of Our Lord," *Journal of Theological Studies* 9, no. 33 (1907): 53–59; Devin White, "Jesus at Fifty: Irenaeus on John 8:57 and the Age of Jesus," *Theological Studies* 40, no. 1 (2020): 158–63.

> Lastly, he came even to death so that he might be *the firstborn from the dead,* himself *holding the primacy in all things,* the Author of life, prior to all and going before all [Luke 3:23].[38]

Irenaeus argues for an older Jesus by emphasizing the importance of the incarnate Son recapitulating every stage of human growth, as well as the necessity of his reaching the age of maturity—a *senior*—to have credibility as a public teacher.[39] Furthermore, he notes that, in John 8:57, the Jews said to Jesus, "You are not yet fifty years old and you have seen Abraham?" Surely if Jesus had been in his thirties, Irenaeus reasons, they would have said, "You are not yet *forty* years old."[40]

One may debate whether Irenaeus actually held this unusual timeline, or whether he was simply asserting that Christ assumed all stages of human maturation even by the age of thirty-three—a demonstration of God's power to grant maturity and vigor at any age. We can be certain, however, that Irenaeus sought to refute certain docetic claims regarding the authenticity of Jesus's maturation by showing how Jesus indeed "recapitulates" or "reassumes" all stages of human growth. First, recapitulation in Christ restores the integrity of the human person as *body and soul*: Jesus was not human merely "in appearance" (*putativus*) but fully human in all stages of growth.[41] Second, Jesus sanctifies each stage by restoring its integrity and giving it full participation in God. Irenaeus writes: "For in what way would we be able to share in divine adoption [*huiothesia*], if we had not received through the Son communion from Him and in Him; if his Word had not, by becoming flesh, shared communion [in God] with us? Thus, he passed through every age, restoring [*apokatastasis*] for all the communion with God."[42] A human being does not, therefore, need to pass through all possible experiences in life, but rather to share in the restoration and communion already established by Jesus for each stage of human growth. Third, Christ's recapitulation of the human stages of growth precludes moral indifferentism. Jesus not only sanctifies each age, bringing it into communion with God, but also acts as

---

38 Irenaeus, *Against the Heresies* II, 22, 5 (SC 294, 220–22, lines 8–21; ACW 65, 74).
39 See Steenberg, "Children in Paradise," 16.
40 See Irenaeus, *Against the Heresies* II, 22, 5–6 (SC 294.2, 222–28).
41 See Irenaeus, *Against the Heresies* II, 22, 4 (SC 294.2, 220, lines 96–98). See also *Against the Heresies* III, 18, 6 (SC 211, 360–62, lines 1–3).
42 Irenaeus, *Against the Heresies* III, 18, 7 (SC 211.2, 366–67, lines 2–7).

its model. He shows each period of life what it is to be pious and just, what it means to be a teacher of the truth, and, most of all, how to be obedient to the Father. In short, he reveals the maturing virtues to the world.

After Adam and Eve's transgression, humanity lived in a state of destructive disobedience, but the incarnate Son subjects humanity to God and thereby restores full participation in the divine likeness: "He assigned humanity to be the imitator of God and established upon him the paternal law that man might see God; and he allowed man to receive the Father."[43] By recapitulating or living through these stages—even within his brief thirty-three years—Jesus "accustomed" (*adsuescere*) man to see God and God to dwell in man.[44] In effect, the recapitulation of the five ages—from infancy to maturity—"accustoms" the scope of each person's freedom to imitate Christ and obey the divine law, thereby restoring free participation in the divine likeness.

FROM IMAGE TO LIKENESS: ORIGEN AND BASIL

The movement from divine image to divine likeness requires grace, but God also calls for the cooperation of man. Many Fathers emphasize the importance of this synergy. For instance, the third-century theologian Origen of Alexandria (185–254) offers this account of man's maturation:

> The highest good, then, towards which every rational being hastens, which is also called the end of all things, is defined even by many among the philosophers in this way, that "the highest good is to become as far as possible like God." But this is not so much a discovery of theirs as, I think, taken by them from the divine books. For Moses, before all others, points to it when he describes the first creation of the human being, and saying *And God said, "Let us make the human being in our image and likeness."* Then he adds afterwards: *And God made the human being, in the image of God he made him; male and female he made them and he blessed them.* The fact that he said, *in the image of God he made him* and was silent about the *likeness*, indicates nothing else except that the human being obtained the dignity of the *image* in his first creation, but the perfection of the *likeness* was reserved for him at the consummation; that is, that

---

43 Irenaeus, *Against the Heresies* III, 20, 2 (SC 211.2, 390–92, lines 13–17).
44 Irenaeus, *Against the Heresies* III, 20 (SC 211.2, 392, lines 16–17).

he might acquire it for himself by the exercise of his own diligence in the imitation of God, so that while the possibility of attaining perfection was given to him in the beginning through the dignity of the *image*, he should in the end through the accomplishment of the works, complete in himself the perfected *likeness*.[45]

In Origen's description, man acquires the divine likeness through an *imitatio Dei*, an imitation of God through the exercise of moral virtue. The "likeness," therefore, indicates a "consummation" or "perfection" of the already gifted divine image. *Theōsis* emerges through the daily exercise of freedom to form a more perfect expression of the divine.

The Cappadocian bishop Basil of Caesarea (330–79) offers another perspective on this use of freedom. He defines Christianity as "likeness to God as is possible for humanity."[46] In turn, he explains the following distinction between the divine image and the divine likeness in man:

> By our creation we have the first [image], and by our free choice [*proairesis*] we build the second [likeness]. In our initial structure co-originates and exists our coming into being according to the image [*kat'eikona*] of God. By free choice we are conformed to that which is according to the likeness [*kath'homoiōsin*] of God. And this is what is according to free choice, the power exists in us but we bring it about by our activity [*energeia*] . . . And in giving us the power to become like God, he let us be artisans of the likeness to God, so that the reward for the work would be ours.[47]

Basil, as we shall see, does not deny the essential action of *God* in the supernatural fulfillment of man; yet he does not lose sight of man's free choice (*proairesis*) in maturation. Our activity (*energeia*), formed by God's activity, transforms the human mode of existence into that of the divine.

---

45 Origen of Alexandria, *On First Principles* III, 6, 1 (Behr, Vol. 2, 440–41).

46 Basil of Caeserea, *On the Origin of Humanity* 1, 17 (SC 160, 210, lines 26–27; PPS 30, 45).

47 Basil of Caesarea, *On the Origin of Humanity* 1, 16 (SC 160, 206, lines 1–7; PPS 30, 43). Basil also argues that both men and women share the divine image and the potential for divine likeness. "The woman also possesses creation according to the image of God, as indeed does the man. The natures are alike of equal honor, the virtues are equal, the struggles equal, the judgment alike . . ." (*On the Origin of Humanity* 1, 18 [SC 160, 212, lines 7–9; PPS 30, 45]).

VIRTUES AND THE LIKENESS OF GOD
Virtues as Divine Qualities: Gregory of Nyssa

The Fathers inherited centuries of reflections on the nature of virtue. Perhaps Aristotle's treatment of virtue remains best known today. His definition of virtue (*aretē:* "an excellence") as "the state (*hexis:* 'habit') which makes a man good and which makes him do his own work well" designates the qualities that perfect or mature the human being.[48] Virtues such as courage or justice therefore give form to the human and distinguish him from other objects in the world.

The Platonic tradition also shaped the Fathers' approach to the virtues in relation to God. Plato, in his dialogues, sought to define virtue and the scope of such virtues as justice and piety. By the conclusion of the *Meno*, for instance, Socrates has taken the reader through a variety of definitions—from virtue as a "kind of wisdom" to a "gift from the gods"—but he refrains from providing a single answer.[49] However, in the *Theaetetus*, Socrates makes an observation that will become fundamental for the Fathers of the Church:

> That is why a man should make all haste to escape from earth to heaven; and escape means *becoming as like God as possible*; and a man becomes like God when he becomes just and pious, with understanding. But it is not at all an easy matter, my good friend, to persuade men that it is not for the reasons commonly alleged that one should try to escape from wickedness and pursue virtue.[50]

"Becoming as like God as possible" through the pursuit of virtue becomes even more pronounced in later forms of Platonism. The third-century Neoplatonist Plotinus made assimilation to God the central theme of his ethics and the deepest desire of the philosopher. On the one hand, he distinguishes assimilation to God from any other form of imitation in the

---

48 Aristotle, *Nicomachean Ethics* 1106a21, trans. W. D. Ross, in *The Complete Works of Aristotle*, vol. 2, ed. Jonathan Barnes (Princeton, NJ: Princeton University Press, 1984), 1747.

49 See Plato, *Meno* 100b, trans. G. M. A. Grube, in *Plato: Complete Works*, ed. John Cooper (Indianapolis: Hackett, 1997), 897. John Rist's account of Plato's development in the dialogue reveals the philosopher to be seeking an objective ground for virtue and ethics, one not defined by the fickleness of human desires. "Plato's original aim in ethics was to fix the meaning of moral language, to offer an account of moral knowledge that would be valid universally and the problem as to whether this is possible remains with us today" (John Rist, *Plato's Moral Realism* [Washington, DC: Catholic University of America Press, 2012], 253).

50 Plato, *Theaetetus* 176a, trans. M. J. Levett and Myles Buryeat, in *Plato: Complete Works*, 195.

material realm: "Likeness to good men is the likeness [*homoiōsis*] of two pictures of the same subject to each other; but likeness to the gods is likeness to the model, a being of a different kind to ourselves."[51] In fact, one cannot even speak of God without acquiring those qualities that reflect the goodness of the divine: "In reality, it is virtue which goes before us to the goal and, when it comes to exist in the soul along with wisdom, shows God; but God, if you talk about him without true virtue, is only a name."[52] Virtues—"excellences"—therefore reflect divine qualities and reveal God to the soul.

Many Fathers would advance this theme in their own writings. Another Cappadocian bishop, Gregory of Nyssa (335–94), in his *Life of Moses*, teaches that virtuous living effects the participation in the infinite perfections of God: "Certainly, whoever pursues true virtue participates in nothing other than God, because he is himself absolute virtue. Since, then, those who know what is good by nature desire participation in it, and since this good has no limit, the participant's desire itself necessarily has no stopping place, but stretches out with the limitless."[53] For Gregory, deification demands not only divine action but also an *imitatio Dei*. Thus, in his sermons on the Beatitudes, he notes the true significance of man's practice of mercy: "Now I know that in many passages of the Divine Scripture holy men call the Divine Power merciful; as does David in the Psalms, Jonas in his prophecy, and the great Moses frequently in the Law. If, therefore, the term 'merciful' is suited to God, what else does the Word invite you to become but God, since you ought to model yourself on the property of the Godhead."[54] Virtues not only perfect or mature the human person; they also divinize through the graced imitation of God's qualities.[55] Yet, how can a mere human come to know and live the divine qualities?

---

51 Plotinus, *Ennead I*, 2, 7, in *Porphyry on Plotinus and Ennead I*, trans. A. H. Armstrong (Cambridge, MA: Harvard University Press, 1966), 147.

52 Plotinus, *Ennead II*, 9, 15, trans. A. H. Armstrong (Cambridge, MA: Harvard University Press, 1966), 285.

53 Gregory of Nyssa, *The Life of Moses* I, 7 (GNO 7.1, 4, lines 10–15; Malherbe and Ferguson, 31).

54 Gregory of Nyssa, *Sermons on the Beatitudes* 5 (GNO 7.1, 124, lines 18–24; ACW 18, 131).

55 See Gregory of Nyssa, *On the Christian Mode of Life* (GNO 8.1, 17, lines 23–25 and 48, lines 1–6; FC 58, 132): "When a just act and grace of the Spirit coincide, they fill the soul into which they come with a blessed life; but separated from each other, they provide no gain for the soul." Hans Boersma notes that "Gregory believes that the final gift of salvation will not be in proportion to the virtue that we have contributed. God's grace far outstrips our virtue." See

"Growing into God": Basil of Caesarea and Gregory of Nyssa

Basil the Great compares the maturation of the soul to the maturation of the body: "Growth is of two kinds, that of the body and that of the soul. But growth of the soul is progress to perfection [*eis teleiōsin*] through things learned, while bodily growth is development from smallness to the appropriate stature."[56] Indeed, man holds the unique privilege of "growing" spiritually as well as materially. "Thus 'grow' [*auxanesthe*] is said to the irrational animals in regard to perfection of body, in regard to the completion of nature; but to us 'grow' is said according to the inner human being, according to the progress which is growth into God [*kata tēn prokopēn tēn eis Theon ousan*]."[57] Man alone possesses the possibility of "growing into God" and becoming like the Creator.

Yet, why does God require the exercise of freedom for deification and not just the gift of grace and the Spirit? Why does God even allow for self-determination with its possibility of sin? Basil responds to these pressing questions:

> Accordingly, God does not love what is constrained but what is accomplished out of virtue. And virtue comes into being out of free choice [*proairesis*] and not out of constraint. But free choice depends on what is up to us. And what is up to us is self-determined. Accordingly, the one who finds fault with the Creator for not fashioning us by nature sinless is not different from one who prefers the non-rational nature to the rational, and what lacks motion and impulse to what has free choice and activity.[58]

If freedom were not to play a role in Christian maturation, it would not be *human maturation*. God so respects human freedom that he allows man both to grow in divine similitude through its right exercise and to suffer the consequences of its abuse.

Hans Boersma, *Embodiment and Virtue in Gregory of Nysa. An Anagogical Approach* (Oxford: Oxford University Press, 2013), 226.

56 Basil of Caesarea, *On the Origin of Humanity* 2, 5 (SC 160, 234, lines 2–3 and 236, lines 4–5; PPS 30, 51).

57 Basil of Caesarea, *On the Origin of Humanity* 2, 5 (SC 160, 236, lines 6–9; PPS 30, 51).

58 Basil of Caesarea, *Homily on Why God Is Not the Cause of Evil* 7 (PG 31, 329–54; PPS 30, 75).

Gregory of Nyssa shares his brother Basil's emphasis on human freedom in Christian maturation. In fact, he even describes the initiation of a life of virtue as a freely elected birth and growth: "We are in some manner our own parents, giving birth to ourselves by our own free choice [*proairesis*] in accordance with whatever we wish to be, whether male or female, molding ourselves to the teaching of virtue or vice."[59] Grace remains essential for maturation, but that grace embraces freedom.[60] The movement from infancy to adulthood requires a synergy between the human and the divine.

Gregory of Nyssa outlines an approach to this "growth into God" through the human appropriation of the names of Jesus. In his treatise *On Perfection*, he shows how the "names" or "titles" of Christ render this assimilation possible. The Scriptures contain many names for Christ, though Gregory focuses primarily on those found in the writings of St. Paul—for example, "the power of God and the Wisdom of God" (1 Cor 1:24), "peace" (Eph 2:14), "light inaccessible" (1 Tim. 6:16), "sanctification and redemption" (1 Cor 1:30), "great high priest" (Heb 4:14), and many others.[61] These names reveal ways in which Jesus makes God imitable. Thus, according to Gregory, "The marks [*xaraktēres*] of the true Christian are all those we know in connection with Christ. Those that we have room for, we imitate, and those which our nature does not approximate by imitation, we reverence and worship."[62]

Gregory then guides the reader through a series of practical reflections on the names that render one "synonymous" with Christ through authentic virtue. For example, the name "peace" means that, "Recognizing Christ as 'peace,' we shall exhibit the true title of Christian in ourselves through the peace in our life." To identify with the Lord means that we "deaden hatred

---

59 Gregory of Nyssa, *The Life of Moses* II, 3 (GNO 7.1, 34, lines 11–14; Malherbe and Ferguson, 55–56).

60 Without the grace of Christ, man cannot even set out on the journey: "By the grace [of Christ], the illusion beguiling man is dispelled, the dishonoring preoccupation with the flesh is extinguished and, by the light of truth, the soul, which received the knowledge, makes its way to the divine and its own salvation." See Gregory of Nyssa, *The Christian Mode of Life* (GNO 8.1, 41, lines 5–9; FC 58, 127).

61 Gregory of Nyssa, *On Perfection* (GNO 8.1, 175, lines 14–20; 176, lines 1–18; 178, 1; FC 58, 96–98).

62 Gregory of Nyssa, *On Perfection* (GNO 8.1, 178, lines 11–13; FC 58, 99).

in ourselves in order to achieve in our life what we believe is in him."[63] In another example, we learn that one even assumes Christ's name of "high priest" through a self-gift to God in all one's deeds.[64] In exploring the practical implications of Christological names, Gregory makes links to all the Scriptures, showing how the totality of God's Word, which always speaks of Christ, helps one in the process of divine assimilation: "For I think that if a person always keeps this in mind, that he is a participant in the revered name, when he is called a Christian according to the teaching of the apostles, he will also necessarily show in himself the power of the other names by which Christ is thought of, since through his life he is a sharer in each of them."[65] One therefore comes to know the divine qualities by coming to know and imitate Christ.

In general, Gregory demonstrates a positive view of change in the human person, since growth in virtue deifies. In fact, in his *Life of Moses*, Gregory posits that the human person never ceases to "move into God." Since God's being is infinite, the assimilation to the divine can never cease. Thus, Christian maturation is a paradox: it is both "a standing still and a moving."[66] When one finally enters God, one has come to the end of the journey in maturity; yet, at the same time, one continues to grow in the depths of the divine attributes. The inexhaustible joy of God becomes the eternal rest of the Christian.

CONCLUSION

This chapter examined the second pillar of Christian maturation, the exercise of human freedom for virtue. This growth takes on an added dimension for Christians, since the virtuous man not only becomes more human; he also becomes *more divine.* Jesus himself effected and revealed this reality through his own life by rendering God imitable in a human mode. When a Christian imitates Christ and acquires his virtues—meekness, courage, patience, and so on—he achieves evermore his end: the likeness of God.

---

63 Gregory of Nyssa, *On Perfection* (GNO 8.1, 183, lines 19–24 and 184, lines 1–5; FC 58, 102).

64 Gregory of Nyssa, *On Perfection* (GNO 8.1, 186, lines 7–20 and 187, lines 1–8; FC 58, 104–5).

65 Gregory of Nyssa, *On Perfection* (GNO 8.1, 209, lines 23–24 and 210, lines 1–4; FC 58, 119–20).

66 Gregory of Nyssa, *Life of Moses* II, 243 (GNO 7.1, 118, lines 1–8; Malherbe and Ferguson, 117).

I would note three other features of this growth in character. First, though this pillar of maturation requires the exercise of human freedom, it is still gifted with grace in the Spirit. The Holy Spirit aids all persons, no matter what age or state of life, in an imitation of Christ. Second, we must be patient with ourselves and with others in this growth in the virtues. Every person must struggle with particular vices, disordered attractions, addictions, and traumas. Meeting these challenges and healing the wounds demand a daily dying to the self, as well as the pursuit of Truth, Goodness, and Beauty. In fact, in the communion of the Church, we should be assisting one another in this formation founded in the love of Christ: the entire Body of Christ benefits from every spark of virtue in the world. Finally, we should always seek the virtues in the context of the Christ-form. Character formation should not become an end unto itself but rather a movement toward genuine maturity by making Christ present in a personal way to all.

Our freedom does not find its full application only in the growth in virtue. There is one further aspect to the way in which human freedom cooperates with the divine will for maturation: the gift of vocation.

TABLE 2.1
Selections illustrating formation in Christ in Gregory of Nyssa's *On Perfection*

TITLES	FORMATION
1. "Christian"	**Discipleship** "When we do understand this [name], we shall, as a consequence, also learn clearly what sort of persons we should be shown to be as a result of our zeal for this way of life and our use of His name as the instructor and the guide for our life" (FC 58, 96).
2. "The power of God and the Wisdom of God" (1 Cor 1:24)	**Worship of God** "When we behold the greatness of the composition of being, we may recognize His unspeakable power through what we comprehend, and, in order that, when we calculate how all things that did not exist before came into being . . . we then worship the incomprehensible wisdom of the One who thought of these things" (FC 58, 10).
3. "Peace" (Eph 2:14)	**Interior and exterior peace** "Therefore, let us also reconcile, not only those fighting against us on the outside, but also the elements at variance within us, in order that no longer may the 'flesh lust against the spirit and the spirit against the flesh' (Gal 5:17)" (FC 58, 103).
4. "True light" (John 1:9) and "sanctification" (1 Cor 1:30)	**Receiving and conforming to the gift of sanctification** "Let us prove by our life that we ourselves stand apart, being ourselves true sharers of His name, coinciding in deed and not in word with the power of his sanctification" (FC 58, 103).

5. "Redemption" (1 Cor 1:30)	**A Mind Focused on Christ** "If, then, we become slaves of the One who redeemed us, we shall look exclusively towards our Master, on the grounds that we no longer live for ourselves, but for the One who possesses us, because He gave His life for us" (FC 58, 103–4).
6. "Passover and High Priest" (1 Cor 5:7; Heb. 4:14):	**Self-sacrifice** "For it says: 'He delivered himself up for us, an offering and a sacrifice' (Eph 5:2). Through these words we learn this, that the person looking towards that One delivers himself as an offering and sacrifice and Passover, and will show himself to God as a living sacrifice, 'holy, pleasing to God,' becoming a reasonable 'service'" (FC 58, 104).
7. "A rock" (1 Cor 10:4)	**Fidelity and perseverance** "This word assists us in the firmness and permanence of our virtuous life, that is, in the steadfastness of our endurance of suffering, and in our soul's opposition and inaccessibility to the assaults of sin" (FC 58, 108).
8. "Hope" (Col 1:27)	**Hope in Christ** Upon the foundation of Christ "we build, putting down the principles of our life as a kind of foundation, and, through our daily achievements, we erect pure thoughts and actions upon it" (FC 58, 109).

CHAPTER 3

VOCATION AND COMMITMENT

John Paul II wrote that a vocation "indicates that there is a proper course for every person's development to follow, a specific way in which he commits his whole life to the service of certain values."[1] In turn, a *Christian* vocation, motivated by the greatest value of love for God and neighbor, requires the full dedication of self to a divine call and mission. The person *receives* the gift of maturity through grace and freely *assimilates* the self to God through growth in virtue, but a mature personality emerges through *the free response to vocation*. The saints of the early Church and the saints of all times demonstrate the truth of self-surrender to God's loving call: they shine forth as the most vivid persons of history.

This chapter explores the early Church's understanding of Christian commitment and maturity. However, before examining some ideas from the Fathers, this chapter considers important insights from the Scriptures.

---

1 John Paul II, *Love and Responsibility,* trans. H. T. Willetts (New York: Farrar, Straus, and Giroux, 1981), 256.

THE SCRIPTURES AND VOCATIONAL COMMITMENT

The Old Testament: Relationship and God's Sovereignty

The Hebrews generally divided the life cycle into three phases: childhood, youth, and the period from maturity to old age.[68] Though some debates linger regarding the exact ages that marked these periods, one may make some general estimations. Leviticus 27:1–8, for instance, provides specific ages of transition: (1) infancy—one month to five years; 2) childhood and youth—five to twenty years; (3) maturity and old age—twenty to sixty years.[2] Thus, one reached maturity at the age of twenty, when new responsibilities transformed a youth's life.

In turn, one can glean some characteristics of each stage from these texts. For example, youth may possess beauty and strength, but they lack wisdom and often fail to apply themselves to essential tasks: "The glory of young men is their strength, but the beauty of old men is their gray hair" (Prov. 20:29); "But the youth did not draw his sword; for he was afraid, because he was still a youth" (Judg. 8:20). The mature and elderly may experience ever-decreasing strength, but they also possess the gifts of wisdom and experience: "Remember also your Creator in the days of your youth before the evil days come and the years draw nigh when you will say, 'I have no pleasure in them.'" (Eccl 12:1); "Wisdom belongs to the aged and understanding to the old" (Job 12:12).

The mature man and woman discovered their roles and commitments not so much through a process of interior self-discovery as through their relationships in the community and with God. This idea conflicts radically with our notion of absolute autonomy and individual expression. Yet, the Hebrew youth achieving the mature status did not perceive a conflict between his freedom and his place in the community. The acceptance of social roles—fatherhood, motherhood, work, and so on—along with the ethical and cultic obligations stemming from their unique covenantal relationship with God, gave form to individual lives. Robert Devito notes that "individual responsibility, constituted in relationship rather than diminished

---

2 On these divisions and related scripture passages, see Hans Walter Wolff, *Anthropology of the Old Testament*, trans. Margaret Kohl (Philadelphia: Fortress Press, 1974), 121–22.

by it, was always compatible with the sovereignty of God."[3] Indeed, true life comes from a relationship with God, and authentic maturity comes from freely embracing this relationship along with its obligations: "The living, the living, give thanks to you, as I do this day; the father makes known to the children your faithfulness" (Isa. 38:19).[4]

However, the constraints of both the physical and social frameworks for maturation could never limit God's choice and call. In fact, in the Old Testament, God often defies conventions and expectations regarding "maturity." For instance, many biblical stories involve the granting of authority to the younger over the older members of a family. Jacob, through subterfuge, obtains his father's blessing instead of Esau, and continues to receive divine favor (Gen. 27:1–40). Samuel, to his surprise, is told to anoint David, the youngest of Jesse's sons (1 Sam 16:1–13). Solomon became king over his younger brothers (1 Chr 22:6–10). God also calls the elderly and gives them vigor normally found in youth: Moses "was a hundred and twenty years old when he died; his eye was not dim, nor his natural force abated" (Deut. 34:7). And all who "wait for the Lord shall renew their strength, they shall mount up with wings like eagles, they shall run and not be weary, they shall walk and not faint" (Isa. 40:31). Finally, God calls even to the faint of heart to heroic lives, as demonstrated by the missioning of Isaiah and Ezekiel (Isa. 6:1–3; Ezek. 2–3:1–3). These examples and more teach a fundamental truth: God's choice, call, and gifts matter more than any physical or social definitions.[5]

The Child Jesus in the Temple: Embracing the Father's Mission

The Scriptures record stories of Jesus's conception and birth that confirm his authentic humanity. Luke offers intimate details that show the infant Jesus truly to be Emmanuel, God-with-us: "And she gave birth to her first-born son and wrapped him in swaddling clothes, and laid him in a manger, because there was no place for them in the inn" (Luke 2:7). Matthew calls the infant

---

3 Robert DiVito, "Old Testament Anthropology and the Construction of Personal Identity," *Catholic Biblical Quarterly* 61, no. 2 (1991): 236.

4 "Death," therefore, means ceasing to praise God: "Do the shades rise up to praise you?" (Ps 88:10). On the centrality of relationships with the community and with God, see Wolff, "Anthropology," 106–7.

5 Frederick Greenspahn, *When Brothers Dwell Together: The Preeminence of Younger Siblings in the Hebrew Bible* (Oxford: Oxford University Press, 1994), 13–14; 151–60.

Jesus a *paidion,* which means "young child" (Matt. 2:13; Matt. 2:20–21). This *paidion* remained fully dependent on his parents for sustenance, shelter, and even protection from hostile powers; as an infant, he grew in the heart of a loving family and a community rooted in the Hebrew faith.

Only Luke gives us a striking story of Jesus as a child verging on youth (Luke 2:41–52). Mary and Joseph discover that Jesus is not with the caravan as they make their way home from Jerusalem. The frantic parents return and discover Jesus conversing with the teachers in the temple. Mary asks him, "Son, why have you treated us so? Behold, your father and I have been looking for you anxiously." Jesus responds, "How is it that you sought after me? Did you not know that I must be in my Father's house?" Luke concludes the story by stating, "And he went down with them and came to Nazareth, and was obedient to them; and his mother kept all these things in her heart. And Jesus increased in wisdom and in stature [*hēlikia*], and in favor with God and man."

What are we to make of the twelve-year-old Jesus conversing with the teachers? On the one hand, we clearly see signs of his youth: his dependence on and obedience to his parents; his growth in wisdom, stature, and favor with God and man. On the other hand, we see that Jesus demonstrates a maturity far beyond his age: he converses with the teachers, listening attentively and asking penetrating questions; he responds to a mission from his Father that draws him out of his family circle. The mystery of maturity in the Old Testament—God's choice, call, and gift bringing one beyond the strictures of physical maturation—becomes apparent in this passage. Jesus is fully human in his growth, but as the divine Son he gives form to a new humanity realized only in his perfect response to the Father.

Several other elements come to the fore. First, this passage shows the importance of obedience and vocation in Christian maturation. Jesus justifies his presence in the temple by his loving obedience to his Father: "Why do you seek me? Do you not know that I must be in the things of my Father (*en tois tou patros mou*)?" (Luke 2:49). Jesus leaves his parents because the "things" or "affairs" of his Father lead him back to the temple. His vocation defines his person; his eternal mission from the Father gives form even to his life on earth. Yet, despite the primacy of this vocation, Jesus respects the obligations of his young age and station through free obedience to his parents: "And he went down with them and came to Nazareth, and was obedient to them" (Luke 2:51). In short, Jesus shows us, even as a child (*teknon*), what mature freedom looks like in respect to divine mission and human relationships. Benedict XVI summarizes this revelation: "As Son, Jesus brings a new freedom: not the freedom of someone with no obligations, but the freedom of someone totally united with the Father's will, someone who helps mankind to attain the freedom of inner oneness with God."[6]

Second, at the end of the passage one hears the following: "And Jesus increased in wisdom and in stature, and in favor with God and man" (Luke 2:52). The wording echoes passages from the Old Testament. The first comes from Isaiah's prophecy of God's chosen one: "There shall come forth a shoot from the stump of Jesse, and a branch shall grow out of his roots. And the Spirit of the Lord shall rest upon him, the spirit of wisdom and understanding, the spirit of counsel and might, the spirit of knowledge and the fear of the Lord" (Isa. 11:1–2). The second suggests a reference to the growth of Samuel: "Now the boy Samuel continued to grow both in stature and in favor with the Lord and with men" (I Sam 2:26). Jesus, therefore, both fulfills God's promises to Israel—he is the "root of Jesse"—and recapitulates the prophetic mission seen typologically in Isaiah and Samuel: he has come to prepare the people for his Father.

Yet, this verse also presents the mystery of Jesus's authentic human growth that both models our maturation and makes Christian maturation possible. The word for stature, *hēlikia*, designates both physical growth and psychological-social maturation in time and history. Furthermore, this verse also makes clear that his maturation incorporates both the human and the divine: he finds favor before God and men. Thus, Jesus shows the qualities of authentic human maturity and, through the union of his divine and human natures, makes a new maturity possible in grace. Jesus does indeed grow physically within the parameters of his society, but, as will be demonstrated, he also exercises his divine-human freedom to form something radically new. This "growth in wisdom" implies temporal growth—a human maturation—and the manifestation of a divine quality, Wisdom. Again, Benedict XVI highlights the importance of Jesus's genuine humanity in his maturation: "And yet it is also true that his wisdom *grows*. As a human being, he does not live in some abstract omniscience, but he is rooted in a concrete history, a place and a time, in the different phases of human life, and this is what gives concrete shape to his knowledge."[7]

---

[6] Benedict XVI, *Jesus of Nazareth. Volume 3. The Infancy Narratives,* trans. Philip Whitmore (New York: Image, 2012), 120–21.

[7] Benedict XVI, *Infancy Narratives*, 127.

Origen of Alexandria, commenting on this verse (Luke 2:52), notes the human and graced "maturities" taking place in the one person of Jesus, concluding that Jesus unites and transforms two forms of human maturation: "There are two stages of life [*aetates*] in the Scriptures. One is corporeal, which is not in our power, but in the power of nature, while the other is of the soul, which is within our power, according to which, if we want, we grow daily and come to our maturity [*summitas*]."[8] According to Origen, we see in Jesus the union and perfection of the two *aetates:* the natural human physical maturation—the growth in stature—along with the *spiritual* development through the exercise of human freedom in union with the divine. Though one finds no more stories of Jesus's adolescence and young adulthood, one can be certain that his life dynamically unfolded in history as a recapitulation and elevation of the human. And in his public ministry—in obedience to his Father and prompted by the Holy Spirit—he continues this growth to its very end in the Ascension.

THE FATHERS AND VOCATIONAL COMMITMENT

The following sections examine three vocations and their contribution to maturation: (1) the universal call to holiness, the vocation of every Christian and every state of life; (2) marriage; and (3) priesthood. The monastic life will be considered more fully in subsequent chapters on asceticism and witness.

Maturity in the Universal Call to Holiness

The primary vocation of the Christian stems from the sacrament of Baptism: the universal call to holiness, the vocation to Christian maturity. Many Catholics attribute this insight to the Second Vatican Council, particularly to the document *Lumen gentium.* The Council Fathers wrote:

> The classes and duties of life are many, but holiness is one—that sanctity which is cultivated by all who are moved by the Spirit of God, and who obey the voice of the Father and worship God the Father in spirit and in truth. These people follow the poor Christ, the humble and cross-bearing Christ in order to be worthy of being sharers in His glory. Every person must walk unhesitatingly according to his own personal gifts

---

8 Origen, *On The Gospel of Luke* 20, 6 (SC 87, 286).

and duties in the path of living faith, which arouses hope and works through charity.[9]

Indeed, the Council pronounced these words in the hope that Christians would embrace their baptism as a true calling in the Church and in the world.

Yet, it would be better to say that the Council did not *discover* this important insight but rather *recovered* it and encouraged it in new ways. One finds in the writings of the Church Fathers, despite the differences in time and culture between them and the Second Vatican Council, a consistent exhortation to the faithful to assume their mission and grow in the likeness of Christ. Such entreaties resound most fully in baptismal catechesis—that is, in preached instructions for the catechumens, the "hearers," or those preparing for the sacrament, and neophytes, those recently baptized and still receiving formation in the faith. These sermons also voice this call to mixed audiences and in a variety of occasions, since it is a *universal* invitation to maturity in Christ. Thus, although the implications of this call do not always find their full articulation in the life of the Church, nonetheless one can still say that Vatican II in fact echoes the wisdom and pastoral concerns of the ancients.

※ ※ ※ ※ ※

The brilliant baptismal sermons of the renowned preacher John Chrysostom (347–407) provide evidence for this pastoral concern. Chrysostom makes clear that *all the baptized* —men and women, infants and adults, rich and poor—share the same gifts and responsibilities. He teaches catechumens the dignity of their impending transformation in Christ: "But henceforth do you, the new soldiers of Christ, both men and women—for the army of Christ knows no distinction of sex—cut off every [corrupt] habit of this sort, because you are going to receive the King of the universe. Cleanse your minds so thoroughly that no uncleanness darkens your thoughts."[10] The baptized faithful should rejoice in this new status, since they have become "stars":

> There are stars on earth because of Him who came from heaven and was seen on earth. Not only are these stars on earth, but—a second marvel—they are stars in the full light of day. And the daytime stars shine more

---

9 Vatican Council II, *Lumen gentium*, November 21, 1964, 41.
10 John Chrysostom, *On Baptism* 1, 40 (SC 50, 129, lines 4–13; ACW 31, 39).

brilliantly than those which shine at night. For the night stars hide themselves away before the rising sun, but when the Sun of Justice shines, these stars of day shine forth still more brightly."[11]

Baptism, in fact, represents a rebirth for the Christian, who now matures under the protection of the Mother Church. Indeed, the Church rejoices in the new children who emerge from the sacred waters: "So, too, that spiritual mother, the Church, looks on her children, rejoices, and is glad when she sees herself as a fertile field lush and green with this spiritual crop. Consider, my beloved, the excess of her love."[12] This rebirth and maturation even applies to actual infants who receive the gifts of the sacrament: "It is on this account that we baptize even infants, although they are sinless, that they may be given the further gifts of sanctification, justice, filial adoption, and inheritance, that they may be brothers and members of Christ, and become dwelling places for the Spirit."[13] The Church's divinely adopted children therefore defy the physical limitations of their age and enter a new frame of growth guided and empowered by the Spirit.

Chrysostom emphasizes the importance of freedom and growth in virtue for the baptized. They have acquired this freedom through their new status: "Now you are free and citizens of the Church ... You are not only free, but also holy; not only holy, but also just; not only just, but also sons; not only sons but also heirs; not only heirs, but also brothers of Christ."[14] They see their lives differently as they undertake the way of Christ: "This light clears away the mist from the spiritual eyes of these travelers, puts them on the right road, and makes them walk thenceforth on the path of virtue."[15] Once again, Chrysostom indicates that the new maturation the baptized experience through their enlightened freedom transcends the temporal limitations of their purely physical existence: "For this newness does not know old age nor is it subject to disease. It is not overcome by despondency, nor is it eclipsed by time. It yields to nothing; it is conquered by nothing except sin alone. Sin is for it the weight of years."[16] One *matures* as a free Christian, but

---

11 John Chrysostom, *On Baptism* 3, 1 (SC 50, 150, lines 1–4 and 152, lines 5–7; ACW 31, 56).
12 John Chrysostom, *On Baptism* 4, 1 (SC 50, 181, lines 5–9; ACW 31, 66).
13 John Chrysostom, *On Baptism* 3, 6 (SC 50, 154, lines 1–7; ACW 31, 57).
14 John Chrysostom, *On Baptism* 3, 5 (SC 50, 153, lines 3–8; ACW 31, 57).
15 John Chrysostom, *On Baptism* 4, 20 (SC 50, 193, lines 7–10; ACW 31, 57).
16 John Chrysostom, *On Baptism* 6, 21 (SC 50, 225–26, lines 6–10; ACW 31, 101).

one does not experience the decrepitude of *age*: the physical limitations of human freedom do not apply to the baptized growing in the divine likeness.

Chrysostom offers two striking examples of this universal call to holiness. In one sermon, he holds up the Roman centurion Cornelius (Acts 10:1–33) as a model for the Christian living in the world: "Here is a soldier who has had benefit of no instruction, who was tangled up in the affairs of this life, who has each day a thousand things to distract and bother him. Yet he did not waste his life in banquets and drinking and gluttony, but spent his time in prayer and almsgiving."[17] In fact, Cornelius illustrates the Christian life not only for the laity but for every Christian as such: "But he will be a trustworthy teacher not only for the military but also for all of us, as well as for those who have chosen the monastic life and those dedicated to the service of the Church."[18] Like Cornelius, one may achieve Christian maturity even in the midst of temporal affairs if one only embraces the gifts and mission of baptism.

In another homily, Chrysostom addresses both the neophytes and a group of "rustics," uneducated people from the countryside who came to join the assembly for worship. One gets the sense from this sermon that the regular congregation who gathered for Chrysostom's rhetorical pyrotechnics did not appreciate the bumpkins in their midst. Thus, Chrysostom calls the regulars to account by praising the additions to his flock: "Therefore, let us not look simply at their appearance and the language they speak, while we overlook the virtue of their lives. Let us observe carefully the angelic life they lead and the love of wisdom shown in their way of life."[19] The rustics exhibit Christian virtues and a hunger for God that one cannot find in the highly educated and powerful. "He [the rustic] has exact knowledge of things which the philosophers who take pride in their beard and staff have never even been able to imagine. Can you fail to take this as a clear proof of God's power?"[20] Holiness is not the province of the elite but the *telos* of all persons baptized in the Body of Christ.

---

17 John Chrysostom, *On Baptism* 7, 29 (SC 50, 244, lines 5–9; ACW 31, 116–17).
18 John Chrysostom, *On Baptism* 7, 31 (SC 50, 245, lines 1–4; ACW 31, 117).
19 John Chrysostom, *On Baptism* 8, 4 (SC 50, 249, lines 1–4; ACW 31, 120).
20 John Chrysostom, *On Baptism* 8, 6 (SC 50, 250–51, lines 6–9; ACW 31, 121).

Maturity in the Call to Christian Marriage and Family

In ancient Greek literature one finds the association between marriage (*gamos*) and maturity, or completion (*telos*).[21] The lexicon of the grammarian Hesychius of Alexandria (fifth or sixth century AD) contains some suggestive expressions of this association. For instance, the plural form *teleioi*—"mature," "complete," "fulfilled"—also indicates "those who have been married."[22] A complete or fulfilled household (*telesphoros oikos*) refers to a house of "one who has married and has children."[23] Scholars question whether marriage's association with *telos* in such examples denotes the marriage ritual itself—a rite of completion—or marriage as a transition from adolescence to adulthood. Both interpretations, however, show marriage as a transformation of the human person, a growth or movement to greater fulfillment in society. Marriage "matures" the couple and brings them into a new stage of life.[24]

In a commentary on Dionysius the Areopagite's *Letter 8*, which was attributed to Maximus the Confessor and later demonstrated to be by John of Scythopolis, one finds a further affirmation of marriage as a rite of maturity. The author of the commentary desires to explain *Letter 8*'s use of the expression "preparatory sacred prayers" (*kata proteleious euxas hieras*).[25] John of Scythopolis explains the phrase as follows:

> The term *proteleios* used to be used by the Athenians in reference to the prayers and sacrifices which precede the rite of marriage. This was because they used to refer to the wedding as a *telos*, inasmuch as it fulfils (*teleioun*) human life . . . But above all, they used to refer to the mysteries of a certain of their so-called gods as a *telos* and as a *teletē*, and this because it perfects the initiates and leads them into perfection. The great Dionysius applies the impious words of the Greeks to the true mystery when he uses the adjective *proteleios* to refer to those most perfect prayers which precede the mystery of communion and

---

21 For examples see Du Plessis, *Teleios*, 47–51.

22 Hesychius of Alexandria, *Hesychii Alexandrini Lexicon*, ed. Moriz Schmidt (Jeone, Sumptibustormam Dufti: Libreria Maukiana, 1867), 1442.

23 Hesychius of Alexandria, 1443.

24 See Du Plessis, *Teleios*, 49. See also Z. Philip Ambrose, "The Homeric Telos," *Glotta* 43 (1965): 60–61.

25 Dionysius the Areopagite, *Letter 8*, 6 (PTS 36, 188, lines 1–3).

request purification and an uncondemned partaking of the perfect and perfecting gifts . . .²⁶

In this passage, John both refers to the Greek understanding of marriage as maturation and perfection, and applies the term *telos* to the Mystery of the Eucharist as the true rite of maturation in the Church.

Given John's words above, does this mean the Christian tradition came to reject the idea of marriage as *teleios*? In fact, it has been argued that marriage as maturity or completion may even inform other marriage metaphors found in the New Testament and early commentators. In his *Letter to the Ephesians*, for example, Paul uses the metaphor of marriage for the unity between Christ and the Church: "'For this reason a man will leave his father and mother and cling to his wife, and the two will be one flesh.' This is a great mystery, but I say it refers to Christ and the Church" (Eph 5:31–32). Echoing the covenant and the messianic image from the Old Testament, Paul points to the union of Christ and the Church as a new phase in history and in the lives of Christians. As the man and woman come to a *telos* through the Mystery (*mysterion*) of marriage, so the Church and the Christian come to a *telos* through the union effected in Christ's passion.²⁷

In a later example, the tenth-century bishop Arethas of Caesaria made use of this metaphor in commenting on Revelation 19:7: "Let us rejoice and exult and give him the glory, for the marriage of the Lamb has come, and his Bride has made herself ready." The Church as bride, notes Arethas, now finds fulfillment in Christ: "The spiritual marriage of the Lord is presented by the betrothal [*mnēsteia*] with the Church, and thus it is a perfect [mature] marriage [*teleios gamos*]. And the Holy Apostle alludes to this when writing to the Corinthians: 'I presented you to Christ as a holy bride united to one husband [2 Cor 11:2].'"²⁸ Arethas transfers the idea of human marriage as *telos* to the mature union of Christ with the Church, which Christ consummated on the Cross and now sustains in eternal glory. Thus, marriage as *teleios* serves as a living witness to the maturation of the Church in union with Christ.

---

26 John of Scythopolis (attributed to Maximus the Confessor), *Scholia in Epistulas S. Dionysii Areopagitae* (PG 4, 553D; Rorem and Lamoreaux, 258). For more examples see Hendryk Bolkestein, *Telos ho gamos* (Amsterdam: Noordhollandsche uitgevers-maatschappij, 1933), 23.

27 On marriage as *teleios* as an informing idea behind the scriptural metaphor, see Du Plassis, *Teleios*, 50.

28 Arethas of Caesarea, *Commentary on Apocalypse* 57 (PG 106, 740A).

Marriage therefore forms a couple and their family for maturity in society and, in light of the Christological metaphor, for maturity in the life of the Church. Since each marriage between man and woman is the *image* of Christ's marriage with the Church, each human marriage strives to become the *likeness* of Christ's union with the Church. A married couple assumes their responsibilities as adults in the community, but together they seek the holiness evident in the Christ-Church union of the Eucharist.

This section turns once again to John Chrysostom for vocational insights. While Chrysostom certainly worked within the societal norms and expectations of his times—especially the norms that governed gender roles—nonetheless, his teachings still offer sound pastoral wisdom and practical counsels. For Chrysostom, the universal call to holiness applies to every class and role in society: "Whether you are a slave, or have an unbelieving wife, or are marked with the sign of circumcision, you are called, and that is what matters."[29] Yet marriage represents the primal vocation in God's creation:

> From the beginning, God in His providence has planned this union of man and woman, and has spoken of the two as one: "male and female He created them" and "there is neither male nor female, for you are all one in Christ Jesus." There is no relationship between human beings so close as that of husband and wife, if they are united as they ought to be.[30]

A married couple seeks to imitate Christ in their union and find their fulfillment together in the next life. The husband, for example, follows the example of Christ's sacrifice on the Cross: "And even if it becomes necessary for you to give your life for her, yes, and even to endure and undergo suffering of any kind, do not refuse. Even though you undergo all this, you will never have done anything equal to what Christ has done. You are sacrificing yourself for someone to whom you are already joined, but He offered Himself up for one who turned her back on Him and hated Him."[31] One may say that human marriage and family are an *image* of the Christ-Church union that grows ever more into the *likeness* of the Christ-Church communion:

---

[29] John Chrysostom, *Homily 19 on 1 Corinthians*, 3 (PG 61, 156; PPS 7, 34).
[30] John Chrysostom, *Homily 20 on Ephesians* (PG 62, 135; PPS 7, 43).
[31] John Chrysostom, *Homily 20 on Ephesians* (PG 62, 137; PPS 7, 46).

Paul shows that a man leaves his parents, who gave him life, and is joined to his wife, and that one flesh—father, mother, and child—results from the commingling of the two. The child is born from the union of their seed, so the three are one flesh. Our relationship to Christ is the same; we become one flesh with Him through communion, more truly one with Him than our children are one with us, because this has been His plan from the beginning.[32]

In turn, both husband and wife seek virtue, such that their union might more fully reflect divine love. Chrysostom teaches that the Christian couple's love will mature even after death. He advises the husband to tell his wife "that you love her more than your own life, because this present life is nothing, and that your only hope is that the two of you pass through this life, in such a way that in the world to come you will be united in perfect love."[33] Yet, even now, a virtuous marriage serves as the unifying and sanctifying force of every community: "The love of husband and wife is the force that welds society together."[34]

Unsurprisingly, marriage finds its greatest joy and responsibility in family. Chrysostom tells the couple to help their children to grow in the divine qualities, the virtues, so that they might mature as true Christians:

> Great will be the reward in store for us, for if artists who make statues and paint portraits of kings are held in high esteem, will not God bless ten thousand times more those who reveal and beautify His royal image (for man is the image of God)? When we teach our children to be good, to be gentle, to be forgiving (all these are attributes of God), to be generous, to love their fellow men, to regard this present age as nothing, we instill virtue in their souls and reveal the image of God within them.[35]

Chrysostom does nothing less than call parents to bring out the fullness of the divine image in which their children have been created. This mission prevents parents from ever turning in on themselves: "If the man who buried his one talent gained nothing, but was punished instead, it is obvious that

---

32 John Chrysostom, *Homily 20 on Ephesians* (PG 62, 140; PPS 7, 51).
33 John Chrysostom, *Homily 20 on Ephesians* (PG 62, 447; PPS 7, 61).
34 John Chrysostom, *Homily 20 on Ephesians* (PG 62, 136; PPS 7, 44).
35 John Chrysostom, *Homily 21 on Ephesians* (PG 62, 134; PPS 7, 71).

one's own virtue is not enough for salvation but the virtue of those for whom we are responsible is also required."[36]

Parents should not be daunted before this mission, since God has given and will give them the gifts they need: "Whether you are poor or rich, you can do this; these lessons are not learned from a skillful professor, but from divine revelation."[37] As a Mystery, marriage bestows the grace both to form a family and to give a glimpse of the Kingdom of God on earth.

Maturity in the Call to Priesthood

An examination of the priesthood concludes these reflections on Christian vocation. In earliest Christianity, the priesthood encompassed a variety of roles and functions: liturgical celebrations, ministry of God's word, pastoral care, and governance.[38] This vocation presented a commitment and responsibilities that could frighten even the strongest of men—even a rhetor and ascetic as powerful as Gregory of Nazianzus.

In the year 358, Gregory of Nazianzus, happily ensconced in monastic seclusion in Pontus on the Black Sea, received a summons from his father, the elderly Bishop of Nazianzus, in southwestern Cappadocia. The obedient son returned to discover the real motivations behind his recall: he was reluctantly ordained—on Christmas day, 358 or 359 AD[39]—to the priesthood in order to make him the potential successor to the ailing bishop.

He did not stay for long. Shortly after, Gregory fled the diocese and returned to isolated tranquility. But this time of prayerful retreat opened Gregory's eyes to the importance of his new duties, and he returned to the

---

36 John Chrysostom, *Homily 21 on Ephesians* (PG 62; PPS 7, 72). David Rylaarsdam notes that, according to Chrysostom, Christian households would transform the world: "If society were made up of Christian homes, culture would be transformed. According to Aristotle, households were a basic unity of society. By addressing the formation of families, Chrysostom was articulating a vision that made use of classical norms, but adapted them for Christian purposes." See David Rylaarsdam, *John Chrysostom on Divine Pedagogy: The Coherence of His Theology and Preaching* (Oxford: Oxford University Press, 2014), 222.

37 John Chrysostom, *Homily 21 on Ephesians* (PG 62, 151; PPS 7, 69).

38 For an examination of the wider scope of Christian priesthood in early Christianity, see Joseph Mueller, SJ, "Why Did Ancient Christians Call Their Ministers Priests?" in *New Narratives for Old: The Historical Method of Reading Early Christian Theology*, ed. Anthony Bridgman and Ellen Scully (Washington, DC: Catholic University of America Press, 2022), 273–92.

39 For an overview of Gregory's understanding of priesthood, see Suzette Phillips, "Fit or Unfit for Priesthood? Priestly Ministry According to the Writings of Gregory of Nazianzus," *Logos: A Journal of Eastern Christian Studies* 41/42 (2001): 34–38.

diocese sometime before Easter 362. Needless to say, the people were rather angry about being abandoned by the famous orator and ascetic. In order to reconcile himself with the diocese, Gregory composed a defense for his actions, now known as the *Second Oration or "On the Flight."*

Gregory primarily bases his defense on his fear before the overwhelming responsibilities and awesome dignity of the priesthood. The priest has the duty to unite the souls in his care with God. In fact, he seeks to lead each *image* of God to full maturity, "to provide the soul with wings, to rescue it from the world and give it to God, and to watch over that which is in his image, it abides, to take it by the hand if it is in danger, or restore it, if ruined, to make Christ to dwell in the heart by the Spirit and, in short, to deify [*theon poiēsai*], and bestow heavenly bliss upon one who belongs to the heavenly host."[40] This, according to Gregory, is the most astounding and humbling aspect of the priestly art—that a mere man, wrapped in his own spiritual struggle, is called to lead and sanctify the people for union with God. Unlike Jesus, the priest is a "divinizer" who himself must be "deified." How can a man respond to such a call without trembling?

The priest exercises a variety of ministries as he grows in maturity and leads others to the fullness of Christ. He must preach God's word and teach right doctrine, avoiding the assertion of his own ideas and opinions.[41] He assumes the awesome work of sharing in the very priesthood of Christ—a gift of which no man is worthy:

> Who can mold, as clay figures are modelled in a single day, the defender of the truth, who is to take his stand with angels, and give glory with Archangels, and cause the sacrifice to ascend to the altar on high and share the priesthood of Christ, and renew the creature, and set forth the image, and create inhabitants for the world above, aye and, greatest of all, be God, and make others to be God [*theopoiesonta*]. I know whose minsters we are, and where we are placed, and whither we are guides. I know the height of God and the weakness of man, and, on the contrary, his power.[42]

---

40 Gregory of Nazianzus, *Oration 2*, 22 (SC 247, 118, lines 10–13 and 120, lines 14–15).
41 See Gregory of Nazianzus, *Oration 2*, 35 (SC 247, 132, line 1 and 134, lines 2–13; NPNF II-7, 212).
42 Gregory of Nazianzus, *Oration 2*, 73 (SC 247, 186, lines 12–18; NPNF II-7, 220).

The priest, in short, "conducts souls to their espousals [*numphagōgon tōn psuxōn*]," bringing them to the Bridegroom who makes others divine through the intimate union of God's love.[43]

The priest should tremble before this vocation; yet this fear should not drive him away, but rather inspire him to seek maturity in his own life. He may lead others to the divine likeness if he submits to Christ:

> Since then I knew these things, and that no one is worthy of the mightiness of God, and the sacrifice, and priesthood, who has not first presented himself to God, a living, holy sacrifice, and set forth the reasonable, well-pleasing service, and sacrificed to God the sacrifice of praise and the contrite spirit which is the only sacrifice required of us by the Giver of all; how could I dare to offer to Him the external sacrifice, the antitype of the great mysteries, or clothe myself with the garb and name of priest, before my hands had been consecrated by holy works.[44]

Gregory found the strength to return through the virtues of obedience and trust in God. The prophets trembled—and even ran!—when God chose them, but they discovered that God would make up for their weaknesses. Gregory, inspired by their example, submits to God's will: "I fell down and humbled myself under the mighty hand of God, and asked pardon for my former idleness and disobedience . . . but now I am commissioned to exalt him in the congregation of the people, and praise him in the seat of the elders."[45] He made a commitment before God and the people, and in that commitment he would discover his weakness and his true strength—the strength to shepherd a people to Christ. In his *First Oration*, an Easter sermon, he beautifully summarizes this discovery:

> A Mystery anointed me; I withdrew a little while at a Mystery, as much as was needful to examine myself; now I come in with a Mystery, bringing with me the Day as a good defender of my cowardice and weakness; that he who today rose again from the dead may renew me also by His Spirit; and, clothing me with the new man, may give me to his new creation,

---

43 Gregory of Nazianzus, *Oration 2*, 77 (SC 247, 190, line 2; NPNF II-7, 220).

44 Gregory of Nazianzus, *Oration 2*, 95 (SC 247, 212, lines 1–7 and 214, lines 8–10; NPNF II-7, 223–24). On the need for the priest to grow in virtue see Phillips, "Fit or Unfit for Priesthood?" 350–52.

45 Gregory of Nazianzus, *Oration 2*, 115 (SC 247, 236, line 11 and 238, lines 1–3; NPNF II-7, 227).

to those who are begotten after God, as a good modeler and teacher for Christ, willingly both dying with him and rising again with him.[46]

CONCLUSION

In imitation of Christ, every Christian must embrace a call. The universal call to holiness stems from baptism, and every Christian—single, married, ordained, or religious—lives out this foundational vocation; marriage inspires the family in the journey toward the likeness of Christ's union with the Church; and the priesthood forms the priest and his flock for full communion with the Lord. All these examples demonstrate that Christian maturity requires *a commitment* that leads one out of the self and toward God and neighbor.

This concludes the review of the three pillars of maturity: form and finality; virtue and character; and vocation and commitment. And yet, sadly, remarkably few Christians want to "grow up" in Christ. Why is this the case? The next chapter will consider the reasons for this failure of Christians and, very often, of the Church in the world.

---

46 Gregory of Nazianzus, *Oration 1*, 2 (SC 247, 74, lines 1–8; NPNF II-7, 203).

CHAPTER 4

Satan's Tantrum

[Evil] is the irrational movement of natural powers toward something other than their proper goal [telos], based on an erroneous judgment.

Maximus the Confessor[1]

One cannot resolve the mystery of evil with a trite formula. On the one hand, as a privation,[2] evil exists as a parasite feeding upon the good. Augustine, drawing on this theme, defines evil as an absence or deficit of the good: "For evil has no positive nature, but the loss of good has received the name 'evil.'"[3] Evil, as a "non-thing," deserves no place in the world. On the other hand, evil ravages history as an active force. A perverse intelligence seems to direct its movement through generational cries of anguish and

---

[1] Maximus, *Responses to Thalassius*, Introduction 1, 2, 12 (SC 529, 132, line 214 and 134, line 215; Constas, 82).

[2] On the Neoplatonist approaches to the problem of evil, see Eric Perl, *Theophany: The Neoplatonic Philosophy of Dionysius the Areopagite* (Albany: State University of New York Press, 2007), 53–56.

[3] Augustine, *The City of God* XI, 9 (CCSL 48.2, 330, lines 70–71; WSA I-6, 10).

rage. One cannot dismiss it as a mere "lack" in the fabric of reality. How to reconcile these two experiences of evil—evil as a parasitic "non-thing" and evil as an active force—with the truth of God's goodness?

Jews and Christians have grappled with the problem of theodicy—the problem of reconciling the goodness of God with the experience of suffering and evil—for millennia. The Christian response takes form in the mystery of the Cross, in the innocent God-man who suffers for our sake. Yet, in accounting for the active and systematic nature of evil, Christians have also turned to the Scriptures and tradition to identify the conscious source of evil: Satan or the demonic. Such a turn does not exonerate the deliberate contributions of human beings to the sum of suffering in the world; yet it does attribute the inspiration for seemingly unmitigated evil to spiritual substances of remarkable cunning and wrath.

This chapter will take a different perspective on the demonic and the manner in which human beings sadly adopt the demonic mode of existence. The Fathers of the Church teach that God created the demons as good, as angels, and that these angels fell owing to the corruption of their own will. As Maximus the Confessor wrote, "The demons are not evil by nature, but they have become evil through the misuse of their natural powers."[4] I would propose that one may also call the perversion of the demonic will "elected immaturity"—that is, the deliberate rejection of maturation in Christ. In fact, as this chapter will show, one may describe the tragedy of the demonic rebellion as a "tantrum"—a pathetic, yet deadly, refusal to accept the gift of growing in the divine likeness. The dynamic of the demonic is the free opposition to the three pillars of maturity and a perpetual war against those who embrace the pillars. These infantile beings of pure intellect subject the goodness of the cosmos to their delirium and strive to make human beings like themselves.

REFUSING FORM AND FINALITY

The letter of Jude provides some insights regarding the fall of the angels and the emergence of the demonic. In verses 6–7, we read: "And the angels that did not keep their own position [*archēn*] but left their proper dwelling [*oiktērion*] have been kept by him in eternal chains in the deepest darkness until the judgment of the great day." The verse alludes to certain extrabiblical

---

[4] Maximus, *Centuries on Charity* III, 5 (*Ceresa-Gastaldo*, 146).

traditions regarding fallen angelic beings, especially those found in I Enoch,[5] and it appears within a brief series of examples in which rebellion against God receives a condign punishment.[6] Furthermore, this passage informs us that the demons reject their origin or beginning (*archē*)—the same *Beginning* found in the book of Genesis and the prologue of the Gospel of John: "In the *Beginning* [*archē*] God made heaven and earth"; "In the *Beginning* [*archē*] there was the Word [*Logos*], and the Word was with God, and the Word was God." Maximus the Confessor offers an interpretation of this enigmatic verse:

> The Beginning, which those angels did not keep, is possibly the *logos* according to which they were created; or it is the natural power for deification given to them according to grace; or again, it is the order of the position given to them according to their worthiness of grace. But the dwelling is either heaven; or it is the wisdom which they were created to inhabit according to the habit [*hexis*] of those goods beyond thought—for Scripture knows how to name the house of Wisdom; or the guardianship of the natural goods given to them and of the additional goods of the uncontaminated divinity, which they, rebelling, abandoned . . . Having been shaped willingly and entirely according to this ignorance, they were deprived of the distribution of the blessed, all-illuminating, and uncontaminated light, squandering for non-being the entire spiritual power naturally given to them.[7]

Although Maximus offers various related interpretations of Jude 6, he especially emphasizes the demonic refusal of that which gives them shape or form. First, the *logos* (word or defining principle) of the angels' creation defines *what* each angel is—that is, it provides the limits and potencies of angelic nature. Rejecting this *Beginning* therefore includes a refusal of their *End*, the fulfillment of their nature and what gives them form. The fallen angels-demons-embrace the illogical (*alogikos*, the "nonword") in the false hope of defining themselves. Second, the angels abandon the gift of grace,

---

[5] See I Enoch 20:7-9: "He [Uriel] said, 'This place is a prison for the angels. Here they will be confined forever'" (Nickelsburg and VanderKam, 41–42).

[6] "The reader is hereby struck by the utterly incomprehensible nature of departing from the truth. The angels' fate is commensurate with their privilege." Charles Daryl, "The Angels Under Reserve in 2 Peter and Jude," *Bulletin for Biblical Research* 15, no. 1 (2005): 46. Along with 2 Peter 2:4, one sees here an emphasis on the angelic rebellion through blasphemy by aspiring to the "position" of God. See Kim Paiaoannou, "The Sin of the Angels in 2 Peter 2:4 and Jude 6," *Journal of Biblical Literature* 140, no. 2 (2021): 405.

[7] Maximus, *Responses to Thalassius* 11 (SC 529, 202, lines 12–17 and 204, lines 29–32).

thereby canceling the boon of divine life itself. They want to exist according to their own misguided authority. And finally, through these rejections, the demons became *disordered*—that is, they lost their places in the Holy Order (*hierarchia*) through which they would be assimilated to God. In short, the angels plunge from the origin that defines them and assimilates them to God—a prideful turn from form and finality.

Maximus gives the chilling result of the demonic rejection of the divine Beginning: to reject the Beginning leads to the pursuit of nonbeing. The refusal to mature, to grow in the divine likeness, results in a self-destructive movement toward annihilation. As beings created good, they can never achieve this *nothing*—that is, a total erasure of their being. The *Logos* continues to define them. Yet, privations of their prelapsarian habits (*hexeis*) now deform the grandeur of their former existence.[8] Demons are angels who therefore refuse to be angels. They are now creatures who, though created for glory, prefer the squalor of nihilism; intellects who choose privations over their graced faculties.

Augustine of Hippo offers another enlightening analysis of the demonic rejection of form and finality. In his *De Genesi ad litteram*, Augustine identifies God's creation of the light as the moment when angels come into existence. The angels then receive infused knowledge of God's creation in the six days—that is, the *hexaemeron* first unfolds within the angelic intellect. The cycle of each day in the *Genesis* narrative, in fact, represent the angels' reception of knowledge of creation (Day Knowledge), their acknowledgment of the created gift (Evening Knowledge), and the referral of this creation back to the Creator God who gifts and defines it (Morning Knowledge). Table 4.1 outlines the pattern of God's creation in the angelic intellect.

This pattern—Day, Evening, Morning—applies especially to the angels' reception of their own being and self-knowledge: in coming to know themselves *as creatures* (Evening Knowledge), they must then refer that knowledge back to their Beginning who gives them form (Morning Knowledge). "After acknowledgment of its [the angel's] own proper nature, of its not being

---

8 "Among rational creatures, irrationality, mindlessness, and rashness are privations of reason, mind, and perception. Yet privations are posterior to habits. Therefore, there once existed among the demons, reason, mind, and pious perception" (Maximus, *Centuries on Charity* III, 5 [Ceresa-Gestaldo, 147]).

Table 4.1

...Day...	...Evening came...	...Morning followed...
God gives the angels their being and knowledge of themselves. In subsequent days, angels receive knowledge of God's creatures.	Angels grow in knowledge of themselves and creatures. They know that they are not God.	Angels refer their self-knowledge and knowledge of creatures back to God for the reception of form and the glorification of God.

what God is, it goes back to praising the light which God himself is, and *by which it is formed as it gazes upon it*."[9] They must adhere (*adhaerere*) to God for the reception of their form and for their assimilation to God.[10] Even the celestial powers therefore depend on their participation in God for their stability of nature.

The demonic emerges from an angelic preference for Evening Knowledge—that is, for knowing themselves and creation without reference to their origin and end in God. Augustine writes that "If the angelic nature were to turn to itself, and to take greater pleasure in itself than in the one it is made blessed by sharing in, it would swell with pride and fall."[11] In effect, the demons, by reveling in their own creaturely existence apart from God, come to see themselves and all creation as formless and protean. While unfallen angels, in adhering to God, remain fully what they are by gazing upon their creator, the demons fall into the instability of the passions and spiritual deformation.[12] Their Evening Knowledge becomes a perpetual Night that obscures the truth, corrupts the intellect, and denies the hope of fulfillment.

---

9 Augustine, *The Literal Meaning of Genesis* IV, 22, 39 (CSEL 28.1, 121, lines 19–22; WSA I-13, 264; emphasis added). See also Elizabeth Klein, *Augustine's Theology of Angels* (Cambridge: Cambridge University Press, 2018), 48–49.

10 On the deification and the adherence to God in Augustine, see David Meconi, SJ, *The One Christ* (Washington, DC: Catholic University of America Press, 2013), 67–72.

11 Augustine, *Literal Meaning of Genesis* IV, 24, 41 (CSEL 28.1, 124, lines 13–15; WSA I-13, 265–66).

12 See Augustine, *City of God*, IX, 7–8 (CCSL 47, lines 255–56; WSA I-6, 286–88. See also Ellen Muehlberger, *Angels in Late Ancient Christianity* (Oxford: Oxford University Press, 2013), 52–53.

What does this turn from the divine *telos* mean for demonic existence? First, as suggested by Maximus, the demons have fallen from the Holy Order or hierarchy into disorder. Dionysius the Areopagite, the mysterious fifth-century author of the *Celestial Hierarchy*, defined hierarchy as an order of grace, directed toward the Hierarch who is Christ, which assimilates each member proportionally (*kat'analogian*) to the divine.[13] Demons therefore abandoned the Hierarch and no longer exist in a communion, thereby choosing a vicious parody of their former glory.[14] Their ranks now inspire rivalry and competition, not the harmony of deification.

Second, since the demons no longer look to the source that gives them form, they are now primarily *amorphous*.[15] In the stories of the desert Fathers and Mothers—the ancient monks or solitaries—one hears that the demons have no set mode of appearance; rather, they manifest themselves as deformed beasts. Although such visions terrorized the anchorites, they also demonstrate the demonic inability to sustain a form. In Athanasius's *Life of Antony*, the story of the famous fourth-century desert ascetic, one learns of the arrival of demons into Antony's abode: "The demons, as if breaking through the building's four walls, and seeming to enter through them, were changed into the forms of beasts and reptiles. The place immediately was filled with the appearances of lions, bears, leopards, bulls, and serpents, asps, scorpions and wolves, and each of these moved in accordance with its form."[16] In reality, these fallen powers are impotent: "But because they have no power to act, they do nothing except issue threats. If they had the power, they would not delay, but immediately would perform the evil for which they have a ready inclination—especially evil directed against us."[17] As undefined, they

---

13 See Dionysius the Areopagite, *The Celestial Hierarchy* 1, 1-3 (PTS 36, 8, lines 14-21 and 9, lines 1-15).

14 John Cassian suggests that the demons maintain their hierarchy even after their fall: "The differences of rank, which the adversary powers are said to possess on the model of the holy and heavenly virtues, they either continue to hold now from the station in which each one of them was originally created, or else those who plunged from the heavens laid claim among themselves, in a perverse imitation of the forces that remained there and to the degree that each had fallen into evil, to the formers' grades and titles of rank." See John Cassian. *The Conferences* VIII, 8, 3 (SC 54, 17; ACW 57, 296-97).

15 John Cassian states that demons have lost that which stabilizes them: "For, as you said, discipline and measure can never be observed in undisciplined things." See John Cassian, *The Conferences* VII, 19, 1 (SC 42, lines 260-61; ACW 57, 259).

16 Athanasius of Alexandria, *Life of Antony* 9, 5 (SC 400, 160, lines 21-24; Gregg, 38).

17 Athanasius, *Life of Antony* 28, 6 (SC 400, 214, lines 25-28; Gregg, 52-53).

may tempt humans to follow their mode of existence, but in the end, they cannot make anything good or beautiful, since they have no *real* power in the world. They elected immaturity over fulfillment, and now they twist and turn with the winds of rage.

REFUSING VIRTUE AND CHARACTER

Dionysius the Areopagite explains the connection between the demonic turn from the form and the fall into chronic viciousness. Lacking any stability in form, they now deprive themselves of the stability of character and habit (*hexis*) as well:

> And, furthermore, devils cannot be evil since they owe their origin to God. The Good is the creator and preserver of good things. If they are called evil it is not in respect of their being, since they owe their origin to the Good and were the recipients of a good being, but rather because being is lacking to them by virtue of their inability, as scripture puts it, "to hold on to their original source [*archē*]" (Jude 6). For, I ask you, in what way are the demons evil except in the fact that they have put an end to the habit and the activity of divine good things . . . Their deviation is the evil in them, their move away from what befits them. It is a privation in them, an imperfection, a powerlessness. It is a weakness, a lapse, an abandonment of the capacity they have to be mature [*teleiotēta*].[18]

The horror of the elected immaturity leads to a disintegration of character and personality. The absence of virtues results in decay through the vices.

In considering the demonic rejection of virtue and character, one finds further clarity and inspiration in the traditions of the desert Fathers and Mothers, as well as among those later monastics who would bring their wisdom to the far reaches of the Roman Empire. These ascetics trekked into the desert and wilderness spaces to dedicate themselves to discipline and prayer and, in the new Christian Empire, they replaced the radical witness once manifested in the blood of the martyrs. Although aspects of their radical behavior would require moderation over time, they nonetheless always

---

18 Dionysius, *The Divine Names* 4, 23 (PTS 33, 171, lines 8–26; Luibheid [adapted], 90–91).

conveyed the seriousness of spiritual combat with our disordered attractions and with the ordinary activity of demonic influence.

The most renowned of these figures, the fourth century monk Saint Antony of the Desert, shared his insights regarding the effects of virtues or vices on human beings:

> For virtue exists when the soul maintains its intellectual part according to nature. It holds fast according to nature when it remains as it was made—and it was made beautiful and perfectly straight . . . As far as the soul is concerned, being straight consists in its intellectual part's being according to nature, as it was created. But when it turns from its course and is twisted away from what it naturally is, then we speak of the vice of the soul.[19]

The monk's growth in virtue *perfects* nature and brings him ever closer to the prelapsarian state of humanity.[20]

Yet vice also "twists" humans away from the integrity of their nature and prevents them from actualizing their potential as human beings. Thus, in his great speech on spiritual combat, Antony teaches his brothers how demons attempt to impede humans' progress toward natural maturity and how to respond: "The demons, therefore, if they see all Christians, and monks especially, laboring cheerfully and advancing, first make an attack by temptation and place hinderances [*skandala*] to hamper our way, to wit, evil thoughts [*logismoi*]. But we need not fear their suggestions, for by prayer and fasting, and faith in the Lord their attack immediately fails."[21] Demons, therefore, want human freedom to embrace their own deformed state through the adoption of vices or evil thoughts, though humans can preserve their growth and integrity through dedication to purity and the virtues.

❈ ❈ ❈ ❈ ❈

The fourth-century monk Evagrius Ponticus made explicit links between the demonic and the vices, or "evil thoughts" (*logismoi*). In his writings, he often uses evil thought (*logismos*) and demon interchangeably: he identifies the two as one. The demons, in a sense, *become* a privation; they

---

19 Athanasius, *Life of Antony* 20, 5–6 (SC 400, 188, line 20 and 190, lines 21–28; Gregg, 46).
20 See Athanasius, *Life of Antony* 14, 1–6 (SC 400, 172, lines 1–14 and 174, lines 15–33).
21 Athanasius, *Life of Antony* 23, 1–2 (SC 400, 198, lines 1–7; Gregg, 48).

define themselves by what they take away from themselves and from others. Evagrius therefore counsels his brethren to discern and to respond to the attacks from the vices as a form of combat against demons:

> It is necessary to recognize the differences among the demons, and to note their circumstances of coming. We shall know from the thoughts—and the thoughts from the deeds—which of the demons are rare and which are more preponderous; which kind are unremitting and which are lighter; which burst forth in crowds and which snatch the mind into blasphemy. It is necessary to know these things in order that, whenever the thoughts begin to move the particular material, before we are thrown far from our state, we may say something against them and we may reveal the demon who is present.[22]

Each demon has a specialty, a vice that gives him a parody of genuine form. This diversity of vicious identities, however, does not lead to complete anarchy, since the evil spirits still must work in tandem to drag a human into corruption. Evagrius lists eight principal demons or thoughts that feed on human integrity in a strict order: gluttony, lust, avarice, sadness, anger, acedia, vainglory, and pride.[23] He describes their activity as follows:

> Among the demons who set themselves in opposition to the practical life [*praktikē*], those ranged first in battle are the ones entrusted with the appetites of gluttony, those who make to us suggestions of avarice, and those who entice us to seek human esteem. All the other demons march along behind these ones and in their turn take up with the people wounded by these. For example, it is not possible to fall into the hands of the spirit of fornication, unless one has fallen under the influence of gluttony; nor is it possible to trouble the irascible part, unless one is fighting for food or wealth or esteem ... To put it briefly, no one can fall into a demon's power, unless he has first been wounded by those in the front line.[24]

Demons no longer assimilate themselves to God through the virtues, but they assimilate themselves and human beings to the wounds in the goodness

---

22 Evagrius, *The Praktikos* 43 (SC 171, 598–600).
23 Though Evagrius himself will change the order slightly in certain works.
24 Evagrius Ponticus, *On Thoughts* 1 (SC 438, 148–52, lines 1–17; Sinkewicz, 153).

of the fallen world. Only a vicious hierarchy of destruction gives them any order or place in existence.

Evagrius offers a helpful comparison between the angels and the demons that illustrates the refusal of virtue and character. Angelic thoughts—the thoughts angels inspire in human beings—"are concerned with the investigation of the natures of things and search on their spiritual principles."[25] Angels inspire humans to contemplate the truth of things as given in their forms and *logoi* or defining principles. A human responding to such inspirations could look upon a bar of gold not with avarice, but with the desire to know the gold as a divine gift. Demonic thought, however, "neither knows nor understands these things, but without shame it suggests only the acquisition of sensible gold and predicts the enjoyment and esteem that will come from this."[26] The demons therefore deny form and first principles, leading persons instead to the irrational exploitation of goods. The demon and the vicious human only perceive creation as food for consumption with no genuine end or fulfillment.

REFUSING VOCATION AND COMMITMENT

In Matthew 16:13–20, Peter proclaims Jesus to be the Messiah. Jesus responds, "Blessed are you, Simon son of Jonah, for this was not revealed to you by flesh and blood, but by my Father in heaven." Yet the joy of this moment is short lived. Not long after, Jesus tells the disciples that "he must go to Jerusalem and suffer many things at the hands of the leaders, the chief priests and the teachers of the law, and that he must be killed and on the third day be raised to life" (Matt 16:21). Jesus's prediction does not fit with Peter's vision of the Messiah, and so the zealous apostle rebukes him: "Never Lord! This shall never happen to you!" Jesus's response drowns out the impetuosity of the fisherman: "Get behind me, Satan! You are a stumbling block to me; you do not have in mind the concerns of God, but merely human concerns" (Matt 16:23). Peter, in attempting to impede Jesus's mission from the Father, gave voice to the demonic and became a hindrance or stumbling block (*skandalon*) for the journey toward the Passion and the Cross. In fact, in seeking to have Jesus avoid these tribulations in order to save his life, Peter renewed the trials of Jesus in the desert, when Satan sought to turn Jesus from his

---

25 Evagrius Ponticus, *On Thoughts* 8 (SC 438, 176, lines 1–5; Sinkewicz, 158).
26 Evagrius Ponticus, *On Thoughts* 8 (SC 438, 178, lines 14–21; Sinkewicz, 158).

mission toward "merely human concerns": material goods, power, and the false instrumentalization of God.

Because of the rejection of their divine *telos*, demons also refused their vocation. The name angel comes from the Greek word for "messenger": *angelos*. Thus, the name does not designate so much a genus or species as a mission or vocation. In the Old Testament, when a divine messenger (Hebrew: *mal'akh*; Greek: *angelos*) speaks to a human, the messenger's voice often disappears in favor of God's. This means that the angel identifies so fully with his mission that God assimilates the angelic voice to the divine.[27]

Yet the fallen angels abandoned their vocation within the harmony of the *Logos* in favor of their own words: they ceased to be messengers or *angeloi* and became demons (*diaboloi*, "devils" or "slanderers"). No longer assimilated to the divine voice, they descended into discord, the cacophony of divided hearts (*dis:* apart, divided; *cor:* heart). They now eschew commitment to anything other than themselves and they thus take on the anti-mission of slanderers; they transform language from truth to lies. Such a tragic state emerges from abandoning their Beginning and their call.

The desert Fathers and Mothers accepted their vocation of voluntary exile from the patterns of the world and a life according to the rhythm of Christ. Their mission on behalf of themselves and the Church involved maturation and progress in becoming fully what God called them to be. John Cassian (360–435), who brought his experiences of Eastern monasticism to the West, speaks of the challenges faced by the athletes of the desert:

> It is true that each day we zealously practice meditation in every discipline and make progress, going from uncertain beginnings to a sure and solid skill and coming to know what at first we had known obscurely or been completely unaware of, proceeding by what I could call firm steps in the practice of that discipline and becoming perfectly and easily versed in it. Nonetheless I find that, as I strive laboriously in this purity, I have progressed in this alone: I know what I cannot be [*ut sciam quid esse non possum*]. Hence, I think that nothing but hard work will be my lot as a

---

27 See, for instance, the call of Gideon in Judges 6. We first hear: "And *the angel* of the Lord appeared to him [Gideon] and said, 'The Lord is with you, you mighty man of valor.'" (Emphases mine.) Yet, after Gideon's response, we hear, "And *the Lord* turned to him and said, 'Go in this might of yours and deliver Israel from the hand of Mid'ian: Do not I send you?" Gideon's true interlocutor is not the angel, but God himself. See Judges 6:11–18.

result of such contrition of heart, so that there may always be a reason for weeping. Yet I do not cease to be what I must not be.[28]

The monk strives to be what he cannot be with his own strength, that is, to become fully mature in Christ. His struggle therefore includes heroic discipline, but more importantly it requires divine grace.

Demons seek to exploit the frustration voiced above—"Yet I do not cease to be what I must not be"—and cajole monks into abandoning their vocation. In the writings of Evagrius Ponticus, the demons use the vices not only to corrupt the character of the monk but also to send them back into world:

> But if all alone one should stand ready in the wrestling school of the desert and if the body should in some way happen to be impaired by illness, then does the devil present voluntary exile to the soul as especially difficult, suggesting that the tasks of virtue can be performed not (merely) in a particular place, but by any manner of life, and that at home with the consolation of family it could attain the prizes of freedom from possessions with less weariness.[29]

The barrage of demonic discouragement therefore falsely suggests that the path to maturity can be found in another state of life: one should walk away from vocation in favor of an always undefined future.

How can the monk respond to such seductive enticements? Evagrius wrote a handbook for fighting demons called *The Antirhētikos* in which he provides scriptural responses to particular demons-thoughts. He selects many of these scripture verses to aid the monk in his fidelity toward his vocation. For example:

> **Thought:** Against thoughts that advise us and say, "Do not live severely; through fasting and constant labor you will weary your weak body."
>
> **Response:** "And he labored forever, and he will live to the end, so that he will not see corruption when he sees sages dying (Ps 48:10)."[30]
>
> **Thought:** Against the thought that seeks, on the pretext that profit will fill its need, to be entangled in the affairs of the world.

---

28 John Cassion, *The Conferences* VII, 3, 1 (SC 42, 246; ACW 57, 248).
29 Evagrius Ponticus, *To Eulogios* 3 (Sinkewicz, 30).
30 Evagrius Ponticus, *The Antirhētikos* 1, 14 (Brakke, 56).

Response: "No one serving in the army gets entangled in everyday affairs; the soldier's aim is to please the enlisting officer. And in the case of an athlete, no one is crowned without competing according to the rules (2 Tim. 2:4–5)."[31]

Thought: Against the thoughts that entice us to go out in the world in order to benefit those who see us.

Response: "The words of crafty persons are gentle, but they strike into the depths of the bowels (Prov. 26:22)."[32]

The scriptural verses in these examples unmask the wiles of the demons and encourage the monk to persevere. God's Word also serves as an apotropaic; that is, the sacred verses can drive off evil. Just as Jesus quoted scripture to defeat the Devil in his attempts to distract him from his mission, so the monk—or any Christian—may call upon the holy texts as weapons against infidelity.

CONCLUSION

The fallen angels chose immaturity over fulfillment in Christ. Their refusal of form and finality results in instability and deformation; their rejection of virtue and character leads to personal decay; and their resounding "No!" to vocation shapes a life without meaning or hope. Only their drive to make humans like themselves—corrupt infants in an eternal tantrum—keeps them active, seductive, and dangerous.

We now live in a culture that encourages elected immaturity, and therefore we should not show surprise before the many tantrums that explode around us. A world devoid of form, the unity of the virtues, and self-gift through commitment can only descend into chaos. I will explore this crisis further in the concluding chapter, which treats the hope the Fathers offer us for a restoration of maturity in ourselves and in our society.

---

31 Evagrius Ponticus, *The Antirhētikos* 3, 55 (Brakke, 97).
32 Evagrius Ponticus, *The Antirhētikos* 7, 18 (Brakke, 151).

❋ ❋ ❋ ❋ ❋

PART 2

❋ ❋ ❋ ❋ ❋

The Means of Maturation

CHAPTER 5

Maturation and the Scriptures

This and the following two chapters explore several means for coming to Christian maturity. Christian maturity requires the divine gift—that is, the grace of participation in the Christ-form, and ordered freedom, that is, growth in virtue and a personal response to vocation. In the life of the Church, every Christian and every Christian community receive inspired means for these three elements of growth: the Scriptures, the Sacraments—celebrated in the life of the Church—and asceticism. Thus, God does not abandon humanity to a program of frustrating self-improvement and social amelioration; rather, God actively shepherds his flock through word, sign, communion, tradition, and practice.

Since the Second Vatican Council, the Church has recovered a deeper sense of the power of God's Word, the Scriptures. *Dei Verbum* states: "For in the sacred books, the Father who is in heaven meets His children with great love and speaks with them; and the force and power in the word of God is so great that it stands as the support and energy of the Church, the strength of faith for her sons, the food of the soul, the pure and everlasting source of spiritual life."[1] In fact, the council echoes the belief of the Fathers of the Church,

---

1 *Dei Verbum*, 21.

as demonstrated in these words from Origen of Alexandria: "I think each word of divine scripture is like a seed whose nature is to multiply diffusely ... Its increase is proportionate to the diligent labor of the skillful farmer or the fertility of the earth."[2] The *holiness* of God's Word enters human hearts through reading or hearing, and then it exercises its transformative power. It serves as the way of encounter—"the Father ... meets His children"—and guides all those who apply the labor of their lives to its pattern.

Brian Daley writes that the early Church's approach to the reading of the Scriptures was that of a "hermeneutic of piety"—that is, "a sense that the ultimate test for the adequacy of any explanation of a Biblical passage's meaning is the degree to which that explanation fits with Christian 'religion,' with the Church's traditional understanding of the holiness and uniqueness of the God who reveals himself in the Biblical story, and with the holiness to which all the story's hearers are called in response."[3] Indeed, for the Fathers of the Church one must receive the Scriptures as the very pattern of one's life such that its story may convey the Christ-form. One cannot read God's Word as one would a work of philosophy or the legacy of a lost civilization; one must read it rather as an encounter with the living mystery of God. The Fathers of the Church therefore offer a perspective on engaged reading and hearing that shapes Christian maturation.

MATURITY AND TYPOLOGY: IRENAEUS AND RECAPITULATION IN CHRIST

Irenaeus of Lyons affirms that human nature develops through maturation and growth. Contrary to the gnostics, he teaches that God liberates man not *from history*; instead, God liberates and matures man *within history*.[4] Three Irenaean teachings form the basis for man's historical maturation. First, since all created things are *not God*, they are not perfect by nature. In the case of humans, this means that their perfection must come through temporal growth and movement. Irenaeus writes:

---

2 Origen of Alexandria, *Homilies on Exodus* 1 (SC 321, 42; Heine, 227).

3 Brian Daley, "Is Patristic Exegesis Still Usable? Reflections on Early Christian Interpretation of the Psalms," *Communio* 29 (2002): 202.

4 "Irénée refuse un tel salut; il ne s'agit pas de se libérer du monde, mais de libérer le monde auquel nous appartenons." See A. Luneau, *L'histoire du salut chez les Pères de l'Eglise: La Doctrine des ages du Monde* (Paris: Beauchesene, 1964), 93.

Inasmuch as God is indeed always the same and unbegotten as respects Himself, all things are possible to Him. But created things must be inferior to Him who created them, from the very fact of their later origin; for it was not possible for things recently created to have been uncreated. But inasmuch as they are not uncreated, for this very reason do they come short of the perfect. Because, as these things are of later date, so are they infantile; so are they unaccustomed to, and unexercised in, perfect discipline. For as it certainly is in the power of a mother to give strong food to her infant, [though she does not do so], as the child is not yet able to receive more substantial nourishment; so also it was possible for God Himself to have made man perfect from the first, but man could not receive this [perfection], being as yet an infant.[5]

Given man's natural imperfection—his "infancy"—time itself therefore serves as the field of growth. One matures in history and in the world: "God had power at the beginning to grant perfection to man; but as the latter was only recently created, he could not possibly have received it, or even if he had received it, could he have contained it, or containing it, could he have retained it."[6] As one created "recently," man must grow in his reception of God's gifted *telos*.

Second, sin impedes man's maturation in history. Although created in the image of God and moving toward his likeness, man chose to reject this inheritance, the gift of maturation. Irenaeus writes, "For as, among men, those sons who disobey their fathers, being disinherited [*alienati; allotrioi*], are still their sons in the course of nature, but by law are disinherited, for they do not become the heirs of their natural parents; so in the same way is it with God—those who do not obey Him being disinherited by Him, have ceased to be His sons. Wherefore they cannot receive His inheritance."[7] As we shall see, the sin of Adam resulted in man's perpetually infantile state of rebellion, an elected refusal to come to his fullness.

Third, as a previous chapter has shown, the incarnate Son realizes man's maturation in himself and brings humanity into his fulfillment. In becoming man, the son *accustoms* humanity to grow in the divine likeness:

---

5 Irenaeus, *Against the Heresies* IV, 38, 1 (SC 100.2, 944, lines 3–15 and 946, lines 16–17; ANF 1, 521).

6 Irenaeus, *Against the Heresies* IV, 38, 2 (SC 100.2, 950, lines 45–47; ANF 1, 521).

7 Irenaeus, *Against the Heresies* IV, 41, 3 (SC 100.1, 986, lines 37–39 and 988, lines 40–43; ANF 1, 525).

> For He was made *in the likeness of sinful flesh* that He might condemn sin, and then cast it out of the flesh as condemned; and also, that He might invite humankind to His own likeness, inasmuch as He designated humans as imitators of God, led them to the Father's law that they might see God, and granted them the power of receiving the Father. He was the Word of God who dwelt in humanity, and was made the Son of Man in order that He might accustom [*adsuescere; ethizein*] humankind to receive God, and accustom God to dwell in humanity according to the Father's good pleasure.[8]

Thus, the entire life of the Incarnate Word heals wounded humanity and unites God to restored humanity. One may come to participate in the reality effected by the Son: humanity formed in the divine likeness.

✵ ✵ ✵ ✵ ✵

Given these foundational principles, how do the Scriptures provide us with a means for Christian maturation? In Irenaeus's reading of the Scriptures, one discovers the story of man's maturation within salvation history in four stages. First, *man is created in his infancy*, that is, he must grow into the likeness of God through his relationship with Divine Word. Irenaeus describes the prelapsarian state of Adam and Eve:

> Now having made the man lord of the earth, and everything that is in it, He secretly appointed him as lord over those who were servants [i.e., angels] in it. But they, however, were in their full-development, while the lord, that is, the man, was very little, since he was an infant, and it was necessary for him to reach full-development by growing in this way ... And so beautiful and good was the Paradise, [that] the Word of God was always walking in it: He would walk and talk with the man prefiguring the future, which would come to pass, that He would dwell with him and speak with him, and would be with mankind, teaching them righteousness. But the man was a young child, not yet having a perfect deliberation, and because of this he was easily deceived by the seducer.[9]

---

8 Irenaeus, *Against the Heresies* III, 20, 2 (SC 211, 390, lines 67–71 and 392, lines 72–75; ACW 64, 96).

9 Irenaeus, *On the Apostolic Preaching* 12 (Behr, 47). Matthew Steenberg notes that, "Irenaeus' language of 'child' and 'infant' throughout his corpus is essentially offered as an observation of what he sees as a natural state, a commentary on the necessary and ordinary condition of

The fall, of course, impedes Adam and Eve's full relationship with the Word and permanently stunts their growth. They remain "infants" in their sin, as demonstrated by the Scriptural accounts of humanity's violence and disintegration.

Next, God initiates *a relationship with man under the Law* such that man might recover the fullness of the divine image and come into the likeness. All that takes place in the stories of the Patriarchs, despite the regular deviations of the people from God's way, prefigure the future fulfillment in Christ. From Abraham, to Moses, to David, and to the Babylonian Exile and the promises of the Prophets, God "accustoms" man through words, signs, wonders, and commands. God shepherds wandering humanity toward the Christ. For instance, Irenaeus assumes the classic typology of the Exodus as prefiguring Christ's Passion: "He saved the sons of Israel from this, revealing in a mystery the Passion of Christ, by the slaughtering of a spotless lamb and by its blood given to be smeared on the houses of the Hebrews as a guard of invulnerability: the name of this mystery is the Pasch, source of liberation."[10] The Scriptures therefore offer the history of this "accustoming" of humanity in moral and spiritual growth as preparation to receive Christ.

The third stage occurs through *Christ's recapitulation and perfection of man's salvation history* in the Incarnation and the Paschal Mystery. We have seen in a previous chapter how Irenaeus describes the reality of Christ's recapitulation of all the stages of human growth—from infancy through death—and realizes man's maturity in the Resurrection. Christ's life is also a "compendium," a recapitulation, of the maturation within salvation history: since all the types of salvation history—Adam, Noah, Moses, David, and so on—and the accompanying events point to Christ, Christ himself perfects or matures all that came before. "He [Christ] recapitulated [*anekephalaiōsato*] in Himself the long unfolding of humankind, granting salvation by way of compendium [*syntomō*], that in Christ Jesus we might receive what we had lost in Adam, namely, to be according to the image and likeness of God."[11] Jesus Christ is the New Adam who obeys the Father; the New Moses who achieves the true Exodus from sin and death; the New David who rules and conquers the enemy of death. Christ summarizes and realizes all that took

---

a newly created being rather than a judgment on its moral and social character" ("Children in Paradise," 7).

10 Irenaeus of Lyons, *On the Apostolic Preaching* 25 (Behr, 56).

11 Irenaeus, *Against the Heresies* III, 18, 1 (SC 211, 342, lines 9–12; ACW 64, 87–88).

place in the previous ages, making participation in his life possible: "Really, what way could we be partakers of filial adoption, unless we had received through the Son participation in Himself; unless His Word, having become flesh, had granted us communion in God? For that reason, He also came [that is, lived] through every age [*hēlikias*], restoring to all the participation in God."[12] The New Testament therefore provides the form of Christ's recapitulation and fulfillment of salvation history.

The final stage takes place in *Christ's return*. At the consummation of history, in the second coming of Christ, creation's *telos* comes to pass: "God, therefore, is one and the same, who rolls up the heaven as a book, and renews the face of the earth; who made the things of time for man, so that coming to maturity [*maturescens; akmasas*] in them, he may produce the fruit of immortality [*telesforēsē tēn athanasian*]; and who, through His kindness, also bestows [upon him] eternal things, that in the ages to come 'He may show the exceeding riches of His grace' (Eph 2:7)."[13] Christ's second coming demands wakefulness and preparedness, but it also inspires hope: "He shall, at His second coming, first rouse from their sleep all persons of this description, and shall raise them up, as well as the rest who shall be judged, and give them a place in His kingdom."[14] The Scriptures therefore give the hope of the future age, the promise of full maturity in God.

※ ※ ※ ※ ※

The Scriptures, for Irenaeus, recount a love story between God and humanity that becomes clear in the coming of Christ. Christ does not erase all that came before but rather reassumes it and retells it in its final form. In the words of John Behr, "The apostolic proclamation of the crucified Christ is composed from the texture of Scripture, no longer proclaimed in the obscurity of types and prophecies, but clearly and concisely, in a résumé [recapitulation]: what was prolix becomes condensed, what was incomprehensible becomes comprehensible, the unseen becomes seen, the invisible visible—the Word becomes flesh."[15] The whole story of the Christ—from

---

12 Irenaeus, *Against the Heresies* III, 18, 7 (SC 211, 366, lines 172–78; ACW 64, 91).

13 Irenaeus, *Against the Heresies* IV, 5, 1 (SC 100.1, 424, lines 1–5; ANF 1, 466).

14 Irenaeus, *Against the Heresies* IV, 22, 2 (SC 1001.1, 688, lines 35–38; ANF 1, 494).

15 John Behr, *Irenaeus of Lyons. Identifying Christianity* (Oxford: Oxford University Press, 2013), 138.

Genesis to Revelation—demonstrates the authentic maturation of humanity in God's grace.

A Christian, therefore, can never take the stance of Marcion of Sinope, who rejected the Old Testament, since without the history of Israel *the story of the Christ* would become not only incomprehensible but also ineffective. This does not mean to deny the transformative power of even a single verse of the Scriptures nor does this deny the essential graces of the Incarnation and the Paschal Mystery; yet it does point to the effective unity of the two Testaments in the life of the Church and the life of each Christian. For, just as Christ recapitulates the previous ages in himself, so also each Christian and the Church must relive salvation history through grace. Paul Quay's masterful *The Mystery Hidden for the Ages in God* expresses the full import of Irenaeus's understanding of Scriptures: "Even as Jesus was the perfect Jew, who relived all the stages of the life of Israel, rectifying what was done amiss and perfecting all else, so each Christian who lives by the grace of Christ is able to relive Israel's life in and with Jesus. Only by such a life does he become able eventually to live as befits a son of God, directed in all things by the Holy Spirit."[16] The baptized Christian, in his or her infancy, therefore comes to know and live salvation history through reading and living the Scriptures in a Christological key.

The maturation of Israel, in all its twists and turns, must also become the Christian's maturation. The types who point to Christ—Moses the liberator, David the King, and so on—reveal the movement from immaturity to maturity. Just as "the boy still remains in the man," so the story of Israel remains ever in the person of Christ, not abandoned, but revealed as healed and whole. Personal and communal meditation on the Scriptures now allows the individual Christian and the community to come to the fullness of Christ.

MATURITY AND HISTORY: AUGUSTINE AND THE SIX-DAY CREATION (HEXAEMERON)

In his *Confessions*, Augustine describes how his early encounters with the poorly rendered Latin translations of the Scriptures inspired only his scorn and derision. In his words, immaturity impeded his full appreciation of the text's profundity: "My swollen pride recoiled from its style and my intelligence failed to penetrate to its inner meaning. Scripture is a reality that

---

16 Paul Quay, *The Mystery Hidden for Ages in God* (New York: Peter Lang, 1995), 9.

grows along with little children, but I disdained to be a little child and in my high and mighty arrogance regarded myself as grown up."[17] Augustine desperately needed the formation that the Scriptures offer, but his pride impeded him from becoming a child in the faith and sitting at the Lord's feet to learn scriptural truths. Only after years of wandering and, above all, the experience of listening to Ambrose of Milan's preaching, did Augustine discover the spiritual depths hidden beneath the literal sense of the texts:

> Another thing that brought me joy was that the ancient writings of the law and the prophets were now being offered to me under quite a different aspect from that under which they had seemed to me absurd when I believed that your holy people held such crude opinions; for the fact was that they did not. I delighted to hear Ambrose often asserting in his sermons to the people, as a principle on which he must insist emphatically, *The letter is death-dealing, but the spirit gives life* (2 Cor 3:6). This he would tell them as he drew aside the veil of mystery and opened to them the spiritual meaning of passages which, taken literally, would seem to mislead.[18]

This discovery of the "spiritual sense" of the Scriptures, unlocked through allegory and typology, allowed Augustine to interpret God's Word in ways that aided his own and his congregation's maturation. His preaching and writing on the sacred texts aimed to convey these healing effects of God's love. Jason Byassee writes that Augustine grounds his exegesis in beauty: "By this we mean whether it is 'fitting' with the words on the page, with the figure of Christ, and with the need of the congregation present to have its affections redirected aright once more."[19] One could say that the Scriptures and their proclamation redirect the children of God toward their fulfillment in Christ, to the beautiful splendor of their maturity in God.

※ ※ ※ ※ ※

One example of Augustine's exegesis for maturation is found in his allegorical interpretations of the Hexaemeron, the six days of Creation in *The Book of Genesis*. In several works, he adopts a schema, found in both

---

17 Augustine, *Confessions* III, 5, 9 (O'Donnell, 26; WSA I-1, 80).
18 Augustine, *Confessions* VI, 4, 6 (O'Donnell, 61; WSA I-1, 140).
19 Jason Byassee, *Praise Seeking Understanding: Reading the Psalms with St. Augustine*. (New York: Eerdmans, 2007), 133.

Christian and non-Christian writings, of the six ages of man: each day of the Genesis narrative corresponds to a stage of humanity's maturation in salvation history.[20] These interpretations generally follow the divisions given in Matthew 1:17: "So all the generations from Abraham to David were fourteen generations and from David to the deportation to Babylon fourteen generations, and from the deportation to Babylon to the Christ fourteen generations." Thus, the Scriptures reveal and effect God's restoration of humanity through a historical maturation process—a process of generation that is ongoing in the Church and in the life of the individual Christian.

The version that appears in his *On Genesis Against the Manicheans* makes explicit links to human growth from infancy to adulthood.[21] Table 5.1, on the following page, summarizes the allegorical correspondences and movement.

The table shows how Augustine offers a vision of history, from the fall of humanity to the beginning of renewal in Christ, that would give Christians hope in God's providence and non-Christians the confidence to enter the Church.[22] For instance, in his *Instructing Beginners in the Faith*, a work that provides advice on how to present the faith to inquirers, Augustine gives an account of these six ages to show the movement of salvation history. His presentation serves as an invitation, as if he were to say: "Come find rest in Christ, the fulfillment of history!" History passes, but it is not without form—the Christ-form—and each person may discover hope in its consummation. "Therefore, the person who longs for true rest and true happiness must take his hope away from perishable and transitory things and place it in the word of the Lord, so that, by holding fast to that which remains forever, he together with it may also remain forever."[23]

In fact, Augustine develops his allegory further in *The City of God* to show that the senescence of humanity—the final stages of man's decay from sin—receives a new birth and maturation in the seventh and eighth days.

---

20 For a summary see Luneau, *L'histoire du salut*, 283–85; R. A. Markus, *Saeculum: History and Society in the Theology of St. Augustine* (Cambridge: Cambridge University Press, 1970), 17–21. Some works in which Augustine makes use of these schema are *De Genesi contra manicheos, De diversis questionibus octoginta tribus, De catechizandis rudibus,* and *De Trinitate*.

21 Augustine, *On Genesis Against the Manichees* I, 24, 42 (CSEL 91, 111, lines 1–19 and 112, lines 20–23).

22 For a discussion of the apologetic and catechetical uses of this schema, see Luneau, *L'histoire du salut*, 329.

23 Augustine, *Instructing Beginners in the Faith* 16.24 (CCSL 46, 149, lines 29–33; WSA 5, 65).

Table 5.1

Day / Age	Creation	Maturation in Savlvation History
First day/first age Gen. 1:3	Creation of the light and its separation from the darkness.	From Adam to Noah: the infancy of humanity (*infantia*). Ten generations.
Second day/second age Gen. 1:6	The separation of the waters above from the firmament below.	From Noah to Abraham: the childhood of humanity (*pueritia*). Ten generations.
Third day/third age Gen. 1:9	The separation of the waters under the heavens from the dry land.	From Abraham to David: the adolescence of humanity (*adolescentia*). Fourteen generations.
Fourth day/fourth age Gen. 1:14	The separation of day and night; the creation of the stars in the heavens.	From David to Babylonian captivity: the youth of humanity (*iuventus*). Fourteen generations.
Fifth day/fifth age Gen. 1:20	The creation of flying creatures, sea creatures, etc.	From Babylon to Christ: the old age of humanity (*gravitas*). Fourteen generations.
Sixth day/sixth age Gen. 1:26	The creation of the living soul of man.	From Christ to the consummation of history: the birth of the new man from the old man (*senectus*). No fixed generations; ongoing.

Man's rest and deification, his full maturity in Christ, occurs when God draws history into eternity:

> For we ourselves will be the *seventh day*, when we will be full and remade by his blessing and sanctification. There, at rest, we will see that he is truly God. This is what we wanted ourselves to be, when we abandoned him and separated ourselves from the true God, listening to the words of the seducer: "You will be gods." God would have made us gods by participation in him, not by desertion. What have we done without him, except decay in his anger? Yet, having been remade by him and perfected by a greater grace, we will rest in eternity, seeing that he is God through whom we will be full when he himself will be all things in all things . . . Thus, this seventh age will be our rest, the end of which will have no evening. Yet, the Lord's Day, as *the eternal eighth day*, is made sacred by Christ's resurrection. It prefigures not only the eternal rest of the spirit, but also the fulfillment of the body.[24]

The allegorical schema of the *eight days*, which comprise the seven days of Genesis and the eighth day of the Resurrection, reveals how God never abandoned humanity, instead guiding and nourishing man toward full maturation in Christ. Man moves from the elected immaturity of the fall (*infantia*) to the decay of old age in a fallen world (*senectus*) to a renewal and elevation in the *telos* of the resurrection.[25]

In his various formulations of the eight-day maturation of man, Augustine does not mean to imply that God has ignored the individual person's freedom, such that humanity, collectively and ineluctably, enters the resurrection to life. According to this allegorical schema, the individual Christian must also *personally* mature in communion with the saints. Augustine makes this clear in his *On Genesis Against the Manicheans*,

---

24 Augustine, *City of God* XXII, 30 (CCSL 48, 865, lines 105–15, 141–45; WSA I-7, 553). See also John Gavin, SJ, "Souls and Bodies, History and Eternity: John Scottus Eriugena and the Intermediate State," *Annales Theologici* 29 (2015): 139–44.

25 Augustine summarizes the schema using, once again, the image of human maturation: "But then it can easily be seen in the case of any individual human being that the first two ages, infancy and childhood, cling to the senses of the body; of these there are five: sight, hearing, smell, taste and touch; double the number five, because of the two sexes, male and female, from which such generations arise, and you get ten. But now from adolescence onward, when reason begins in human beings to get the upper hand, the five senses are joined by knowledge and activity, which guide and organize the life we lead." See Augustine, *On Genesis Against the Manichees* I, 24, 42 (CSEL 91, 111, lines 1–10; WSA I-13, 66).

in which he follows the account of the stages of salvation history with a second version that applies the schema to the individual Christian: "We also, one and all, have those six days in our personal lives, distinguished from each other in good works and an upright way of life, after which we should be hoping to rest."[26] Table 5.2 summarizes the individual Christian's growth in recapitulating the days of Genesis.[27]

What does Augustine teach us regarding maturation and the Scriptures? First, Christian maturation *takes place in time and history*. In his *On the Trinity*, having discussed the temporal formation of humanity and the Christian as outlined in the Scriptures, Augustine emphasizes the importance of spiritual growth within history. Since humans, as corporeal beings, change and grow, they can only arrive at their *telos* within the parameters of the temporal:

> To sum up then: we were incapable of grasping eternal things, and weighed down by the accumulated dirt of our sins, which we had collected by our love of temporal things, and which had become almost a natural growth on our mortal stock; so we needed purifying. But we could only be purified for adaptation to eternal things by temporal means like those we were already bound to in servile adaptation . . . So insofar as we are changeable, to that extent do we fall short of eternity. But eternal life is promised us by the truth, from whose transparent clarity our faith is as far removed as mortality is from eternity. So now we accord faith to the things done in time for our sakes, and are purified by it; in order that when we come to sight and truth succeeds to faith, eternity might likewise succeed to mortality . . .[28]

Christianity does not eschew the historical in favor of esoteric knowledge and the purely abstract but recognizes fully both the spiritual and corporeal reality of man. Although maturation concludes in eternity, it unfolds in time.

Second, the Scriptures reveal that God has *entered history for the sake of man's salvation and maturation*. The Greek Fathers of the Church called this God's "condescension"—*sunkatabasis*, "descent to be with"—that in fact begins with the Father's very act of creation, culminates in the Son's Incarnation, and continues even now through the Holy Spirit. The Hexameron

---

[26] Augustine, *On Genesis Against the Manichees* I, 25, 43 (CSEL 91, 112, lines 1–3; WSA I-13, 67).

[27] Quotations from WSA I-13, 67–68.

[28] Augustine, *De Trinitate* IV, 18 (WSA I-5, 169).

Table 5.2

Day	Maturation
First day	The beginning of faith: "we have the light of faith, when we begin by believing visible things, and it is on account of this faith that the Lord was prepared to appear in visible form." (Infancy)
Second day	The awakening of the spiritual life: "we have a kind of solid structure in the discipline by which we distinguish between things of the flesh and things of the spirit, as between the nether and upper waters." (Childhood)
Third day	The turning away from sin: "we separate our minds from the slippery slope and the stormy waves of fleshly temptations . . ." (Youth)
Fourth day	The desire for prayer and the Truth: " . . . we have already been making and discerning spiritual perceptions in the solid structure of discipline, we see what unchangeable truth is, which shines in the soul like the sun . . ." (Adolescence)
Fifth day	Living the Truth: "we begin to produce results on the fifth day, acting in this most turbulent world, as in the waters of the sea, in the interests of brotherhood and good fellowship . . ." (Old Age)
Sixth day	Growth in the virtues: "from the stronghold of our minds, where we already have the spiritual fruit of good thoughts and ideas, we direct all the movements of our spirit so that it may be 'a live soul,' one at the service, that is, of reason and justice, not foolhardiness and sin. In this way too may the man be made to the image and likeness of God . . ." (Senectitude)
Seventh day	Finding rest in God: "because not only is he [God] the one who works these good works in us, ordering us to work them, but it is also he that is rightly said to rest, because at the end of all these works he bestows himself on us as our rest." (Rest)

itself allegorically demonstrates that creation requires the temporal interaction between God and human beings for its fulfillment in the seventh and eight days. History does not unwind in a cycle or spin out aimlessly toward annihilation, but finds its hope in eternity through God's self-emptying gift.

Third, the Scriptures, through a variety of texts and genres, reveal this divine condescension and, in turn, *invite persons and peoples of every time and place to become a full part of that story.* Modern historians may balk at embracing a schema that excludes other cultures and times—not to mention the inclusion of events and miracles that fail to satisfy contemporary criteria for historical validity. Yet, the *story* the Scriptures tell through a variety of texts and genres does not cancel other stories but gives all stories their form. One discovers man's infancy, childhood, adolescence, youth, old age, senectitude, and rest within God's Word—a story that gives confidence and hope—but every age must understand its own story within this form. This becomes evident in the way that Augustine moves from the macrohistory of the Hexaemeron in the formation of the cosmos to the microhistory of the Hexaemeron in the individual Christian. In short, people and cultures, through contemplation of the Scriptures, discover the mutual struggles and hope in a common history grounded in God's promises. Human beings journey together to consummation in Christ.

CONCLUSION

Irenaeus and Augustine together make the case for the Scriptures' contribution to Christian maturation. One may read the story of the salvation history, from Genesis to Revelation, as maturation through the effective, condescending love of God in history. The elected immaturity of humanity becomes a restored growth in the recapitulation of Jesus Christ. In turn, individual Christians and the Church, through the grace of the Spirit, reassume this transformative narrative to arrive at the *telos* of the resurrection. God's Word elevates every human word to the intimacy of divine union.

The Scriptures therefore effect maturation through a communal relationship with God. In the Divine Word, the individual and the community enter into the love story of God's formation of humanity for participation in his glory. The interpretive key of Jesus Christ, who recapitulates and fulfills the promise of God's Word, unlocks this often bewildering collection of texts and genres for a transformative event in the hearts of every generation. God condescended to mature man in history, and God continues this process in every generation through encounters with the Word.

CHAPTER 6

Maturation and the Mysteries

The Greek word *mysterion* designates either something secret or a sign that reveals something hidden. It can also refer to a sacred rite whose symbols only the initiates may know. Thus, early Christians appropriated the word *mysterion* for their own rites in which they shared the saving actions of Christ, especially through the blessed waters of Baptism and the celebration of the Eucharist. The Westerners would call these rites "Sacraments," though one also sometimes finds the Greek word *mysterion* in their sacred vocabulary.

The Mysteries offer the essential grace for the maturation of the Christian. Although the early Christians did not number their Mysteries in the way Latin Christians would later—for example, the seven Sacraments—they nonetheless recognized the particular rites that extend the fruits of the Paschal Mystery in history. Catechetical sermons, *mystagogiai*—post-Baptismal explanations of the rites of initiation—and dedicated treatises convey their understanding of the transformative power of these encounters with Jesus. Given that one becomes the likeness of God through divine gift, the Mysteries serve as the most important means for deification.

This chapter focuses on the Sacraments of initiation: Baptism and the Eucharist. In addition, it will consider two early approaches to repentance and post-Baptismal reconciliation—a topic of some controversy in the early centuries that would lead to another Mystery in the life of the Church. Three Fathers of the Church—Ambrose of Milan, Mark the Monk, and Maximus the Confessor—reveal the depths of these gifts and their effects on the recipients.

THE MYSTERY OF BAPTISM

Baptism received a variety of descriptive names in the early Church, including Illumination, Rebirth, Divine Adoption, and Purification. This Mystery gives the foundational participation in the life of the Trinity and it is therefore more than just a restoration of the Edenic state. Baptism represents a *new* beginning and a *new* becoming—that is, the maturation of the Christian starts in the sacred font and develops from the Christ-form imprinted on the soul. The Orthodox theologian Dumitru Staniloae describes the power of the Trinitarian immersion: "A person goes forth from baptism as a wholly new existence. He is not renewed in one respect only, but his very existence has become 'other.' He is like a newborn but on another plane: the plane of a life lived in common with Christ, a life filled with all the potentialities created by the process of spiritualization. His existence now has another foundation and a different movement..."[1]

Baptism, therefore, is the Christian's real birthday. Jesus himself teaches that one must be reborn to have life in him: "Truly, truly, I say to you, unless one is born again (or "born from above": *gennēthē anōthen*) he cannot see the kingdom of God" (John 3:3). And again: "Truly, truly, I say to you, unless one is born of water and the Spirit, he cannot enter the kingdom of God. That which is born of the flesh is flesh, and that which is born of the Spirit is spirit" (John 3:5–6). This new birth, like physical birth, also marks the unfolding of a life as one grows into the Christ-form: "We were buried therefore with him by baptism into death, so that as Christ was raised from the dead by the glory of the Father, we too might walk in newness of life" (Rom 6:4). Baptism is not static, but it initiates a journey defined by growth and becoming. One celebrates this birthday as the *anagennēsis* or regeneration, a new life and hope: "[He] saved us, not because of deeds done by us in righteousness, but

---

[1] Dumitru Staniloae, *The Experience of God*, vol. 5, *The Sanctifying Mysteries,* trans. Ioan Ionita and Robert Barringer (Brookline, MA: Holy Orthodox Press, 2012), 32.

in virtue of his own mercy, by the washing of regeneration [*palingenesia*] and renewal [*anakainōsis*] in the Holy Spirit" (Titus 3:5).

Rebirth in the Spirit: Ambrose of Milan

Ambrose of Milan describes the fourth-century rites of initiation in Milan in his *On the Mysteries* (*De mysteriis*). He preached this *mystagogia* to the newly Baptized a week after their Baptism at the Easter Vigil to explain the hidden meanings behind each part of the ritual. His exposition draws heavily upon biblical typology to demonstrate the antiquity and transformative power of what had taken place: Baptism is anticipated by the Spirit hovering over the face of the waters in Genesis, the cleansing waters of the flood, and the sweet water that sprang from the rock to quench the thirst of the Israelites. One could not rightly understand these images and the Mysteries without having first experienced their effects: "Now the time warns us to speak of the Mysteries and to set forth the very purpose of the sacraments. If we had thought that this should have been taught those not yet initiated before baptism, we would be considered to have betrayed [*prodidisse*] rather than to have portrayed [*edidisse*] the Mysteries."[2] No longer catechumens, the new Christians needed to learn the full import and responsibilities stemming from their new life.

Ambrose uses a variety of images to convey the effects of the sacrament, including cleansing and rebirth.[3] In fact, the Baptistry is "the sanctuary of regeneration," the womb from which Christians emerge renewed.[4] The Holy Spirit imbues the ordinary waters with the efficacy to liberate and elevate the person to a mode of existence in the form of Christ, who himself descended into the depths in order to raise persons up: "Christ, moreover, on seeing His Church in white vestments—for whom He himself, as you have it in the book of Zecharias the Prophet [Zech. 3:3] had put on 'filthy garments'—that is, a soul pure and washed by the laver of regeneration, says: 'Behold, thou art fair, my love, behold thou art fair, thy eyes are as a dove's,' in whose likeness the Holy Spirit descended from heaven" (Song of Sol. 4:1).[5] In Baptism and

---

2 Ambrose of Milan, *On the Mysteries* 1, 2 (SC 25, 157; FC 44, 5).

3 For an analysis of the primary themes see Everett Ferguson, *Baptism in the Early Church* (Grand Rapids, MI: Eerdmans, 2009), 635–46.

4 Ambrose, *On the Mysteries* 2, 5 (SC 25, 158; FC 44, 6).

5 Ambrose, *On the Mysteries* 7, 37 (SC 25, 176; FC 44, 18).

the accompanying anointing, the Trinity redefines the unfolding of one's life: "God the Father sealed you; Christ the Lord confirmed you and gave you a pledge, the Spirit, in your hearts, as you have learned in the lesson of the Apostle."[6]

Baptism and Maturation: Mark the Monk

This section turns to a perhaps lesser-known figure for a consideration of Baptism as maturation. One finds very few details about the life of the spiritual master and theologian known as Mark the Monk. Scholars generally date his active years to the second half of the sixth century, locating his monastic and hermetic life in such places as Palestine or Egypt.[7] Nearly all, however, affirm the remarkable depth and influence of the surviving corpus that treats topics like Baptism, Repentance, Christology, prayer, and asceticism. Not all his positions remain acceptable to Christians, especially when confronted with Augustinian teachings on the state of postlapsarian humanity. However, when one examines his teachings within the context and controversies of his time, one discovers a dynamic approach to Baptism that emphasizes the maturation of the Christian.

Mark forged his positions on Baptism in part through his critique of the so-called Messalian heresy. It is extremely difficult to determine the primary tenets of this heretical movement. Our information about the group comes almost entirely from the opponents and critics, except for an associated collection of homilies attributed to Saint Macarius of Egypt—the Pseudo-Macarian corpus—that some scholars have deemed examples of "mitigated Messalianism."[8] Furthermore, Columba Stewart has shown that much cultural and linguistic confusion may have occurred in translating the Messalian beliefs from their Semitic origins into the Greek language and

---

6 Ambrose, *On the Mysteries* 7, 42 (SC 25, 178; FC 44, 20).

7 For an overview of the limited biographical details, see Marcus Plested, *The Macarian Legacy: The Place of Macarius-Symeon in the Eastern Christian Tradition* (Oxford: Oxford University Press, 2004,) 75–76; Owen Chadwick, "The Identify and Date of Mark the Monk," in *History and Thought of the Early Church* (London: Variorum Reprints, 1982), 125–30.

8 For a brief overview of the history of condemnations and assessments, see Aelred Baker, "Messalianism: The Monastic Heresy," *Monastic Studies* 10 (1974): 135–41. On ancient lists of Messalian doctrines, see Plested, *The Macarian Legacy,* 23.

milieu.⁹ Thus, the Semitic forms of Christian confession, with their emphasis on the affect and personal experience of the divine, received much vitriol when ineptly shared with the followers of the Greek intellectualist tradition.

The name "Messalian" comes from the Syriac for "those who pray"— *euchiteis* in Greek—and the general condemnations for the sect's beliefs appear throughout the fourth and fifth centuries. Opponents especially condemned two purported Messalian positions: (1) The Messalians supposedly taught that a demonic presence inhabits the soul from birth and, even after Baptism, this interior malevolence cohabits the soul along with grace. Baptism, therefore, does not achieve the full liberation of the person from sin and evil, and only extreme asceticism and prayer could free one from the evil power for full union with God. Thus, some scholars have compared the Messalians with the Pelagians in their pessimistic views and emphasis on asceticism for liberation from sin.¹⁰ (2) They overemphasized visions and mystical experiences, which included the possibility of seeing the very form of God.¹¹

Mark, in responding to the Messalian positions, emphasized both the completeness of Baptism and the authentic freedom to grow in the divine likeness. Kallistos Ware writes that "He sees the entire Christian life as nothing else than the progressive realization . . . of the grace that we received originally in Baptism."¹² Baptism therefore serves as both the ground and the ever-expanding source of Christian maturation.

Mark unfolds three principal themes regarding Baptism and maturation. First, *Baptism is Christian maturation and a gift*. Mark seeks to respond to the Messalian understanding of Baptism—that is, Baptism is deficient and only reaches its fulfillment through radical ascetical practice—while also addressing the fundamental problem of why people continue to sin even after Baptism. A disciple voices this issue to him as follows: "Some say that

---

9 See Columba Stewart, OSB, *"Working the Earth of the Heart": The Messalian Controversy in History, Texts, and Language to AD 431* (Oxford: Oxford University Press, 1991).

10 See Theodoritus Polyzozogopoulos, "The Anthropology of Diadochus of Photice I," *Theologiai Athinai* 55, no. 4 (1984): 185.

11 The collection of homilies attributed to either Macarius of Egypt or, for some, to Symeon of Byzantium, contains some of the features associated with Messalianism—for example, the vocabulary for "feeling" (*aisthēsis*) and "experiencing" (*peira*) the divine—but they do not exhibit the more egregious condemned doctrines.

12 Timothy Ware, "The Sacrament of Baptism and the Ascetic Life in the Teaching of Mark the Monk," in *Studia Patristica* 10 (Berlin: Akademie-Verlag, 1970), 441.

holy baptism represents maturity [*teleion*], and rely on Scripture that says, 'Get up, be baptized, and have your sins washed away'... At the same time, they also discover that the same sinful activity persists in themselves after baptism. With regard to these two positions, what should we say, or whom should we believe?"[13] Surely, some would say, if we sin after Baptism, Baptism cannot achieve its immediate effects in the soul.

In response, Mark affirms the manner in which Baptism brings about a true liberation from sin and participation in the divine life. After Adam and Eve's fall, all humanity remains subject to the power of death, which Mark defines in stark terms: "Death is alienation from God. When the first human being died, that is, when he was alienated from God, we too were unable to live in God. On account of this the Lord came in order to give us life through the washing of new birth and to reconcile us to God, which he has done."[14] Baptism is *teleios*—complete, full, mature—because this divine gift overcomes death as alienation and restores the divine image, the human, to its union with the Creator. Christian maturity does not therefore depend entirely on asceticism, but on the perfect grace of the Mystery: "But, for those who say they acquire maturity [*teleiotēs*] through spiritual struggles, the law of liberty is useless, and all the legislation of the New Testament is abrogated ... And God's grace is no longer grace, but rather is a reward for our spiritual struggles."[15] Though one may call Baptism a rebirth, it is also maturation in its graced reformation and elevation of the recipient: "So we are not nullifying God's grace. Heaven forbid!"[16]

Second, *Baptism is freedom in maturation*. In his response to the Messalians, Mark now asserts that we continue to sin after Baptism, not because the Mystery is deficient but because we personally fail to live out the commandments. "[If] we are held in the grip of sin even after baptism, it is not because baptism is imperfect [or lacking in maturity (*ateles*)], but because we neglect the commandment and by our own free will are addicted to sensual pleasures."[17] Here one finds Mark's apparent deviation from Augustine's teaching on original sin, since he goes so far as to say that Baptism restores

---

13 Mark the Monk, *On Baptism* 1,1 (SC 445, 293, lines 1–14; PPS 37 [adapted], 290).
14 Mark the Monk, *On Baptism* 2,12 (SC 445, 372, line 23; PPS 37, 318).
15 Mark the Monk, *On Baptism* 1, 2 (SC 445, 300, lines 26–34; PPS 37, 291).
16 Mark the Monk, *On Baptism* 1, 2 (SC 445, 302, lines 36–37; PPS 37, 292).
17 Mark the Monk, *On Baptism* 1, 2 (SC 445, 302, lines 38–41; PPS 37, 292).

one to the state of Adam and thereby allows for a sinless life through the proper exercise of freedom. One cannot attribute disordered attractions to the wounds of original sin but only to the misuse of human liberty.[18] Baptism returns one to a state of *posse non peccare*, the capacity not to sin.[19]

We should, however, despite this apparent clash with Western Christian doctrine, refrain from condemning Mark's teachings *in toto*. The context of his arguments demanded a firm emphasis on the perfection of Baptism and the attribution of actual sins not to the deficiency of the Mystery, but to the recipient. Mark does not simply denounce the "Pelagianism"—that is, the teaching that man must perfect himself solely through obedience to the commandments and the practice of discipline—of the Messalians to fall into a Pelagianism of his own. All post-Baptismal maturation depends entirely on the divine grace gifted through the sacred font, not on human strength. Mark therefore understands all maturation to stem from God's initiative, especially from the action of the Holy Spirit.

Mark's fundamental insight lies in his dynamic interpretation of Baptism. Baptism is not an isolated, static moment in the life of the Christian, but a transformation that ignites and sustains the potential of human freedom. This Mystery encompasses all three pillars of human maturation: form, freedom, and vocation. "The gift [*dōrea*] [of maturity] is variously revealed to us according to the various ways we keep the commandments."[20] The Mystery is both maturity and becoming mature, a now and a not yet. Dumitru Staniloae echoes Mark's teaching: "The new life is a gift from above that comes to us

---

18 "Afterwards, to the extent that each person who has mystically received grace falls short and does not perfectly carry out the commandments, he is controlled by sin—which is not Adam's sin, but rather the sin of someone who is negligent and careless because he has received the power to do the work but has not successfully completed it." See Mark the Monk, *On Baptism* 1, 5 (SC 445, 338, lines 168–74; PPS 37, 306).

19 "It also clearly shows that the errors you call 'the sin of Adam' are errors due to free will, for the Scripture talks about 'using your freedom as a pretext for evil, and 'grieving the Holy Spirit' and 'enacting the desires of the flesh and of the senses' and 'having started with the spirit, are you now ending with the flesh?', and 'we are debtors not to the flesh, to live according to the flesh'... Therefore it is not Satan, nor the sin of Adam, but us that the Scripture blames." See Mark the Monk, *On Baptism* 2, 9 (SC 445, 358, lines 42–48; 360, lines 49–53; PPS 37, 313). See also the following statement: "If then those who followed Adam were able not to sin as Adam did when he transgressed, it is clear that we too are able to do so. Why, then, do we make excuses by wishing away our sins, and why do we prattle about the injustice of God, as though God unjustly allows us to be warred upon by the evils of others?" (Mark the Monk, *On Baptism* 2, 17 [SC 445, 392, lines 55–60; PPS 37, 325]).

20 Mark the Monk, *On Baptism* 2, 17 (SC 445, 394, lines 72–74; PPS 37, 326).

through baptism but it is a gift that must be preserved and developed by our own diligence... The gift is also a duty."[21]

Finally, though Mark stresses the responsible exercise of freedom after Baptism, he also highlights the ongoing *reception and activity of the Holy Spirit in the Baptized*. Baptism confers the initial indwelling of the Spirit—the end of alienation—and the new maturation in Christ. Obedience to Christ's commandments requires the Spirit, since the dynamism of Baptism depends on the Spirit's ongoing activity:

> From this we know that the grace of the Spirit that has been given to us as a gift is perfect and has been given to us so we may fulfill all the commandments. This grace receives no increase from us, but herself provides increase to us by means of growth (*auxēsis*) in Christ, empowering us until death to do her works "until all of us come to the unity of the faith and of the knowledge of the Son of God, to maturity, to the measure of the full stature of Christ" (Eph 4:13).[22]

Thus, Mark hardly places humanity in the impossible situation of self-maturation; rather, he shows how Baptism in fact establishes an indispensable union with the life of the Spirit that allows for authentic freedom.

THE MYSTERY OF THE EUCHARIST
The Gift of the Altar: Ambrose of Milan

The newly baptized, dressed in their white robes, now leave the baptistry to join the Church's celebration of the Eucharist. They move seamlessly from font to feast, from rebirth to communion. Sharing in the Body and Blood of the Lord completes their entrance and establishes their new existence within the rhythm of the liturgical year. "The cleansed people, rich in these insignia, hasten to the altar of Christ, saying: 'And I shall go unto the altar of God, who gives joy to my youth' (Ps 42:4)."[23]

Ambrose continues his *mystagogia* with an exposition on the incredible event that takes place on the altar. He notes the occasions in the Old Testament in which God intervened to transform nature: Moses's rod became a serpent; the waters of the Red Sea parted; and water sprang forth from the

---

21 Staniloae, *The Experience of God*, 38.
22 Mark the Monk, *On Baptism* 1, 5 (SC 445, 348, lines 274–82; PPS 37, 309).
23 Ambrose, *On the Mysteries* 8, 43 (SC 25, 178 and 180; FC 44, 20).

rock to quench the Israelites. Yet, all these miracles pale before the transformation of the bread and wine. Even the manna that sustained the wandering tribes in the desert cannot rival the true Bread from Heaven: "Consider now whether the bread of angels is more excellent or the flesh of Christ, which indeed is the body of life. That manna was from heaven, this is above the heavens; that was subject to corruption, if it were kept for a second day, this is foreign to every corruption, because whosoever shall taste in a holy manner shall not be able to feel corruption."[24]

Thus, the people receive not ordinary nourishment, but the very life of the Christ in themselves: "The Lord Jesus himself declares: 'This is my body.' Before the benediction of the heavenly words another species is mentioned; after the consecration the body is signified. He Himself speaks of His blood. Before the consecration it is mentioned as something else; after the consecration it is called blood. And you say 'Amen,' that is, 'It is true.' What the mouth speaks, let the mind within confess; what words utter, let the heart feel."[25] The "sacrament *is* Christ" and it feeds the spirit.[26] Ambrose, in his *On the Sacraments*, proclaims that the new Christians now share both in the grace and the communion of those who partake of the great Mystery:

> You have come, then, to the altar; you have received the grace of Christ; you have obtained the heavenly sacraments. The Church rejoices in the redemption of many, and is glad with spiritual exultation that the members of her household are at hand dressed in white. You have this in the *Canticle of Canticles*. Rejoicing, she invokes Christ, having prepared a banquet, which seems worthy of heavenly feasting. And so she says "Let my beloved come into His garden and eat the fruits of his apple trees." What are these apple trees? You were made dry wood in Adam, but now through the grace of Christ you flower as apple trees.[27]

The recipient of this holy food matures to flower and bear fruit—for this life and for eternity.

---

[24] Ambrose, *On the Mysteries* 8, 48 (SC 25, 182; FC 44, 23).

[25] Ambrose, *On the Mysteries* 9, 54 (SC 25, 188; FC 44, 26). See also *On the Sacraments* 5, 14 (SC 25, 108).

[26] Ambrose, *On the Mysteries* 9, 58 (SC 25, 190; FC 44, 27).

[27] Ambrose, *On the Sacraments* 5, 14 (SC 25, 126; FC 44, 313).

The Eucharist and Communal Formation in the Likeness: Maximus the Confessor

Maximus the Confessor composed *The Church's Mystagogy* in part as an extension of an earlier treatise, *The Ecclesiastical Hierarchy*, by Dionysius the Areopagite. His work presents allegorical interpretations of a church's structure and the parts of the Holy Synaxis—the rite of the Eucharist—to reveal how the Mystery both forms the Church and matures the human person.[28] He offers multiple original interpretations for all the elements of the liturgy, thereby revealing the layered depths as they present themselves to participants.

Two major themes come to the fore in Maximus's treatise. First, the celebration of the Eucharist *unifies the people of God for the growth into the divine likeness*. Sin alienated human beings from God and from one another, scattering them into the ever-expanding fragmentation of nonbeing. The Eucharist, the crown of the Baptismal gift, heals the divisions and draws all into a deeper reflection of the divine likeness. The Church, as the space of the sacred Mystery, reveals the power of God's restoration and elevation of humanity:

> It will be shown that the holy Church of God works the same things and in the same way as God does around us, as an image relates to its archetype. For, from among men, women, and children, nearly boundless in number, who are many in race and class and action and language and occupation and age and persuasion and trade and manners and customs and pursuits, and again, those who were divided and the most different from one another in expertise and worth and fortune and features and habits, those who are in the holy Church and are regenerated by her and are recreated by the Spirit—to all he gives equally and grants freely one divine form and designation, that is to be and to be called Christ.[29]

The Eucharist, therefore, unfolds as a *communal* Mystery, a realization of the Church in her mission to give form and freedom to humanity. It summarizes

---

28 For an overview of the work, see V. L. Dupont, "Le dynamisme de l'action liturgique: Une etude de la Mystagogie de Saint Maxime le Confesseur," *Revue des Sciences Religieuses* 65 (1991): 363–98.

29 Maximus, *Mystagogia* 1 (PPS 59, 53).

the Paschal Mystery and anticipates the fulfillment of the Resurrection.[30] Thus, the rite as a whole demands the full participation of the people through an attentiveness to all its elements and the reception of all its meaning.

Second, Maximus teaches that the Eucharist forms the recipient into the likeness of Christ. "The Mystery transforms those who partake in a worthy manner into itself and, by grace and participation, renders them similar to the one who is good as the cause of everything that is good."[31] Although the entire rite transforms the community, the individual reception of the Eucharist remains an intimate moment for each person and further establishes union through the common form in the Lord.

Maximus, claiming to cite an elder mentor, makes the case for the regular participation in the Divine Synaxis. Only in the heart of the Church does each "infant in Christ" receive the gifts to grow fully into the life of God:

> For this reason, the blessed elder believed—and he never ceased to exhort us—that it is necessary for every Christian to attend the holy Church of God and never to be absent from the holy synaxis that is performed in the Church. He believed this firstly because of the holy angels who abide in the Church, who register those who enter each assembly and report to God, and who offer intercessory prayers on their behalf. He believed this secondly because of the grace of the Holy Spirit that is always invisibly present but is present in a special way during the time of the holy synaxis. This grace remakes, reshapes—and to speak truly—transforms each one found there into something more divine in a way that is proportionate to him. And this grace leads each one to that which is signified by the mysteries performed during the holy synaxis, even if he does not perceive it with his senses because he is still an 'infant in Christ' and he is unable to see into the depth of what is occurring.[32]

Any celebration of the Mystery of the Eucharist, may include beginners (the faithful), the advanced (the virtuous), and the mature (*teleioi*), and each group will proportionally receive the divine likeness to the degree of his or

---

30 His allegorical interpretations of each part of the rite follow the descent of the Logos in the Incarnation—the first entrance of the Holy Synaxis—to the eschatological fulfillment of the second coming, when Christ will "remake us into himself . . . by stripping away the properties of corruption in us, and he will graciously give to us the archetypal mysteries that are represented here through sensible symbols." See Maximus, *Mystagogia* 24 (PPS 59, 88).

31 Maximus, *Mystagogia* 21 (PPS 59, 80).

32 Maximus, *Mystagogia* 24 (PPS 59, 85).

her readiness.[33] Yet, in the end, all are maturing infants before God, receiving the essential nourishment God offers in the heart of the Church.

THE MYSTERY OF REPENTANCE: AMBROSE AND MARK THE MONK

One finds the practice of post-Baptismal repentance throughout Patristic writings, though not necessarily in its contemporary form of individual confession. The Mystery of Repentance and Reconciliation therefore finds its roots in the ancient discovery that God's mercy extends beyond just the singular moment of Trinitarian immersion. The maturing Christian requires this Mystery, since he or she needs liberation from sin for the full and effective participation in the Eucharist.

Ambrose, in his *Concerning Repentance,* teaches the need for and the means of repentance. In this treatise he opposes the Novatianists, those holding the restrictive positions of the third-century priest-theologian, Novatian, who denied post-Baptismal forgiveness to those who lapsed during persecution.[34] Ambrose counters the Novatianist refusal of mercy with the Church's authority and responsibility to preach the forgiveness of sin in the name of Christ: "The Church holds fast its obedience on either side, by both retaining and remitting sin; heresy is on the one side cruel, and on the other disobedient; wishes to bind what it will not loosen, and will not loosen what it has bound, whereby it condemns itself by its own sentence."[35]

Ambrose connects the Mysteries of Baptism, the Eucharist, and Repentance as gifts bestowed upon the Church for salvation in Christ.[36] Regarding the relationship between Repentance and Baptism, J. Warren Smith notes that Repentance "is the product of baptismal grace as well as the precondition for it. Since sin prevents us from knowing our corruption and being suitably contrite, we are dependent upon Christ's compassion for us in our

---

33 Maximus, *Mystagogia* 24 (PPS 59, 93).

34 See J. Patout Burns, *Cyprian the Bishop* (New York: Routledge, 2002), 25–78.

35 Ambrose, *Concerning Repentance* I, 2, 7 (SC 179, 56–58; NPNF II-10, 330).

36 "So, then, He gave them [the Apostles] all things, but there is no power of man exercised in these things, in which the grace of the divine gift operates." See Ambrose, *Concerning Repentance* I, 8, 35 (SC 179, 82; NPNF II-10, 335).

sin, as he was for Lazarus."³⁷ One first approaches the font in the state of a penitent, as one who must turn west to renounce the Devil and then turn east toward the Risen Jesus. After Baptism, one sustains the state of repentance for both past sin and for those transgressions emerging from the abuse of freedom. A penitent, however, always finds him or herself in the presence of the merciful Christ.

The Baptized, as those crucified with Christ and dead to sin, should not hesitate to bring their subsequent sins to the Church for remission and mercy. "Let us then not be ashamed to confess our sins unto the Lord. Shame indeed there is when each makes known his sins, but that shame, as it were, ploughs his land, removes the ever-recurring brambles, prunes the thorns, and gives life to the fruits."³⁸ On the one hand, one must come to the priests who hold the authority to bind and loose. They have received the apostolic authority to convey the grace of divine forgiveness.³⁹ On the other hand, God's mercy also descends upon the penitent through the collective prayers of the Church. One is "redeemed from sin by the weeping of the multitude, and is purged in the inner man. For Christ granted to His Church that one would be redeemed by the means of all."⁴⁰ One experiences repentance and forgiveness as both a personal reconciliation with Christ and with the whole Church.

※ ※ ※ ※ ※

Mark the Monk counters the idea that one may progress beyond the need for repentance. Even the mature require post-Baptismal reconciliation:

> But you will undoubtedly say to me, "What need do those who are truly pleasing to God and who are drawing near to maturity [*teleion*] still have for repentance [*metanoias*]?" That there have been—and are—such people, I fully agree, but be wise and listen, and you will understand how even such persons as these have need of repentance . . . Even if there were such virtuous people, even they are children of Adam and

---

37 J. Warren Smith, *Christian Grace and Pagan Virtue* (Oxford: Oxford University Press, 2011), 204.

38 Ambrose, *On Repentance* II, 1, 5 (SC 179, 134; NPNF II-10, 345).

39 "The office of the priest is a gift of the Holy Spirit, and His right it is specially to forgive and to retain sins." See Ambrose, *On Repentance* I, 2, 8 (SC 179, 58; NPNF II-10, 346).

40 Ambrose, *On Repentance* I, 15, 80 (SC 179, 119; NPNF II-10, 342).

undoubtedly were born under the sin of transgression, and thus have been condemned and sentenced to death, unable to be saved without the Lord.[41]

Though Mark may teach, contrary to Augustine, that after Baptism one acquires the potential not to sin, he nonetheless realizes that such an achievement lies beyond the capacity of most people. "It follows that for both those who are great and those who are not, repentance is unfinished [*atelestos*] until death."[42]

While Ambrose highlights the Church's role in aiding the penitent, Mark emphasizes the mission of the penitent on behalf of the Church. One repents for one's own sins *and* for those of the community. "If the Devil does not cease waging war against us, neither should repentance ever be idle. The saints are also compelled to offer it on behalf of their neighbors. Without active love, the saints are unable to reach perfection [*teleiōthēnai*]."[43] Alexis Torrance calls this "Christ-like repentance"—that is, an imitation of Christ's own assumption of humanity's sin and acceptance of the Cross.[44] The penitent cannot redeem as Christ redeemed, but he nonetheless may offer his own repentance in union with Christ for the sake of his neighbor. Daily penance through "subjugating thoughts, praying without ceasing, and patiently enduring afflictions that occur" liberates one from pernicious thoughts and contributes to the conversion of one's neighbor through love.[45]

CONCLUSION

The Mysteries of Baptism, the Eucharist, and Repentance serve as essential means for receiving the Christ-form. Through the writings of Ambrose, Mark the Monk, and Maximus, we see here that the Mysteries both convey the gift of maturation and furnish the ground for free participation in the divine life.

---

41 Mark the Monk, *On Repentance* 10 (SC 445, 246, lines 1–14; PPS 37 [adapted], 159).

42 Mark the Monk, *On Repentance* 11 (SC 445, 248, lines 1–2; PPS 37, 160).

43 Mark the Monk, *On Repentance* 11 (SC 445, 250, line 17; PPS 37, 160).

44 Alexis Torrance, "Repentance as the Context of Sainthood in Mark the Monk," in *Studies in Church History*, vol. 47, *Saints and Sanctity,* ed. Charlette Methuen and Andrew Spicer (Cambridge: Cambridge University Press, 2011), 87.

45 Mark the Monk, *On Repentance* 7 (SC 445, lines 1–4; PPS 37, 154).

Furthermore, the Mysteries transform both the individual *and* the community: one never shares in the Mysteries as an isolated monad but as one member of the Body of Christ. One can only receive the Mysteries within the life of the Church: Baptism brings one into the Body of Christ; the Eucharist unites the participants in the sacred banquet; and Repentance and Reconciliation take place in and for the Church. Maturity through the Mysteries anticipates the full communion of the saints that will occur with the resurrection—the *telos* of God's glory.

CHAPTER 7

MATURATION AND ASCETICISM

Asceticism has acquired a bad reputation in the modern age. People associate ascetic disciplines with dour monks, self-flagellation, and sexual repression. Fasting, we hear, promotes negative body images; self-denial augments depression; continence depreciates the goodness of human desires. Deranged contemporary ascetics, in their declaration of war against their own bodies, reveal a lingering dualism in the life of the Church. As the triumph of the sexual revolution and consumerism unfolds, how can one assume such antiquated views and practices?

This chapter proposes that a healthy form of asceticism remains essential for Christian maturation. Kallistos Ware boldly defends its importance: "Without asceticism, none of us is authentically human."[1] Our primary teacher for this theme is Maximus the Confessor, who offers a balanced understanding of disciplines that aim at the maturation of the human person.

---

1 Kallistos Ware, "The Way of the Ascetics: Positive or Affirmative?" in *Asceticism,* ed. Vincent Wimbush and Richard Valantasis (Oxford: Oxford University Press. 2002), 13.

DEFINING ASCETICISM

Modern scholars debate the very definition of asceticism. The Greek word *askēsis* means "exercise or training," which applies both to physical and spiritual disciplines. Practices such as withdrawal from the world, fasting, elected poverty, and bodily self-denial exist in all times and cultures, and they have come to define both personal and communal lives. Anthony Saldarini rightly notes that the goals—both implicit and explicit—may vary: "Ascetical attitudes, commitments, and behavior are a specification of the vaguer, more general category of 'discipline,' which may encompass activities and attitudes oriented toward virtue, knowledge, achievement, social standing, survival, religion, and productive activity, among others."[2] Thus, the new "secular monks," with their dedication to "wellness" and transcendental meditation, show that asceticism does not belong exclusively to the religious.[3]

Sadly, many scholars generally pass over the spiritual and religious motives of asceticism in search of other agendas. For example, through withdrawal (*anachōrēsis*) from society, the ascetic protests cultural norms, while at the same time acquiring a moral authority and power. Some scholars maintain that psychological problems, from anorexia to obsessive-compulsive disorder (OCD), plagued the desert monks and led to loathsome practices. And yet, many still admit that such disciplines also serve as a form of education for concentrated efforts in community building, scholarship, and psychological well-being.[4] In short, scholars remain mixed in their assessment of both modern and ancient asceticism.

Certainly, some elements of these analyses ring true: ascetics do indeed promote countercultural attitudes toward the vices of the age, while at times advocating extreme exercises bordering on self-harm. One may also note the status of the "holy man" in antiquity and his voice for societal reform, along

---

2 Anthony Saldarini, "Asceticism in the Gospel of Matthew," in *Asceticism in the New Testament,* ed. Leif Vaage and Vincent Wimbush (New York: Taylor and Francis, 1999), 14.

3 Andrew Taggart, "Secular Monks," *First Things,* March 2020, https://www.firstthings.com/article/2020/03/secular-monks.

4 For an overview of some positions, see Saldarini, 12–16. Kallistos Ware notes that, "A certain measure of ascetic self-denial is thus a necessary element in all that we undertake, whether in athletics or in politics, in scholarly research or in prayer. Without this ascetic concentration of effort, we are at the mercy of exterior forces, or of our own emotions and moods; we are reacting rather than acting" (Ware, "Ascetics," 3).

with the ascetic's capacity for creative concentration.[5] This chapter, however, principally considers asceticism to be the essential cooperation (*synergia*) with divine grace that leads to Christian maturity. This approach assumes the biblical context of the fall of humanity and the redemption of Christ, as well as such anthropological features as human freedom, the wounds of sin, and the empowerment of divine grace. Most of all, it understands asceticism as a series of disciplines directed at the *transformation*, not the elimination, of fallen human nature through freedom and grace, with the goal of sharing in the very life of the Trinity.

ASCETICISM AND THE COMMANDMENT OF LOVE

Can one find warrant for ascetic practices in the Scriptures? The Old Testament does contain many examples of what one would consider spiritual disciplines, though not all scholars agree on their significance.[6] Fasting, for instance, serves as an act of penance (e.g., 1 Sam. 7:6), an expression of mourning (e.g., 1 Sam. 31:13), or a purification for encountering God (e.g., Exod. 27-28; Dan. 9:1). Spiritual preparation could require periods of sexual abstinence (e.g., Exod. 19:14-15), while extended continence gives prophetic witness before impending destruction (Jer 16:1-2). One could "separate himself to the Lord" through the Nazarite vow, which involved dietary restrictions and symbolic acts such as not cutting one's hair (Num. 6; Judg. 13:4-5). In Jesus's own time, such Jewish communities as the Therapeutae and the Essenes separated themselves from society in search of deeper communion with God and in preparation for the coming age.[7] In general, however, all these practices aimed at the fulfillment of the *Shema Yisrael*, the

---

5 See, for example, Peter Brown, "The Rise and Function of the Holy Man in Antiquity," *Journal of Roman Studies* 61 (1971): 80-101.

6 For an overview of passages and interpretation, see James Montgomery, "Ascetic Strains in Early Judaism," *Journal of Biblical Literature* 51, no. 3 (1932): 183-213; Steven D. Fraade, "Ascetical Aspects of Ancient Judaism," in *Jewish Spirituality I. From the Bible through the Middle Ages*, ed. Arthur Green (New York: Crossroad, 1986), 253-88.

7 Fraade notes that, "Ancient Jewish 'asceticism' . . . cannot be interpreted simply as a reflex of specific historical events or foreign influences, both of which are important to consider, but as a perennial side of Judaism as it struggles with the tension between the realization of transcendent ideals and the confronting of this-worldly obstacles to that realization" (Fraade, "Ascetical Aspects," 260).

commandment of love: "Hear [*shema*], O Israel: The Lord our God is one Lord; and you shall love the Lord your God with all your heart, and with all your soul, and with all your might" (Deut. 6:4–5). Asceticism, in all its forms, helped forge the relationship with God.

Jesus himself practices disciplines, though he qualifies them considerably. He withdraws and fasts in preparation for his public ministry (Matt 4:1–12) but scandalizes some for not imitating the radical witness of John the Baptist (Luke 7:33–34). He embraces poverty and simplicity of life, even demanding the same from his disciples (Matt 8:20; Luke 9:1–6). Obedience to the Father gives shape to Jesus's mission: "Truly, truly, I say to you, the Son can do nothing of his own accord, but only what he sees the Father doing; for whatever he does, that the Son does likewise" (John 5:19); "Father, if you are willing, remove this chalice from me; nevertheless not my will, but yours, be done" (Luke 22:42). Jesus practices separation (*anchōrēsis*) from his family and home, calling his disciples to do the same for the formation of a new eschatological family (Matt 12:46–50). Yet Jesus summarizes all these practices in his New Commandment: "A new commandment I give you, that you love one another; even as I have loved you, that you also love one another. By this all men will know that you are my disciples, if you have love for one another" (John 13:34–35).[8]

※ ※ ※ ※ ※

Love (*agapē*) gives form to human existence and draws creation into union with the Creator. Maximus, in a letter to the courtier John the Curcularius, composed a magnificent encomium to divine and human love. "For nothing is more truly Godlike than divine love, nothing more mysterious, nothing more apt to raise up human beings to deification."[9] When love animates one's life, all things are ordered toward nature—what Maximus calls the *logos*, or principle, of nature that gives form to the human—and toward God. "Love alone, properly speaking, proves that the human person is in the image of the Creator, by making his self-determination submit to reason, not

---

8 For additional examples and analysis, see Saldarini, 11–27; David Rensberger, "Asceticism and the Gospel of John," in *Asceticism in the New Testament,* ed. Leif Vaage and Vincent Wimbush (New York: Taylor and Francis, 1999), 29–48.

9 Maximus, *Letter 2* (PG 91, 393B; Louth, 85).

bending reason under it, and persuading the inclination to follow nature and not in any way to be at variance with the *logos* of nature."[10]

Maximus does not speak of *agapē* as an abstraction. The gift of divine charity demands full obedience to the commandment to love in word and deed. All other virtues emerge from this gift. "I mean love of humankind, brotherly and sisterly love, hospitality, love of the poor, compassion, mercy, humility, meekness, gentleness, patience, freedom from anger, long-suffering, perseverance, kindness, forbearance, goodwill, peace towards all. Out of these and through these the grace of love is fashioned, which leads one to God who deifies the human being that he himself fashioned."[11] God created man with a mission: to unite all things through his love and to bring them into the Father's house.

Human beings failed in this mission. Succumbing to the temptation of the Devil, *philautia*, or self-love, overwhelmed *agapē*. The perversion of the greatest gift imprisoned man's heart, and the expansiveness of love shrank to fit the confines of the human ego. All persons became rivals for the goods of the creation, and the fog of sin obscured the Light of the World. "Thus, humankind has brought into being from itself the three greatest, primordial evils, and (to speak simply) the begetters of all vice: ignorance, I mean, and self-love, and tyranny, which are interdependent and established through another. For out of ignorance concerning God there arises self-love. And out of this comes tyranny towards one's kin: of this there is no doubt."[12] Elsewhere, Maximus affirms the goodness of Creation, but then laments how self-love has made it the source of disintegration and division: "Yes, everything that has been made by God is good and fair, so that we who use them may be pleasing to God. Yet, we, in our weakness and material-mindedness, preferred material and worldly things above the commandment of love; and clinging to them we fight with men, though love for every man must be preferred above all visible things, even the body."[13] This is the true death that stems from the sin of Adam: the alienation from God and neighbor, the eclipse of love.

---

10 Maximus, *Letter 2* (PG 91, 396C; Louth, 86–87).
11 Maximus, *Letter 2* (PG 91, 405A; Louth, 91–92).
12 Maximus, *Letter 2* (PG 91, 397A; Louth, 87).
13 Maximus, *The Ascetic Life* (CCSG 40, 17, lines 116–23; ACW 21, 107).

The Incarnation overcame man's incarceration. Maximus begins his book on asceticism by stating that the Son became flesh to save humanity from destruction and death.[14] Such a reversal of *philautia*, of self-love, required the healing of the human heart and the destruction of pride through perfect obedience to the New Commandment of love. Jesus alone, fully God and fully man, could accomplish this. Not even the Devil's machinations could impede Jesus from demonstrating love in all that he did, right up to his self-gift on the Cross. "This then was the Lord's purpose, that as man He obey the Father until death, for our sake, keeping the commandment of love; that against the devil He fight back, in being subject to attack from him by means of those whom he egged on, the Scribes and the Pharisees. This by being conquered deliberately, He conquered him who hoped to conquer and snatched the world from his dominion."[15] Christ, therefore, restores the human capacity to receive divine love and establishes the freedom to obey the New Commandment—the commandment that heals and unites all to the Trinity.

Christian asceticism, the art of Christian maturation, acquires its form from the restored commandment of love. In fact, the baptized, as adopted children in God's grace, must incarnate divine love through the daily discipline of charity. "God takes form in each, through his great love for humankind, out of the virtue that is present in each through the ascetic struggle. For the 'hand' of each just man: that is his ascetic struggle in accordance with virtue, in which and through which God receives his likeness to human beings."[16] All other motives for asceticism—creative concentration, social critique, liberation from communal corruption—cannot take precedence over the love revealed in the Lord himself.

SPIRITUAL EXERCISES

Part 1 has already demonstrated the primacy of the first pillar for Christian maturation, the gift of the Christ-form. God alone, through the action of grace, deifies the human person and realizes the supernatural end for which

---

[14] "The goal of the Incarnation was our salvation" (Maximus, *The Ascetic Life* [CCSG 40, 5, lines 5–6]).

[15] Maximus, *The Ascetic Life* (CCSG 40, 29, lines 243–46 and 31, lines 247–48; ACW 21, 110–11).

[16] Maximus, *Letter 2* (PG 91, 403B; Louth, 90).

man is created. The Sacraments, therefore, as the conveyers of Christ's saving actions in history, take primacy over any works of man. Receptivity, not rapacity, must define human existence.

Yet the gratuity of Christian maturation does not cancel human freedom and responsibility. On the contrary, human beings, having emerged from the saving font of Baptism, now assume an existence of graced activity.[17] Deification unfolds as a pure gift—the first pillar—and as a daily application of freedom in imitation of Christ, the second and third pillars.[18] Freedom, having escaped the prison of *philautia*, expands through liberation in the New Commandment. No longer warring against nature, and now rebuffing the whispered enticements of the demonic, the human person acquires a new movement (*kinēsis*) toward the authentic end: participation in the very life of God.

Maximus highlights three general ascetic activities. First, one must willingly embrace the trials of life as both education and purgation.[19] Maximus does not mean to suggest an indifference to the natural evils of the world, especially an indifference to the suffering of one's neighbor. But God has allowed the inevitable occasions of pain and the dissatisfaction with fleeting pleasures to serve as a propaedeutic and a katharsis.[20] This category therefore designates a mature, ascetical attitude toward the divine concession in the fallen order of Creation: God *allows* the pleasure-pain dialectic for a radical awakening of authentic freedom. For example, the suffering of the hedonist, drowning in unquenchable desires for pleasure, may become both a clarion call and an occasion of reorientation:

> For the infinitely-wise God, who providentially directs the course of our lives, often allows us to use things naturally according to our own impulses in a way what leads to our correction. We see this at times

---

[17] "So then one must keep whatever He has commanded, every man that is baptized in the name of the life-giving and deifying Trinity. It is for this reason that the Lord joined to right faith the keeping of all the commandments: He knew that one, apart from the others, was not able to save man." See Maximus, *The Ascetic Life* (CCSG 40, 7, line 38 and 9, lines 39–43; ACW 21, 104).

[18] On the various tensions in Maximus's thought, including the priority of grace and the necessity of activity, see Paul Blowers, "The Dialectics and Therapeutics of Desire in Maximus the Confessor," *Vigiliae Christianae* 65 (2011): 430–31.

[19] Maximus, *Ambiguum 8* (PG 91, 1104C; Constas I, 144–45).

[20] Pain (*odunē*) and pleasure (*hēdonē*) define the postlapsarian state. See Maximus, *Responses to Thalassius* 61 (SC 569, 108, lines 205–11).

among those who become frenzied in their abuse of material things, for by means of the very confusion and turmoil which both surrounds and is generated by these things, God redirects irrational lust for the things of this life to a natural object of desire.[21]

The mature Christian therefore sees the trials of life as redemptive, especially as transformed by Christ's own rejection of disordered pleasure and his acceptance of the Cross.

Second, having now recognized his pitiful state and need for healing, the human being applies himself to those exercises that redirect the self to the New Commandment directed toward love (*agapē*). These practices aim especially at freedom from disordered attachments (*apatheia*) and a reorientation of the passions for the primacy of love. Maximus defines a blameworthy passion as "a movement of the soul contrary to nature"; that is, it directs the will toward those things that can neither satisfy nor fulfill man for his true end.[22] Asceticism, informed by grace, transforms human desires for healing and maturation. The disciplines heal the wounds of passionate disintegration—the fragmentation of the person in the pursuit of fruitless desires—bring sanity to human nature, and direct the heart toward the source of all love.[23]

Finally, Maximus recommends the imitation of "those who are advanced."[24] This begins with the *imitatio Christi*.[25] Yet, the saints and martyrs

---

21 Maximus, *Ambiguum 8* (PG 91, 1104C; Constas I, 144–45).

22 Maximus, *Centuries on Charity* I, 35 (Ceresa-Gestaldo, 60).

23 Andrew Summerson, in an important study of Maximus's *Ad Thalassium*, notes the relationship between *apatheia* and transformed eros, which lead toward man's *telos* in eternal well-being: "*Apatheia* is less a fixed target than a process of purification that one undergoes. Nevertheless, any process requires some sort of finality. Hence, for Maximus, *apatheia* fueled by erotic love for the divine, finds its completion in eternal life." See Andrew Summerson, *Divine Scripture and Human Emotion in Maximus the Confessor: Exegesis of the Human Heart* (Leiden: Brill, 2021), 120.

24 Maximus, *Ambiguum 8* (PG 91, 1105A Constas I, 147).

25 See, for example, *On the Ascetic Life* for the necessity to imitate (*mimēsasthai*) and follow Christ: Maximus, *On the Ascetic Life* (CCSG 40, 9–14). Kallistos Ware highlights the two-fold imitation of Christ: "The imitation of Christ has two aspects. It involves both death and resurrection (cf. Rom 6:3–5), both cross-bearing and glorification. We are to imitate the Savior first and foremost in his *kenosis*, in his self-emptying and humiliation; but we are to imitate him also by participating in his divine life." See Kallistos Ware, "The Imitation of Christ According to Saint Maximus the Confessor," in *A Saint for East and West*, ed. Daniel Haynes (Eugene, OR: Cascade, 2019), 72.

provide a variety of models for radical discipleship, each one incarnating different virtues of the Christ-form. Part 3 of this book considers the importance of these witnesses.

※ ※ ※ ※ ※

Within these general categories, three disciplines come to the fore: fasting, almsgiving, and prayer. Each practice coincides with one of the three powers of the tripartite soul, a Greek psychological model that Maximus most likely inherited from Evagrius Ponticus and other sources.[26] Thus, the application of these disciplines restores a natural balance to the soul and opens the person to maturation in the Spirit.

The human soul consists of three distinct faculties meant to work in harmony: the desirous or concupiscible faculty (*epithumia*), the spirted or irascible faculty (*thumos*), and the rational faculty (*logos*). When governed rightly by reason, the balanced soul directs the person toward natural goods and, informed by grace, toward fulfillment in God. However, when these powers become disordered and seek fulfillment in lesser goods, they disintegrate the person through the arousal of the passions.[27] This understanding of human psychology therefore exonerates Creation itself from being the source of evil, and places the responsibility for its corruption—and healing—on the proper orientation of man: "The vices, whether of the concupiscible, the irascible, or the rational element, come upon us with the misuse of the faculties of the soul. Misuse of the rational faculty is ignorance and folly, of the irascible and concupiscible faculty, hate and intemperance. Their right use is knowledge and prudence. If this is so, nothing created and given existence by God is evil."[28]

The first discipline, fasting, facilitates the reorientation of the concupiscible faculty of the soul (*epithumia*). The concupiscible faculty, when properly ordered, directs the human person toward the genuine goods of nature and, most of all, toward eternal rest in God. After the fall, however, the unified orientation toward God shattered into competing desires for sensible goods, which very often overwhelmed the governing faculty of reason.

---

26 See, for example, Evagrius Ponticus, *Praktikos* 15 (SC 171, 4, lines 1–4).

27 "Every passion always consists of a combination of some sensible object, sensation, and a natural power, by which I mean anger, desire, or reason as turned aside from their natural functions." See Maximus, *Responses to Thalassius* 16 (SC 592, 228, lines 69–72; Constas, 132–33).

28 Maximus, *Centuries on Charity* III, 3 (Cesera-Gestaldo, 144; Berthold, 61).

Maximus catalogues the deleterious results of this fragmentation: "Such a soul consequently becomes oblivious of things that are naturally good and turns and invests all of its energy solely into what can be perceived by the senses, and so discovers angry passions, desires, and unseemly pleasures."[29] Man now became engrossed in the fruitless quest for transient pleasures; the soul yearns for things that can never truly satisfy its longings.[30]

Fasting, as a response to disordered desire, in no way implies hatred for Creation or condemnation of the body. Maximus's general principle regarding the goodness of created things precludes any such conclusions: "It is not food which is evil but gluttony, not the begetting of children but fornication, not possessions but greed, not reputation but vainglory. And if this is so, there is nothing evil in creatures except misuse, which stems from the mind's negligence in its natural cultivation."[31] The body, too, demands respect and care, though it harms itself through the misuse of created goods and pleasures. Fasting, therefore, should not harm the body but rather align the corporeal with the spiritual: "'No one,' says the Apostle, 'hates his own flesh,' of course, 'but mortifies it and makes it his slave,' allowing it no more than 'food and clothing' and these only as they are necessary for life. So in this way one loves it without passion and rears it as an associate in divine things and takes care of it only with those things which satisfy its needs."[32]

Fasting, in fact, limits one's possessions and rightly orders the desiring faculty. Maximus explains that, "having simplified myself for God by the undivided identification of my will with his, it is because I have fittingly brought the irrational powers of the soul—I mean anger and desire—under the control of reason [*logos*], and through reason have led them into intimate association with the intellect, so that anger [*thumos*] is transformed into love [*agapē*] and desire [*epithumia*] into joy [*chara*]."[33] Separation from superfluous material things—not only food but also any other excess goods—therefore allows for the concentrated pursuit of the *unum necessarium* (the one thing necessary). In a lapidary phrase, Maximus summarizes this teaching:

---

29 Maximus, *Ambiguum 10* (PG 91; 1112C; Constas I, 160–61).

30 "When the concupiscent element of the soul is frequently aroused it lays up in the soul a fixed habit of pleasure." Maximus, *Centuries on Charity* II, 70 (Cesera-Gestaldo, 126; Berthold, 57).

31 Maximus, *Centuries on Charity* III, 4 (Cesera-Gestaldo, 144; Berthold, 62).

32 Maximus, *Centuries on Charity* III, 9 (Cesera-Gestaldo, 146; Berthold, 62).

33 Maximus, *Ambiguum 6* (PG 91, 1068A; Constans I, 71).

"Let us prove that we eat to live and let us not be convicted of living to eat."[34] Genuine living means abandoning the complications of sensual goods and finding one's nourishment in the generous gifts of God.

Almsgiving contributes to the healing of the spirited faculty of the soul (*thumos*).[35] In its positive sense, the spirited part acts as the drive for the human person, inspiring one to overcome inertia and to pursue genuine goods. However, when let loose from the governing faculty of reason, *thumos* couples with *epithumia* to provoke hatred and intemperance.[36] One perceives persons as rivals for limited pleasures, and responds with tyranny, the imposition of the self upon the other. Anger reigns in the war of domination.

Why, then, does almsgiving tame unbridled *thumos*? The drive to pursue sensual goods makes the world a field of competition where greed draws all things to the self. Maximus notes that, "The passion of greed is revealed when one is happy in receiving but unhappy in giving."[37] The obsession with possession therefore closes the heart to others, including God: "And no one that does not separate himself as was said before, from passion for worldly things, can love genuinely either God or his neighbor. Indeed, at the same time to attend to the material and to love God, simply cannot be."[38] To restore one's proper view of God and neighbor, one must redirect the drive from receiving to giving, from consumption to self-gift. Almsgiving—through both the donation of goods and acts of service—drives one out of the ego and toward those who are in need. The spirited faculty becomes *love* through almsgiving,[39] a movement that, coupled with right desire, leads to the source of all love: God.[40]

---

34 Maximus, *Commentary on the Our Father* (CCSG 23, 62, lines 612–13; Berthold, 114).

35 Maximus, *Centuries on Charity* I, 79 (Cesera-Gestaldo, 80; Berthold, 43–44).

36 "Misuse of the rational faculty is ignorance and folly, of the irascible and concupiscible faculty, hate and intemperance." Maximus, *Centuries on Charity* III, 3 (Cesera-Gestaldo, 144; Berthold, 61). See also Lars Thunberg, *Microcosm and Mediator* (Chicago: Open Court, 1995), 201.

37 Maximus, *Centuries on Charity* I, 76 (Cesera-Gestaldo, 78; Berthold, 43).

38 Maximus, *On the Ascetic Life* (CCSG 40, 15, lines 99–104; ACW 21, 106).

39 Maximus, *Ambiguum* 6 (PG 91, 1068A; Constas I, 73).

40 "The disposition of love is made manifest not only in the sharing of money but much more in sharing the word of God and physical service." Maximus, *Centuries on Charity* I, 26

Finally, prayer restores both the rational faculty of the soul (*logos*) and the overarching faculty of the intellect (*nous*). Prayer, indeed, is a discipline that requires daily perseverance and maturation. It includes not only recitation but also a spiritual ascent to the intimate experience of God.

Why does Maximus associate prayer with the purification of reason and intellect? The primary wound of Adam's sin is alienation from, or ignorance (*agnoia*) of, God.[41] Befuddled and beguiled by sensual goods, man forgets his first Good, the loving Creator. In turn, as noted previously, this expands the ego at the expense of God and neighbor: "For out of ignorance concerning God there arises self-love."[42] The mind becomes bereft of its true Good and reason sinks into the fog of competing images: "Our nature, which descended into the earth, whose bars were its eternal barriers, that is, carried off into a desert barren of all feeling for God, where its habit of mind was devoid of the vital movement of the virtues, and had absolutely no sense of goodness, and took no thought of the movement of its desire toward God."[43] Without God, man views all things through the haze emitted by a broken heart; the light of hope leaves him in the dark of despair.

Prayer restores man's highest faculties through an intimate encounter with the One he forgot. It "withdraws the mind from all thoughts and presents it, stripped, to God Himself."[44] Maximus certainly advocates for the recitation of such prayers as the Psalms and the Lord's Prayer for this encounter with God and the healing of the mind.[45] Yet he particularly emphasizes the ascent from the distractions of material things, through the contemplation of

---

(Cesera-Gestaldo, 58; Berthold, 38).

41 On the importance of this theme, see Summerson, 40–43.

42 Maximus, *Letter 2* (PG 91, 397A; Louth, 87).

43 Maximus, *Responses to Thalassius* 64 (SC 569, 200, lines 95–100; Constas, 490).

44 Maximus, *On the Ascetic Life* (CCSG 40, 42, lines 360–63; ACW 21, 114). He further notes the deifying power of prayer: "Thoughts are directed to things. Now, of things some are sense-perceptible, some mental. The mind, then, tarrying with these things carries about with itself thoughts of them; but the grace of prayer joins the mind to God, and joining to God withdraws it from every thought. Then the mind, associating only with him, becomes God-like" (CCSG 40, 47, lines 420–21 and 49, lines 422–26; ACW 21, 116).

45 "One beats back passionate thoughts, for example, by psalmody, prayer, or uplifting of the mind, or by some other suitable occupation." See Maximus, *Centuries on Charity* IV, 48 (Cesera-Gestaldo, 214; Berthold, 80).

material things as signs of the spiritual, as well as of invisible realities—that is, the divine *logoi* or principles that define and sustain all created things—to the ineffable experience of the Trinity.[46] The mind, through contemplation, traverses the barriers erected by the fallen mind's obsession with material goods and finds itself drawn into the love of Father, Son, and Spirit.

One matures in the practice of prayer. Maximus, inspired by Origen and Evagrius, divides the spiritual life into three stages: (1) the active life of purgation and the reorientation of the faculties (*praktikē*); (2) natural contemplation, consisting in the contemplation of natural signs and symbols (*physikē*); and (3) the gifted contemplation of the Trinity (*theologia*).[47] In life, one does not remain definitively in one of these stages, though one cannot come to *theologia* without having gone through the previous two.

In one of his *Centuries on Charity,* he reduces the three stages to two, the active and the contemplative states. The separation from the world gives way to a contemplative movement into God, where one receives the formation of divine *logoi*:

> There are two supreme states of pure prayer, one corresponding to those of the active life, the other to the contemplatives. The first arises in the soul from the fear of God and the upright hope, the second from divine desire and total purification. The marks of the first type are the drawing of one's mind away from all the world's considerations, and as God is present to one, as indeed he is, he makes his prayers without distraction or disturbance. The marks of the second type are that at the very onset of prayer the mind is taken hold of by the divine and infinite light and is conscious neither of itself nor of any other being whatever except of him who through love brings about such brightness in it. Then, when it

---

46 "The pure mind is found either in simple ideas of human things or in the natural contemplation of visible realities, or in that of invisible realities, or in the light of the Holy Trinity." See Maximus, *Centuries on Charity* 1, 97 (Cesera-Gestaldo, 86; Sherwood, 46). See also *Centuries on Charity* II, 61: "It is said that the supreme state of prayer is when the mind passes outside the flesh and the world and while praying is completely without matter and form. The one who preserves this state without compromise really 'prays without ceasing'" (Maximus, *Centuries on Charity* II, 61 [Cesera-Gestaldo, 122; Berthold, 55]).

47 See, for example, *Ambiguum 20*, in which Maximus speaks of progress (*proodos*) and ascent (*anabasis*) through practical philosophy, natural contemplation and theological wisdom, that is, a gifted experience of "all that is perceived by the senses"—heaven itself. Maximus, *Ambiguum* 20 (PG 91, 1240B-C; Constas I, 412–15). See also Evagrius, *The Praktikos* (SC 171, 498, lines 1–2).

is concerned with the properties [*logoi*] of God, it receives impressions of him which are clear and distinct.[48]

The practice of prayer, therefore, overcomes the ignorance of God and restores the proper orientation of intellect and reason. In the end, however, one should note that, though prayer is a discipline, the mystical union with the Trinity comes as a pure gift—one is "taken hold of by the divine and infinite light"—that one cannot grasp at will. True knowledge or acquaintance with God (*gnōsis*) can only come from God's free outpouring of love.

Prayer, fasting, and almsgiving are not the only disciplines that Maximus recommends. For instance, in his *Centuries on Charity*, he also emphasizes vigils, sleeping on the ground, service to others, and manual labor.[49] In general, however, these practices should never harm the body; instead, like the exercises of good athlete, they should train the body to act in accord with the spirit, ever directed toward the goal of love.

CONCLUSION

Asceticism both requires freedom and enhances freedom. One freely engages in selected disciplines in the desire to grow in love for God and neighbor; one grows in freedom through separation from disordered attractions and a greater concentration of will. *Synergia*, or the cooperation between divine grace and the human will, in turn, allows for the growth in virtue and the divine likeness. Without asceticism, the human person remains within the prison of the ego and enslaves himself to the empty promises of the world.

Christian maturity clearly needs asceticism. Physical and spiritual exercises cannot achieve deification on their own, but God, always respecting the gift of freedom, allows the human being to share in the redemptive struggles that Christ himself embraced. Every saint in history has taken on appropriate disciplines, and the fruits of their labors—the divine life—demonstrate the necessity of taking on the disciplines and becoming an athlete of God.

---

48 Maximus, *Centuries on Charity* II, 6 (Cesera-Gestaldo, 92; Berthold, 47).
49 Maximus, *Centuries on Charity* II, 57 (Cesera-Gestaldo, 121; Berthold, 55).

❋ ❋ ❋ ❋ ❋

PART 3

❋ ❋ ❋ ❋ ❋

Expressions of Maturity

CHAPTER 8

WITNESS

Clement of Alexandria (d. 215) extolled martyrdom as the fulfillment of the Christian life: "We call martyrdom maturity [or perfection] [*teleiōsin*], not because the man comes to the end of his life as others, but because he has exhibited the mature [*teleion*] work of love." Yet, he notably extends the application of the word "martyr"—"witness"—to all forms of Christian fidelity: "If the confession to God is martyrdom, each soul which has lived purely in the knowledge of God, which has obeyed the commandments, is a witness both by life and word, in whatever way it may be released from the body—shedding faith as blood along its whole life till its departure."[1] Christian maturity, therefore, demands a life of witness through one's daily confession of God in all circumstances.

This chapter considers three forms of martyrdom as maturity: witness by blood (i.e., dying for the profession of one's faith); witness by confession (i.e., those who suffer for the faith but are not killed); and the quotidian witness as exemplified by monasticism. Oliver Nicholson notes the unifying theme for these forms: "The core of martyrdom would seem to be witness, a complex activity which sustains and is sustained by a state of complete and

---

1 Clement of Alexandria, *Stromateis* IV, 4, 14–15 (SC 463, 78, lines 15–17 and 80, lines 6–11; ANF 2, 411–12; translation adapted). On Clement's careful separation of martyrdom and Christian confession from reckless suicide, see G. W. Bowersock, *Martyrdom and Rome* (Cambridge: Cambridge University Press, 1995), 67–69.

immediate dependence upon God."[2] The accounts of martyrs, confessors, and monks from the early Church can vary in their historical accuracy and even hagiographical excesses.[3] And yet, both the core historicity of these accounts and the genres of their transmission—which indeed include some embellishments—share the intention of contributing to the maturation of future Christians: the texts themselves act as dynamic witnesses and inspire imitation through their examples. In short, the accounts of these radical saints provide essential models of how to live maturely in a world that often opposes truth with hostility and violence.

MARTYRS AND MYSTERIES

"We multiply whenever we are mown down by you; the blood of Christians is seed."[4] So Tertullian famously boasted regarding those who lost their lives during Christian persecutions, and his assertion finds support in the subsequent conversion of the Roman Empire to faith in Christ.

Today, however, many unjustly decry Tertullian and other early Christian writers for their rhetorical excess and historical distortions. For some critics, Christian paeons to supposedly fictional martyrs functioned as gross propaganda for the extension of Christian power, while other scholars condemn the very idea of martyrdom as suicidal self-surrender to violence.[5] Yet, while one may acknowledge the ancients' adoption of certain hagiographical tropes and, at times, an unhealthy zeal for death at the hands of persecutors, one need not fall into the opposite extreme by rejecting Christian martyrologies as harmful fabrications. The sobering words of such theologians as Clement of Alexandria and Augustine, who strongly condemned suicide and the heedless capitulation to violence, reveal that ancient Christians

---

2 Oliver Nicholson, "Preparation for Martyrdom in the Early Church," in *The Great Persecution: Proceedings of the Fifth Patristic Conference,* ed. Vincent Twomey and Mark Humphries (Dublin: Four Courts Press, 2009), 88.

3 Nicholson, "Preparation for Martyrdom," 62.

4 Tertullian, *Apology* 50 (LCL 250, 226–27).

5 For an example, Candida Moss writes, "Martyrdom mattered to people, and the love people felt for the martyrs led to pious exaggeration and well-intentioned forgery." See Candida Moss, *The Myth of Persecution: How Early Christians Invented a Story of Martyrdom* (New York: HarperOne, 2013), 19. For critical reviews of and responses to Moss's thesis, see Luke Timothy Johnson, "Persecuting the Persecuted," *Commonweal* 140, no. 13 (August 2013): 28–30; Ephraim Radner, "Unmythical Martyrs," *First Things,* May 2013, 53–55, https://www.firstthings.com/article/2013/05/unmythical-martyrs.

themselves acknowledged the need to distinguish authentic martyrdom from suicide.[6] Furthermore, genre does not automatically annul history; stylized encomiums do not cancel genuinely courageous acts of fidelity. If anything, the wave of Christian persecutions in the twentieth and twenty-first centuries lends ever greater credence to the ancient narratives of anti-Christian violence.

John Chrysostom, one of the greatest preachers of antiquity, made martyrdom a frequent theme in his sermons.[7] Martyrdom, he teaches, establishes an identification with Christ in his Passion and death: "For since the Master's rib was pierced, from that time on you see countless ribs being pierced. I mean who wouldn't strip for these contests with much pleasure, when they are about to share in their Master's sufferings, and conform to Christ's death?"[8] Yet, one should not pursue martyrdom as an end unto itself, since love, not recklessness, makes saints: "For while love creates disciples of Christ even without martyrdom, martyrdom without love wouldn't have the capacity to effect this."[9] One's witness, therefore, comes from a participation in Christ's greatest act of love, the laying down of his life on the Cross.

The spectacle of martyrdom functions as the great equalizer, since anyone may share in the passion of the Lord: "[The] theater is opened up with complete safety to every status, every age group, and each gender, so that you might learn in full the generosity and ineffable power of the one who set up the contest, and see the apostolic remark certified in practice: 'His power is perfected in weakness' (2 Cor 12:9)."[10] Since one becomes a witness through God's grace, fidelity within such tortures stems from complete dependence

---

6 See, for instance, Augustine's condemnation of suicide, especially as extolled by the Romans, in *City of God* I, 19–20 (CCSL 47, 20–23; WSA I-6, 20–24).

7 For an overview of his understanding of martyrdom, see Michail Galenianos, "The Value of Martyrdom in Times of Persecution According to St. John Chrysostom," *International Journal of Orthodox Theology* 6, no. 1 (2015): 51–62.

8 John Chrysostom, *On the Holy Martyrs* 5 (PG 50, 709; PPS 31, 223).

9 John Chrysostom, *On St. Romanus* 3 (PG 50, 608; PPS 31, 230).

10 John Chrysostom, *On Maccabees* 1, 4 (PG 50, 619; PPS 31, 139).

on God. Anyone, from a child to an elder, may become a revelation of God's power before men.[11]

Yet Christians do not require persecutions to become martyrs: "Aren't you now sad that no opportunity for martyrdom is presently available? On the contrary, let us, too, train ourselves for an opportunity for martyrdom. They despised life. You, despise luxury! They threw their bodies on the fire. You, now throw money in the hands of the poor! They trampled on the burning coals. You, extinguish the flame of desire!"[12] Christians do not restrict their witness to the confines of the arena; they extend it to every aspect of their lives. Thus, a Christian should not look to the martyrs simply for inspiration in times of persecution but for a model of divinely inspired perseverance in everyday life. Through God's power, all persons may emerge victorious in the daily battle against temptation.

Laying down one's life for Christ radically matures and perfects a person. In a homily on Saint Romanus, a fourth-century martyr, John Chrysostom speaks of the horrifying tortures applied by the persecutors, including the removal of Romanus's tongue. The saint had become an "infant"—that is, an *infans* or nonspeaker. Yet, in reality, this loss of physical speech did not infantilize him; rather, it opened him to genuine growth. Through God's power, Romanus spoke with the authority of an adult: "'Out of the mouth of infants and babes you have furnished praise' (Ps 8:2–3a). And so then [it was] out of infants and babes, now out of a tongueless mouth. Then [it was] an immature creature, now a vacant mouth. The root in the children was tender, but the fruit perfected. Here even the root [the tongue] itself was removed and the production of fruit not hindered. For voice is a tongue's fruit."[13] As a mature tree produces fruit, so Romanus produced the gift of witness that nourished new generations of Christians in their own discipleship.

---

11 This becomes especially evident in John Chrysostom's treatment of the Maccabees as Christian martyrs—those graced to give witness to Christ before his coming. The mother who watched her seven sons expire (2 Macc. 7) receives special praise as an elderly woman in the arena. John calls his audience to recognize the divine power within these martyrs: "Please don't mention the dust, nor think about the ash, nor the bones that have been consumed by time, but open wide the eyes of faith and see God's power that accompanies them, the grace of the Spirit that clothes them, the glory of heaven that surrounds them." See John Chrysostom, *On the Maccabees* 1, 1 (PG 50, 617; PPS31, 137).

12 John Chrysostom, *On the Holy Martyrs* 7 (PG 50, 710; PPS 31, 224–25).

13 John Chrysostom, *On Saint Romanus* 10 (PG 50, 611–12; PPS 31, 236).

The remarkable story of Saint Perpetua serves as a further illustration of John Chrysostom's insights. Perpetua—along with her co-witness, Saint Felicity, and some other faithful Christians—died in the arena in third-century North Africa. The pages of her own journal reveal how her martyrdom gave witness to God's power acting in her weakness: how she, a noble woman, stood with Felicity, a slave, in defiance of social classes to join in common witness to the faith; and how the giving of her life became the fulfillment of her initiation into the faith through Baptism and the Eucharist. In fact, Perpetua's martyrdom points back to the Mysteries that convey Christ's saving actions and open one to the full gift of the Spirit—that is, authentic maturity.

Perpetua begins her narrative with a profession and a Mystery. When her father, out of love, attempts to convince her to renounce her faith, Perpetua points to a vase and asks her father if it could be called by another name than what it is. When he responds, "No," she states, "In the same way, I am unable to call myself other than what I am, a Christian."[14] Then, in one simple phrase she notes, "In the space of a few days we were baptized."[15] The delay in Baptism for catechumens was not unusual at this time, and its reception just before death not uncommon. One may also safely speculate that her Baptism included the reception of the Eucharist as a normal part of the rite.[16] Thus, she establishes from the start that the events of her passion will manifest her Christian identity and that her perseverance stems not from her strength but from God through the gift of the Christian Mysteries.

One of Perpetua's visions demonstrates how martyrdom is, in fact, a public enactment of what takes place in Baptism and the reception of the Eucharist. She sees herself before a ladder strewn with sharp weapons—knives, swords, daggers, hooks—and she confronts a giant serpent at the foot of the ladder. Without fear she declares, "In the name of Jesus Christ, he will not hurt me," and proceeds to ascend by first stepping on the serpent's head. When she reaches the top, she finds herself in an enormous garden and meets

---

14 *The Passion of Perpetua and Felicity*, 3 (Heffernan, 106 and 126).

15 *Passion of Perpetua and Felicity* 3 (Heffernan, 106 and 126).

16 "Since an agape meal later takes place in the prison (17.1), there is no reason to think that Perpetua did not have her first eucharist on house arrest or even in prison if that is where the baptism did indeed take place." See Elizabeth Klein, "Perpetua, Cheese, and Martyrdom as Public Liturgy in the *Passion of Perpetua and Felicity*," *Journal of Early Christian Studies* 28, no. 2 (2020): 181.

an old man in shepherd's clothes milking sheep. The man says, "You are welcome here, child," and gives her some cheese, which she dutifully eats. Those standing around her say, "Amen," at which point Perpetua awakens and finds herself still eating an "unknown sweet."[17] The vision is replete with biblical imagery that suggests both a victory over sin and a new life with Christ: the Garden of Eden from Genesis; the crushing of the serpent's head promised to Eve (Gen 3:15); the dragon defeated by Michael (Rev. 12:3); Christ as the Good Shepherd (John 10:11–18); and the difficult path to eternal life (Matt 7:13). Thus, the vision gives hope that the ladder of suffering that Perpetua will endure in the arena will conclude not only in a restored life in Paradise but also in a new life nourished by Christ himself.

In addition to the biblical allusions, one may discover significant Eucharistic images in this scene. The cheese, according to Elizabeth Klein, represents the solid food of the Eucharist that fulfills the promise of her Baptism.[18] The cheese also symbolizes maturation, since it begins as milk, the food of infants, and becomes solid food (cheese), the nourishment of adults. Klein notes that "Here the completion of Perpetua's heavenly initiation is compressed into a wonderfully rich image (the milk-into-cheese): she is a child, now born of God; she was a catechumen but now a martyr; she receives milk *cum* solid food, baptism, and Eucharist."[19] Through martyrdom, the Mysteries received at the start of the narrative—Baptism and the Eucharist—unfold to their true conclusion in Paradise. Klein explains the full import of the vision as follows: "The eucharistic cheese is the reward of Perpetua's martyrdom; it is the sweetness of the life of paradise and the promise of heaven on earth, since she wakes up still chewing. It is therefore not only spiritual combat in *this* life that is expressed as a sort of liturgical drama, but the liturgy gives Perpetua access to the eternal. The liturgy gives her a glimpse of the order and meaning of the universe from God's perspective."[20]

The vision of one of her companions, Saturus, continues this theme of martyrdom as the manifestation of the Mysteries. Saturus sees himself, along with Perpetua and others, being carried east by four angels to a garden. Other martyrs guide them through a door in a wall of light, and they are dressed

---

17 *Passion of Perpetua and Felicity*, 4 (Heffernan, 107 and 127).

18 Klein argues against previous interpretations of the cheese, such as linking it to the practice of receiving milk and honey in the rite of Baptism. See Klein, "Perpetua," 192–93.

19 Klein, "Perpetua," 200.

20 Klein, "Perpetua," 201.

in white robes while a choir continuously chants the Trisagion: "Holy, Holy, Holy." An aged man with "white hair and a youthful face" and a group of elders stand before them. He strokes their faces with his hand, and the elders who are present give them the sign of peace and tell them "Go and play [*ite et ludete*]."[21]

Once again, the vision recalls scriptural images: the garden in the east—that is, Eden; the righteous dressed in white robes (Rev. 6:2, 19:11–14); the Trisagion of the heavenly court (Isa. 6:1); and the encounter with the Father who gives them a paternal caress.[22] The vision also alludes to the Mysteries, since the martyrs wear white baptismal robes and receive the closing liturgical command, "go" (*ite*), which concludes the rites.[23] The martyrs return to an innocence—"Play!" (*ludite*)—which echoes the rebirth of Baptism. In short, martyrdom once again becomes the presentation and the fulfillment of the Mysteries that both restore and mature the Christian for eternal life in the Father's house.

Those baptized in the name of the Trinity who suffer for the faith not only give witness to God's power; they also show the world the hope for true maturity. Their fortitude displays the wonder of God's providence in the midst of tribulation, and it enacts the Mysteries in a dramatic representation of the Lord's Passion. Perpetua's story concludes with these words: "For these new deeds of courage too may witness that one and the same Holy Spirit is always working among us even now, along with God, the Father almighty, and his Son, our Lord, Jesus Christ, to whom is glory and endless power for ever and ever. Amen."[24]

CONFESSORS AND CREEDS

The title "Confessor" designates a Christian who suffers for the faith but is not killed by his persecutors. This hardly means that such figures give an easier form of witness. Confessors often underwent arrest, torture, and disfigurement as the price for their fidelity. Yet they also acquired an important

---

21 *Passion of Perpetua and Felicity*, 11–12 (Heffernan, 114–15 and 130–31).

22 See Heffernan, "Commentary," in *Passion of Perpetua and Felicity*, 289.

23 See Heffernan, "Commentary," 290.

24 *Passion of Perpetua and Felicity*, 21 (Heffernan, 124 and 135). On the ancient associations of martyrdom with the liturgy, see John Baldovin, "Relics, Martyrs, and the Eucharist," *Liturgical Ministry* 12 (2003): 9–19.

status in the Christian community and could exercise authority even after their release from confinement.[25] Thus, these witnesses boldly proclaimed their belief in Christ through their ongoing participation in the Passion and their history of inspired fortitude.

Maximus, the brilliant Greek-speaking theologian and spiritual master, acquired the title of Confessor for his defense of the two activities and wills of Christ—a defense that would lead to his arrest, as well as the loss of his tongue and right hand. Sadly, his suffering stemmed from an internecine conflict among Christians. In a complicated series of events, the post-Chalcedonian Church found herself divided among those who adhered to the two natures of Christ, divine and human, and those who professed a single nature of Christ after the union of human and divine. In desperate attempts to unify the fractured Church, emperors put forward compromise formulae and did not refrain from force in order to gain universal adherence. In the 630s and 640s, Maximus found himself drawn into a conflict regarding two such compromises put forward by the Patriarch Sergius and the Emperor Heraclius: Monoenergism allowed for the two-nature language, but asserted that Christ acted from a single activity (*energeia*), while Monothelitism posited a single will (*thelēsis*) for the Son incarnate. Maximus understood the serious implications of such positions, since they canceled the integrity of Christ's human nature and, as a result, denied humans an authentic union with God. In the words of Brian Daley, Maximus realized that "it is only if that [human] nature remains fully and operatively human in everything it does as a spiritual and material being even while being shaped by obedience and submission to the divine, that the 'ownership' of Jesus' humanity by the Word has revelatory and saving significance for other human beings."[26]

In 648, the Patriarch of Constantinople, Paul II, with the sanction of Emperor Constans II, issued the *Typos*, which sought to suppress all discussions regarding the one or two wills of Christ and forge unity around an open question. Maximus refused to remain silent regarding such a fundamental teaching, and even boldly participated in the Lateran Synod of 649, under the leadership of Pope Martin, which affirmed the two activities and wills of

---

25 Such a status could at times challenge even designated ecclesial authority, as in the case of Cyprian's struggles with such figures in the aftermath of the Decian persecution. See Burns, *Cyprian the Bishop*, 41–44.

26 Brian Daley, SJ, *God Visible: Patristic Christology Reconsidered* (Oxford: Oxford University Press, 2018), 219.

Christ. Such audacity did not go unpunished, beginning with the arrest of Pope Martin and his death in exile in 655. Maximus also went to trial in 655 and was exiled to Bizya in Thrace. He was tried again in 662, and exiled with others to Lazica, in modern Georgia. He died on August 13, 662.[27]

The transcript of the first trial in 655 reveals that Maximus faced trumped up charges of sedition—he was accused of supporting two failed uprisings in 645 and 649—along with his refusal to conform to the *Typos*. At the start, Maximus affirms that he is a Christian, to which the authorities reply, "And how, if you are a Christian, can you hate the emperor?" Thus, the profession of the Christian faith, in their opinion, requires full support of the emperor. Maximus carefully responds, "And what's the evidence for that? After all, hatred is a hidden disposition of the soul, just as love is too."[28] Maximus at no time denies the emperor's authority within his own sphere and demands that his interlocutors support their charges of disloyalty with evidence.

Regarding the doctrinal issues, the authorities appeal to Maximus to accept the *Typos* since it only requires silence, not the acceptance of positions he deemed heretical. Maximus, however, will have none of it: "According to divine Scripture, silence is also annulment. For God said through David: 'There is no speech, nor are there words, whose sounds are not heard.' Therefore, unless the words concerning God are spoken and heard, they don't exist at all, according to Scripture."[29] Maximus asserts an important principle: Christian maturity *requires a confession of faith*. While the Christian must certainly act prudently before hostile forces, he or she cannot cower forever behind the veil of silence. In fact, not to speak of the natural wills and activities of God and man, as the *Typos* required, undermines the opening words of the Creed, which proclaim God the Father as the Creator. Maximus continues:

> I mean that God wouldn't be a maker were he deprived of a natural will and activity, if he made heaven and earth by an act of will and not

---

27 For brief biographies of Maximus, see Blowers, *Maximus the Confessor*, 9–63; Pauline Allen, "Life and Times of Maximus the Confessor," in *The Oxford Handbook of Maximus the Confessor*, ed. Pauline Allen and Bronwen Neil (Oxford: Oxford University Press, 2015), 3–18.

28 "Record of the Trial," 1, in *Maximus the Confessor and his Companions: Documents from the Exile*, ed. and trans. Pauline Allen and Bronwen Neil (Oxford: Oxford University Press, 1999), 48–49.

29 "Record of the Trial," 4, 54–55.

through compulsion, if what David says in the Spirit is true: "Whatever the Lord willed, he did in heaven and on earth, in the seas and in all the deeps." But if the saving faith should be annulled simultaneously with erroneous belief for the sake of an arrangement, this kind of so-called arrangement is a complete separation from God and not a union.[30]

Suppressing all talk about the wills and activities in Christ would therefore also lead to confusion regarding divine volition itself—God becomes a "depersonalized" entity at odds with the scriptural depiction of divinity. This clear violation of the Creed echoes a similar tactic used during the Arian controversy in the fourth century by some authorities, who sought unity in silence:

> This is what the Arians too once proposed in writing at the time of Constantine the Great, when they said: "Let's remove the words *homoousion* ["consubstantial," the Nicene position] and *heteroousion* ["of a different substance," the Arian position] and let the churches unite." Our God-bearing Fathers didn't accept this; instead, they chose to be persecuted and to die rather than pass over in silence an expression which indicated the one supersubstantial godhead of the Father and the Son and the Holy Spirit.[31]

The mature Christian does not allow confusion and error to fester, but steps forward from the silence and gives witness to the Truth.

Such a bold defense does not deny the authority of the state to govern, but it does clearly prohibit the emperor from interfering in the Church's magisterial authority. When asked whether the emperor is a priest—one who shares in ecclesial authority—Maximus responds with a resounding, "No!" How could the emperor claim such a role? The emperor "neither stands beside the altar and after the consecration of the bread elevates it with the words: 'Holy things for the holy'; nor does he baptize, nor perform the rite of anointing, nor does he ordain and make bishops and presbyters and deacons; nor does he anoint churches, nor does he wear the symbols of the priesthood, the pallium and the Gospel book as [he wears the symbols] of imperial office, the crown and purple."[32] The Confessor therefore both defends the truth and

---

30 "Record of the Trial," 4, 56–57.
31 "Record of the Trial," 4, 56–57.
32 "Record of the Trial," 4, 56–57.

marks out the priestly mission of the Church before an often overextended state power.

The Greek word for "to confess," *homologein*, means "to speak together" or "to speak the same language" (*homos*: the same; *logos*: word). In confessing, therefore, one does not offer a personal opinion or slogans. He speaks the language of the faith; he does not babble in popular idioms. "I don't have a teaching of my own," Maximus states, "but the common one of the catholic church. I mean that I haven't initiated any expression at all that could be called my own teaching."[33] Maturity may require that one step forward, in the manner of Maximus, onto the public stage and confess the creed to power, such that the light of truth might transform the world.

MONKS AND MORALS

After the Great Persecution under Emperor Diocletian and the Tetrarchy, the Church soon found herself inaugurating the fourth century with an unaccustomed favored status. The age of the martyrs and confessors, for the most part, had come to an end and the danger of complacency became the new threat to the faith. Yet, new witnesses in the form of ascetics set out for the deserted places to seek communion with God and pray for the world. These Christian athletes enthralled the Church with their heroic exploits as transmitted in monastic lives, recorded stories and sayings, and treatises on the spiritual life. Anthony, Pachomius, Hilarion, Theodora, and many others inspired Christians by the thousands, either to seek out the monastic lives themselves or to live more authentically their vocation in the world.

One delightful collection of monastic tales is the *Spiritual Meadow* of John Moschos. Little is known about the author, a wandering monk who died in Rome around 619.[34] In his travels he encountered many practitioners of *anachōrēsis*—that is, withdrawal from society to dedicate oneself to the ascetic life—and he compiled their stories for the wider Christian community. In his introduction, John explains the title of his work:

> I have called this work *meadow* on account of the delight, the fragrance and the benefit which it will afford those who come across it. For the

---

33 "Record of the Trial," 6, 60–61.

34 For biographical data and details on the manuscript tradition, see Henry Chadwick, "John Moschus and his Friend Sophronius the Sophist," *Journal of Theological Studies* 25, no. 1 (1984): 41–74.

virtuous life and habitual piety do not merely consist of studying divinity; not only of thinking on an elevated plain about things as they are here and now. It must also include the description in writing of the way of life of others . . . So I have emulated the most wise bee, gathering up the spiritually beneficial deeds of the fathers."[35]

One may therefore categorize this work as a collection of "beneficial tales" (*diēgēseis psykōpheleis*), anecdotes meant to inspire a more devout and faithful Christian life through wonder and delight.[36] The figures behind these stories gave witness to God's power, but in this work the tales become the witnesses for generations of Christians.

First and foremost, these monks give witness to their dependence on God for all things. Among the sayings of the elders, one finds sound advice regarding the treatment of the body and purified motives: "The strength of man does not lie in his physical constitution, for that is subject to change. It lies rather in his intention, assisted by God. Let us therefore care for our souls as we do for our bodies, children."[37] Although the tales of the anchorites often astound the public with dramatic feats of self-denial and discipline, one should nonetheless not read these stories as demonstrations of human strength. Rather, the ascetics attribute their growth to God alone, who fulfills their desire for union: "Let us gather together the cures of the soul: piety, righteousness, humility, submission. The greatest physician of souls, Christ our God, is near to us and is willing to heal us; let us not under-estimate him."[38]

The monks attribute their perseverance in the life entirely to Christ. When a demon tempts Abba Stephan to abandon his vocation, he responds, "I do not accept what you say: I know who you are. You do not want to see anybody saved, but Christ, the Son of the living God, he will overthrow you."[39] When elders come to converse with him, Stephan remains in silence. Perturbed, the elders call him out of his apparent stupor and Stephan replies, "Forgive me, but I did not know what you were talking about until just now. But I can tell you what is the matter with me; I can see nothing else, either

---

35 John Moschos, *The Spiritual Meadow* (PG 87.3, 2852C; Wortley, 3–4).

36 See Brenda Llewellyn Ihssen, *John Moschos' Spiritual Meadow: Authority and Autonomy at the End of the Antique World* (Burlington, VT: Ashgate, 2014), 11–13.

37 John Moschos, *The Spiritual Meadow* 144 (PG 87.3, 3008B; Wortley, 117).

38 John Moschos, *The Spiritual Meadow* 144 (PG 97.3, 3008B; Wortley, 117).

39 John Moschos, *The Spiritual Meadow* 62 (PG 87.3, 2916A; Wortley, 48).

by night or by day, but our Lord Jesus Christ hanging on the cross."[40] Abba Stephan lives a life dedicated to knowing and serving Christ, not the demons of the world or the distractions of men.

The monks also model Christian love through almsgiving and charity. Abba Leontius, the Cilician, spent his life in the monastery of St. Mary in Jerusalem. Whenever a blind beggar came, he would put a coin directly into the hand of the mendicant; but if a seeing person came seeking alms, he would place the coin on a step or pillar to be picked up. When asked why he did this, the monk replied, "Forgive me father, but it is not I who gives. It is my lady the Mother of God who provides for both me and for them."[41] Abba Leontius clearly lives ever within the Communion of Saints, among whom Mary is queen, and shares the love he experiences through a selfless sharing of his meager goods. He takes no credit for his works but humbly remains hidden so that all is attributed to God.

Even the miracles associated with these figures point to the mercy and protection of God. A Roman monk named Pardos had been a muleteer. One day, in his previous life, a demon provoked a mule from Pardos's pack to trample a child to death, and Pardos assumed the blame. Guilt-stricken, he fled into the wilderness in shame. On several occasions, he tempts a lion to consume him in order to end his life, but the lion refuses to comply. And then Pardos understood: he received divine protection from the beast because God had forgiven him of any negligence, and he was now free to live an exemplary ascetic life that grew from an experience of divine mercy.[42]

The monks also had to practice mercy in response to God's love. Once a demon, disguised as a young man, came to offer Abba Isaac help with his work in weaving mats. Isaac rejected the offer, and the demon simply gloated, "You are mine ... Because three Sundays running you have received holy communion whilst being at daggers-drawn with your neighbor." The shocked monk immediately went to reconcile with his neighbor. When he returned to his cell, he discovered that the demon had unraveled all his weaving out of anger for his failure to win a new soul for Hell. A small price to pay for salvation![43]

---

40 John Moschos, *The Spiritual Meadow* 64 (PG 87.3, 2916B; Wortley, 48–49).
41 John Moschos, *The Spiritual Meadow* 61 (PG 87.3, 2913C; Wortley, 47).
42 John Moschos, *The Spiritual Meadow* 101 (PG 87.3, 2960CD; Wortley, 81).
43 John Moschos, *The Spiritual Meadow*, 161 (PG 87.3, 3028D-3030A; Wortley, 132-33).

Like martyrs and confessors, the monks also gave witness to the Truth. Many stories teach the importance of receiving the Eucharist only in those churches that shared right doctrine regarding the one person and two natures of Christ.[44] Other accounts give striking lessons on the general importance of orthodoxy. Abba Cyriacos, for example, once encountered Mary outside his cell. The Blessed Mother told him that she would never enter his abode, since he had associated himself with heresy. Shocked, Cyriacos searched his cell and discovered that a scroll he had borrowed also contained some writings of the heretic Nestorius. Needless to say, he removed the tainted scroll and restored himself to good graces with Mary.[45] While tales like this may bring a smile to modern faces, they nonetheless make the point that orthopraxis requires orthodoxy.[46]

These "beneficial tales" inspire not only monks but all Christians. One need not flee the world in order to discover God. Yet, every baptized person must grow in dependence on God, give witness to Christ, practice charity, and defend essential truths. The mature Christian discovers delight in assuming the missions exhibited in John's meadow.

CONCLUSION

Not all mature Christians become martyrs, confessors, and monks in the strict sense. Yet they must all give witness in both times of peace and during periods of tribulation. The exceptional figures exhibited in this chapter serve to show that, in the end, all testimony comes from God's power. Like the perfect martyr, John the Baptist, one demonstrates maturity by pointing away from the self and proclaiming, "Behold the Lamb of God, who takes away the sin of the world!" (John 1:29). The Christian must decrease, and Christ must increase. In this testimony, one discovers the delight of God.

---

[44] See, for example, John Moschos, *The Spiritual Meadow*, 79 (PG 87.3, 2936D-2938A; Wortley, 63–64) and *The Spiritual Meadow*, 199 (PG 87.3, 3088BC; Wortley, 177–78).

[45] John Moschos, *The Spiritual Meadow* 46 (PG 87.3, 2900D-2901C; Wortley, 37).

[46] The monks also showed awareness of the tragedy of schisms. Abba Palladios bemoaned, "Believe me children, heresies and schisms have done nothing for the holy church except to make us love God and each other very much less than before." See John Moschos, *The Spiritual Meadow* 74 (PG 87.3, 2925D; Wortley, 56).

CHAPTER 9

Teacher

Every Christian is a disciple—that is, a student (*discipulus*) of Christ. One does not mature to the point of no longer needing instruction from the Wisdom of God. In the early dialogue *On the Teacher*, Augustine's son, Adeodatus, concludes that even the teacher always remains at the feet of the Master who speaks within the intimacy of the soul: "But as to the truth of what is said, I have also learned that He alone teaches who made use of external words to remind us that He dwells within us. With His help, I shall now love Him all the more ardently as I advance in learning."[1] God's Word instructs through the Scriptures and the saving Mysteries, but the signs—words, bread, wine, water, and so on—facilitate the interior encounter with the Trinity and draw the disciple into the joy of divine life.

Paradoxically, however, the mature disciple must also become a master. Augustine makes two striking observations in his *Teaching Christianity*. On the one hand, all that the Christian teaches comes from God: "None of us, though, should claim our understanding of anything as our very own, except possibly of falsehood."[2] Humility must always check the human tendency to *own* and *use* knowledge for subjecting the world to one's will. On the other hand, humans possess formative knowledge through the act of sharing it:

---

1 Augustine, *On the Teacher* 14, 46 (CCSL 29, 203, lines 34–40; FC 59, 60–61).
2 Augustine, *Teaching Christianity*, Prologue 8 (CCSL 32, 5, lines 227–29; WSA I-11, 104).

"Every kind of thing, you see, which does not decrease when it is given away, is not yet possessed as it ought to be, while it is held onto without also being given out to others."[3] The disciple does not lose the Truth through giving it away; he cannot deplete a reservoir fed by the eternal spring of divine love. Instead, by teaching what he receives from the Gospel, the student-master makes the gift of divine instruction part of himself. Every mature Christian becomes a *paidagōgos*, a servant who leads the children of God (*pais*: child; *agein*: to lead) to the joy of the Truth, while also rejoicing in the expanding wonder of God's love.

The pedagogues in this chapter show how the mature Christian assumes the role of teacher. Augustine of Hippo composed several works that address the challenge of sharing the faith in a fallen world, while Macrina the Younger and John Cassian provide examples of spiritual motherhood and fatherhood—the authentic modes of Christian instruction. They, through the wisdom they received, lead us to the joy of the Father's House.

AUGUSTINE THE MASTER

No Father of the Church reflected more on the nature of Christian instruction than Augustine of Hippo. A highly trained and gifted rhetorician, he taught students the art of public speaking and ascended to the heights of his profession in assuming an imperial appointment in Milan. But it was a Christian teacher, Ambrose, who finally broke through Augustine's swollen ego and exposed him to the wonders of divine Truth. Augustine recalls: "Unknowingly I was led by you [God] to him [Ambrose], so that through him I might be led, knowingly, to you. This man of God welcomed me with fatherly kindness and showed the charitable concern for my pilgrimage that befitted a bishop."[4] Augustine's eventual return to the Christian faith and Baptism inaugurated decades of teaching, the fruits of which continue to echo in our own time.

The Confessions: *Teaching the Way*

The most widely known of Augustine's pedagogical works is his *Confessions*. In this work, the Bishop of Hippo did not seek to put himself on display,

---

3 Augustine, *Teaching Christianity* I, 1, 1 (CCSL 32, 10–11; WSA I-11, 106).
4 Augustine, *Confessions* V, 13, 23 (O'Donnell, 56; WSA I-1, 131).

but to give away—to teach—his gifted experience of God. Reinhard Hütter distinguishes the modern autobiography from the saint's praise of God: "Because the end of the narrative is no longer the saint's own end, but her or his end in Christ, the saint will abandon any self-deceptive attempt at owning his or her experiences . . . The typical modern version of such a form of self-deceptive ownership would be the 'autobiography'—authorship as the achievement of one's self by oneself. Saints do not write autobiographies—and Augustine's *Confessions* is not an autobiography but precisely its doxological disowning and suspension."[5]

In the *Confessions*, Augustine gives his life away through a joyous act of glorification (*doxa*). As a young rhetorician, shattered through his adherence to the incoherent customs (*consuetudines*) of the world, Augustine sought to reach the divine through his own efforts and imagined a protean God that affirmed his own unstable immaturity: "What could be prouder than my outlandish delusion, whereby I laid claim to be by nature what you are? I was subject to change, as was obvious to me from the fact that I was clearly seeking to be wise in order to change for the better, yet I was prepared even to think you changeable rather than admit that I was not what you are."[6] Only in his Baptism does he discover true rest through the full rendering of his life as an act of praise. All he is comes from God and finds fulfillment through an outpouring of praise:

> To you, then, Lord, I lie exposed, exactly as I am. I have spoken of what I hope to gain by confessing to you. My confession to you is made not with words of tongue and voice, but with the words of my soul and the clamor of my thought, to which your ear is attuned; for when I am good, confession to you consists in not attributing my goodness to myself, because though you, Lord, bless the person who is just, it is only because you have first made him just when he was sinful. This is why, O my God, my confession in your presence is silent, yet not altogether silent: there is no noise to it, but it shouts by love. I can say nothing right to other people unless you have heard it from me first, nor can you even hear anything of the kind from me which you have not first told me.[7]

---

5 Reinhard Hütter, "Experience and its Claim to Universality," *Communio* 37 (2010): 207.
6 Augustine, *Confessions* IV, 15, 26 (O'Donnell, 23; WSA-1, 108).
7 Augustine, *Confessions* X, 2, 2 (O'Donnell, 119; WSA I-1, 240).

The *Confessions*, in articulating God's glory as evinced in Augustine's own life, also teaches others to find rest in divine praise. Augustine's life consisted of personal experiences—from his infancy, to his absorption in the discordant pleasures of the world, to his desperate meanderings through Manicheism, skepticism, and Neoplatonism. Yet his life still reflected the universal experience of the restless heart, the hunger to abide in the One who satisfies beyond all measure. Thus, his "doxological disowning" also *teaches* the Way and leads others to their own experience of God. "I confess not only before you in secret exultation tinged with fear and secret sorrow infused with hope, but also in the ears of believing men and women, the companions of my joy and sharers in my mortality, my fellow citizens still on pilgrimage with me, those who have gone before and those who will follow, and all who bear me company in my life."[8] The *Confessions* is not a solipsistic bid to live forever through eloquence, but an invitation to insert one's own story into the chorus of lives glorifying God. In fact, it is Christ who lovingly makes Augustine's life into a demonstration of God's love; the Master tells the story of Augustine's life to Augustine, and Augustine glorifies God by giving God's gift to his neighbors. "You arouse us so that praising you may bring us joy, because you have made us and drawn us to yourself, and our heart is unquiet until it rests in you."[9]

Teaching Christianity: *A Formation in Joy*

Teaching Christianity has greatly influenced the approach to education and the liberal arts in the West, though many have debated its intended scope. Its contributions to the philosophy of language and semiotics continue to intrigue modern scholars in those fields. Augustine wrote the majority of the work in 396, but did not complete it until some twenty years later in 426-27. Thus, it represents both the early and mature thought of the master teacher, rhetorician, and shepherd.

John Cavadini notes that the younger Augustine sought to convey the ascent to God in more philosophical terms—as can be seen, for instance, in the Platonic influence on Augustine in his work *On the Teacher*—but in *Teaching Christianity*, he develops a rhetorical synthesis that reorients human beings from the deleterious use of ephemeral things to the genuine

---

8 Augustine, *Confessions* X, 4, 6 (O'Donnell, 120–21; WSA I-1, 240).
9 Augustine, *Confessions* I, 1, 1 (O'Donnell, 3; WSA I-1, 39).

enjoyment of God.[10] In fact, this shift to joy not only includes God but also one's neighbor, created in the image and likeness of God. Cavadini notes that, "Our enjoyment of God is not the result of philosophy or inward ascents but an enjoyment' whose content and substance are continual acts of charity performed toward whatever neighbor chance or circumstance sends us."[11] On the one hand, *Teaching Christianity* shows how to escape deceptive signs that move one to put the world before God. It points the way to finding joy both in God and in the neighbor as the image of God. On the other hand, it instructs the Christian on *how to teach* this joy through preaching God's Word and living Christ's way.

In this work, Augustine makes the fundamental distinction between using (*uti*) and enjoying (*frui*): "Enjoyment, after all, consists in clinging to something lovingly for its own sake, while use consists in referring what has come your way to what your love aims at obtaining, provided, that is, it deserves to be loved."[12] In fact, only the Trinity may be truly enjoyed for its own sake, while one uses all other things for the sake of coming to rest in God.[13] Human beings do stand out as an exception—one does not "use" persons as one would material objects in the world; yet one still "enjoys" other persons not for their own sake, but as they reflect the image of God. Thus, the mature Christian learns to order his loves (*ordo amorum*): he understands what may be rightly used, and what must be truly enjoyed. This ability to discern between the two belongs to sound Christian formation. Augustine summarizes this as follows:

> But living a just and holy life requires one to be capable of an objective and impartial evaluation of things; to love things, that is to say, in the right order, so that you do not love what is not to be loved, or fail to love what is to be loved or have a greater love for what should be loved less, or an equal love for things that should be loved less or more, or a lesser or greater love for things that should be loved equally. No sinner, precisely

---

10 John Cavadini, "The Sweetness of the Word: Salvation and Rhetoric in Augustine's *De doctrina christiana*," in *De doctrina Christiana: A Classic of Western Culture*, ed. Duane W. H. Arnold and Pamela Bright (Notre Dame, IN: University of Notre Dame Press, 1995), 168.

11 Cavadini, "The Sweetness of the Word," 170.

12 Augustine, *Teaching Christianity* I, 4, 4 (CCSL 32, 8, lines 1-3; WSA I-11, 107).

13 See Augustine, *Teaching Christianity* I, 5, 5 (CCSL 32, 9, lines 1-18; WSA I-11, 108).

as sinner, is to be loved; and every human being, precisely as human, is to be loved on God's account, God though on his own.[14]

As a master of the rhetorical arts, Augustine does not hesitate to endorse the essential elements of oratory and other cultural resources for conveying the Christian message.[15] But he remains personally aware of the seductive nature of signs—"those things ... which are used in order to signify something else"—and customs (*consuetudines*), since they can envelop one in a fog of false desires. Augustine laments, "This, precisely, is the wretched slavery of the spirit, treating signs as things, and thus being unable to lift up the eyes of the mind above bodily creatures, to drink in the eternal light."[16] We too often come to prefer the artificial universe of our own making, and even seek to impose it on others. John Cavadini observes, "In effect we use culture, the realm of signs and signification, to construct ourselves as the creators and this is the perverse sweetness which 'delights' us—it is our own pride, and we are worshiping ourselves."[17] The student of rhetoric and pedagogy, even for the sake of the Gospel, must look always to the eternal light, not to the illusions of the world, for his formation; he must not remain chained in the slavery of the spirit.

If one strives to rightly order one's loves—the mark of maturity—one also becomes a teacher. The Scriptures, above all, give the essential formation for the Christian pedagogue: "Now a person is all the more or the less able to speak wisely, the more or less progress he has made in the holy scriptures. I don't mean just in reading them frequently and committing them to memory, but in understanding them well and diligently exploring their senses."[18] Thus, the Christian teacher does not just teach facts about the faith; rather, he facilitates the liberation of persons from the world's deceptions and the personal encounter with the living God. He conveys the essence of the Scriptures, since they have become part of him through years of prayer and

---

14 Augustine, *Teaching Christianity* I, 27, 28 (CCSL 32, 22, lines 1-9; WSA I-11, 118).

15 "But for the needs of this life, they should not neglect these humanly instituted arts and sciences which are of value for a proper social life." See Augustine, *Teaching Christianity* II, 39, 58 (CCSL 32, 72, lines 12-13; WSA I-11, 159).

16 Augustine, *Teaching Christianity* III, 5, 9 (CCSL 32, 83, lines 16-19; WSA I-11, 173).

17 Cavadini, "The Sweetness of the Word," 170.

18 Augustine, *Teaching Christianity* IV, 5, 7 (CCSL 32, 120, lines 19-21; WSA I-11, 204).

reflection. In the end, however, it is the Holy Spirit who breathes the required eloquence into the burning heart of the teacher:

> By all means let the man who wishes both to know and to teach, learn all things that were to be taught, and acquire proficiency in speaking, as befits a man of the Church. But the actual moment he is due to speak, let him reflect that what really suits the good mind much better is what the Lord said: "Do not give thought to how or to what you are to speak; for it will be given to you in that hour what you are to speak; for it is not you who are speaking, but the Spirit of your Father who is speaking in you" (Matt 10:19-20). So if the Holy Spirit is speaking in those who are handed over to persecutors on Christ's account, why not also in those who are handing Christ over to the learners?[19]

How appropriate that Augustine likens the true teacher to the great witness—that is, the martyr—since both humbly give their lives for love of God and love of neighbor.

Instructing Beginners in the Faith: *Teaching in Love*

Augustine composed this short work between 400 and 405 at the behest of the deacon Deogratias, who sought advice on how to preach the faith specifically to inquirers—that is, those considering the catechumenate.[20] Deogratias put forth concerns not only regarding the content but also the style of one's presentation. In particular, he asks how one may inform and attract an audience without boring them. Augustine shared the frustrated deacon's concerns: the teacher must develop the ability to overcome weariness (*taedium*) in the audience and instill enjoyment (*hilaritas*) in the

---

19 Augustine, *Teaching Christianity* IV, 15, 32 (CCSL 32, 139, lines 16-25; WSA I-11, 219).

20 For an overview of the history and form of *De catechizandis rudibus*, see Lorenzo Perrone, "Confessio e Narratio. Introduzione al *De catechizandis rudibus* di sant'Agostino," *Salesianum* 65 (2003): 161-64.

Gospel.[21] "[Our] greatest concern," he writes, "is much more about how to make it possible for those who offer instruction in faith to do so with joy."[22]

Augustine provides much practical advice, suggesting the use of humor and even the provision of chairs for the inquirers' comfort.[23] He gives the primary topics that belong to the first encounter: the unity of the Catholic Church, the temptations that lead to sin, and the Christian way of life.[24] One learns the importance of adjusting the presentation toward the different degrees of education in the audience.[25] The work contains two sample narratives of salvation history, a long and a short, both of which are designed to demonstrate divine providence in Creation and the movement of all things toward consummation in God's love. Augustine even addresses the problem of catechists exhausted by the efforts of teaching: "You may, however, be dejected because you have had to leave aside another activity which in your view was more essential and upon which you were already intent. The result is that you are in a grumpy mood [*tristis*] and thus give your instruction in a disagreeable [*insuaviter*] manner."[26] Teaching the faith, Augustine counsels, must take priority, even when an inquirer comes at an inconvenient time: "If . . . a very pressing situation arises and disrupts our schedule, we should willingly bend to it so as not to be broken, and the schedule that God has preferred to our own should now be the one to which we adhere, for it is right after all that we should follow his will rather than he ours."[27]

Yet, above all, Augustine emphasizes the relationship of love forged between the teacher and the beginner. "For there is nothing," he writes,

---

21 Catherine Chin notes that *taedium* or boredom was an issue that concerned many rhetoricians in antiquity. See Catherine Chin, "Time, Narrative, and Pedagogy in *De Catechizandis Rudibus*," *Augustinian Studies* 37, no. 1 (2006): 45.

22 Augustine, *Instructing Beginners in the Faith* Prologue 2, 4 (CCSL 46, 124, lines 66–69; WSA 5, 8).

23 Augustine, *Instructing Beginners in the Faith* I, 13, 19 (CCSL 46, lines 142–44; WSA 5, 48–50).

24 See Augustine, *Instructing Beginners in the Faith* I, 13, 18 (CCSL 32, 142; WSA 5, 47–48).

25 See Augustine, *Instructing Beginners in the Faith* I, 9, 13 (CCSL 32, lines 135–36; WSA 5, 33–35).

26 Augustine, *Instructing Beginners in the Faith* I, 14, 20 (CCSL 32, 144, lines 1–3; WSA 5, 51).

27 Augustine, *Instructing Beginners in the Faith*. I, 14, 20 (CCSL 32, 144–45, lines 14–20; WSA 5, 51).

"that invites another's love more than to take the initiative in loving."[28] By exhibiting love, patience, and interest in the other, the teacher infuses his discourse with the presence of God's love. Thus, though the rhetorical talents of the pedagogue may delight the student, only love can bring one to the personal encounter with God. "Keeping this love before you then as a goal to which you direct all that you say, recount every event in your historical exposition [of God's saving plan] in such a way that your listener by hearing it may believe, by believing may hope, and by hoping may love."[29] In the end, the teacher's stumbling words must concede to the truth of the Gospel and the priority of love: "We should rather let the very truth of the explanation that we provide be like the golden thread which holds together the precious stones in an ornament but does not spoil the ornament's lines by making itself too obvious."[30] When the beginner encounters God, he will no longer see the teacher, but the One who is calling him home.

The teacher also personally benefits from his humble instruction of the seekers. When one shares the faith in love, one delights anew in the truths of Christianity. Just as the emergence of speech in an infant astounds the parents, so the language of the Spirit in a neophyte fills the teacher with awe: "And this we experience the more intensely, the closer our friendship with one another is, for the more the bond of love allows us to be present in others, the more what has grown old becomes new again in our own eyes as well."[31] Thus, the mature Christian *must*, in his or her way, become a teacher, since the sharing of faith renews and strengthens one's own. Teaching forges a communion of love and nourishes hope in the promises of the faith.

SPIRITUAL MOTHERHOOD AND SPIRITUAL FATHERHOOD

Augustine stressed the importance of the relationship of love between the Christian teacher and the students—a relationship best described as spiritual motherhood and fatherhood. Every Christian man, no matter what vocation, exercises a form of fatherhood toward all those around him; every Christian

---

28 The Latin reads: "Nulla est enim maior ad amorem invitatio quam praevenire amando." See Augustine, *Instructing Christians in the Faith* I, 4, 7 (CCSL 32, 127, lines 10–11; WSA 5, 17).
29 Augustine, *Instructing Beginners in the Faith* I, 4, 8 (CCSL 32, 129, lines 78–80; WSA 5, 21).
30 Augustine, *Instructing Beginners in the Faith* I, 6, 10 (CCSL 32, 131, lines 26–31; WSA 5, 26).
31 Augustine, *Instructing Beginners in the Faith* I, 12, 17 (CCSL 32, 141, lines 12–15; WSA 5, 36).

woman becomes a mother who nourishes the hungry with her love. This most visibly takes form in the family, the domestic Church. Yet, when Christians strive to fulfill the promise of Baptism, spiritual maternity and spiritual paternity emerge in wonderful and even startling ways.

Saint Macrina the Younger

In 379, Gregory of Nyssa returned to the family estate in Annisa, on the coast of the Black Sea, to see his beloved sister, Macrina the Younger, for the last time. When he saw the once vigorous ascetic on the verge of death, he could not control himself: "As we met each other, the sight of my teacher [Macrina] reawakened the grief within me for she was already ill and close to death. She, however, like those who are skilled in the equestrian art, first allowed me to be swept along for a little while by the violence of my grief and, after this, tried to restrain me, guiding the disorder of my soul with her own ideas as if with a bridle."[32] In the dialogue that follows this scene, Macrina demonstrates why Gregory calls her "teacher." Her exposition on the soul and the resurrection is deeply learned, steeped in philosophical and theological insights; yet her main teaching is one of *hope*: death, for those who live in the Lord, is not the end, but a step into the eternal love of God. She mothers her brother even from her deathbed, soothing his grief with the sweet wisdom that God had granted her.

Saint Macrina has been called the fourth Cappadocian—that is, a saint who deserves to be ranked with the three greatest Greek theologians from the region of Cappadocia, now in modern Turkey: Basil the Great, Gregory of Nazianzus, and Gregory of Nyssa. She was the oldest of nine children in a wealthy and established family. Yet wealth in no way corrupted Macrina and her siblings. The Church recognizes five of them as saints: Macrina, Basil, Gregory, Naukratios, and Peter. One certainly must attribute such holiness to God's grace, but Macrina herself played no small part in the school of sanctity that boasted such alumni. Although she never married—she claimed a "widowed" status after her betrothed died—she became the mother of many children, beyond simply her revered siblings. She does indeed deserve the

---

32 Gregory of Nyssa, *On the Soul and the Resurrection* (GNO 3.3, 1, line 10 and 2, lines 1–7; FC 58, 198).

title "fourth Cappadocian," since she formed Basil and Gregory in the true Christian philosophy: the Way of Christ.[33]

Macrina received an exceptional Christian education based principally on the Scriptures—Gregory notes that "she had the Psalter with her at all times, like a good and faithful traveling companion"[34]—and she quickly surpassed all her mentors in her Christian maturity. She sought to grow in virtue and dedicated herself to living a monastic vocation within her own home.

Such a formation began to shape the lives of those around her. She became a pedagogue for her whole family, inspiring them with her asceticism and passion for God. When her brother Basil, driven by worldly ambitions, returned from his studies in Athens, Macrina showed him a better use for his talents: "Macrina took him over and lured him so quickly to the goal of philosophy that he withdrew from the worldly show and began to look down upon acclaim through oratory and went over to this life full of labors for one's own hand to perform, providing for himself, through his complete poverty, a mode of living that would, without impediment, lead to virtue."[35] She even inspired her widowed mother to enter the new monastic community that she had established on the estate, making the enterprise a true family affair: "Macrina's life became for her mother a guide towards the philosophical and unworldly way of life, and, turning her aside from all that she was used to, she led her to her own standard of simplicity. She prepared her to put herself on a level with the community of virgins so that she shared with them the same food and lodging and all the other things one needs in daily life, and there was no difference between her life and theirs."[36] Her brother Peter became "a co-worker with his sister and mother in every phase of their

---

33 In his *Life of St. Macrina*, Gregory of Nyssa shares her story because "such a life should not be lost sight of in time and, that having raised herself to the highest peak of human virtue through philosophy, she should not be passed over in silence and her life rendered ineffective." This philosophy is the wisdom of Christ. See Gregory of Nyssa, *Life of St. Macrina* 1 (SC 178, 140, lines 24–26 and 142, lines 27–29; FC 58, 163).

34 Gregory of Nyssa, *Life of St. Macrina* 3 (SC 178, 150, lines 23–26; FC 58, 165). On the nature of Macrina's education, see Andrew Louth, "St. Makrina: The Fourth Cappadocian?" *International Journal of Orthodox Theology* 9, no. 2 (2018): 17–18.

35 Gregory of Nyssa, *Life of St. Macrina* 6 (SC 178, 162, lines 8–13; FC 58, 167–68).

36 Gregory of Nyssa, *Life of St. Macrina* 11 (SC 178, 174, lines 4–7 and 176, lines 8–13; FC 58, 170).

angelic existence."[37] And, of course, Gregory attributes his own vocation to his sister, "the teacher" of divine wisdom.

Macrina's final prayer, recorded by her brother, summarizes the meaning and hope found in the Christian faith. In the first part of this lengthy prayer, she expresses the scope of salvation history: "You have made the end [*telos*] of life here the beginning of a true life for us."[38] Her final breath praises Jesus's victory: "You opened up for us a path for the resurrection. For those who fear you, you gave as a token the sign of the holy cross for the destruction of the Adversary and the salvation of our life."[39] She then, in the second part, entrusts herself to God's mercy: "You who have the power on earth to forgive sins forgive me so that I may be refreshed and may be found before you once I have put off my body, having no fault in the form of my soul, but blameless and spotless may my soul be taken into your hands as an offering before your face."[40]

Spiritual maternity marked the life of Macrina. She sacrificed wealth and prestige to give birth to souls inspired by hope. She nourished, protected, and loved a community into life. The esoteric teachings in her dialogue with Gregory on the Resurrection hardly convey the true nature of her pedagogy, since her life, having become a prayer to God, taught as only a mother could: with the gentle determination of love.

John Cassian

Saint Benedict of Nursia, in his *Rule*, enthusiastically endorsed the writings of John Cassian as a source that summons "us along the true way to reach the Creator."[41] Although the birthplace of John remains unknown, sources recount that he and his companion Germanus traveled through the Egyptian desert, "where the most experienced fathers of the monks and every perfection dwelled."[42] The fruits of their conversations with the great ascetics

---

37 Gregory of Nyssa, *Life of St. Macrina* 12 (SC 178, 184, lines 28–30; FC 58, 172).

38 Gregory of Nyssa, *Life of St. Macrina* 24 (SC 178, 218, lines 3–4; FC 58, 180).

39 Gregory of Nyssa, *Life of St. Macrina* 24 (SC 178, 218, line 15 and 220, lines 16–17; FC 58, 180).

40 Gregory of Nyssa, *Life of St. Macrina* 24 (SC 178, 224, lines 41–46; FC 58, 181).

41 Benedict of Nursia, *Rule*, 73 (Fry, 95).

42 John Cassian, *Conferences,* I, 1 (SC 42, 78; ACW 57, 41). For the life of John Cassian, see Columba Stewart, *Cassian the Monk* (Oxford: Oxford University Press, 1998), 3–26.

come to us in the *Conferences* and *Institutes*, writings that inspired both John's own monastic foundation in Gaul and the work of such renowned monks as Benedict.

The dialogues found in the *Conferences* exhibit the power of spiritual fatherhood in their stories of Christian mentoring.[43] In each conference, a master of the desert teaches John and Germanus vital lessons of Christian living through both words and witness. The reader discovers the nature of paternal authority, patience, and love among these renowned figures. Their students listen with rapt attention not because these men had acquired learning through formal institutions, but because the monks had sat for years at the feet of the Lord. They were *abbas*, fathers, because they shared intimately in the life of *the* Father, their loving Creator, and they handed on that patrimony to their spiritual children.

Abba Moses, for instance, shares the essential pillars of maturity with his disciples. The monk, he teaches, must orient himself by the end or *telos* of his vocation: "The end of our profession, as we have said, is the kingdom of God or the kingdom of heaven; but the goal or *scopos* is purity of heart, without which it is impossible for anyone to reach that end. Fixing our gaze on this goal, then, as on a definite mark, we shall take the most direct route."[44] Abandoning the *telos* leads to demonic instability, a life enthralled with the ephemeral goods of the world: "It is inevitable that the mind which does not have a place to turn to or any stable base will undergo change from hour to hour and from minute to minute due to the variety of its distractions, and by the things that come to it from outside it will be continually transformed into whatever occurs to it at any given moment."[45] While the *telos* is the Kingdom of God—beatitude, the vision of God—the goal or means is "purity of heart," which one may equate with love. It unfolds progressively through asceticism and ever more intimate experiences of the divine.[46] Thus, Abba Moses teaches the maturation through fidelity to vocation, movement toward the

---

[43] On the practice of spiritual mentoring, see Christine McCann, "Spiritual Mentoring in John Cassian's *Conferences*," *American Benedictine Review* 48, no. 2 (1997): 212–23; John Levko, SJ, "The Relationship of Prayer to Discretion and Spiritual Direction for John Cassian," *St. Vladimir's Theological Quarterly* 40, no. 3 (1996): 155–71.

[44] John Cassian, *Conferences* I, 4, 1 (SC 42, 81; ACW 57, 43).

[45] John Cassian, *Conferences* I, 5, 3 (SC 42, 83; ACW 57, 44).

[46] See Stewart, *Cassian*, 43–47.

telos of God, and the importance of growing in the virtues—above all, in the purity of heart.

When the two friends visit Abba Chaeremon, the aged ascetic begs them off, claiming to be no longer capable of offering wisdom. They know better, stating, "Yet we ask that you break your silence a little and instead deign to fill us with those things by which we may be able to embrace—more by admiration than by imitation—the virtue that we see in you."[47] They recognize a true father when they see one. Abba Chaeremon gives them sound advice regarding the ascent to maturity through the initial fear of God, then through desire for the Kingdom of God, and finally through the disposition for the Good itself and the love of virtue.[48] These degrees define the movement into the joy of divine adoption, the sharing in God's very life: "If, by God's help and not relying on his own laborious effort, anyone deserves to possess this state, he will begin to pass from the condition of a slave, in which there is fear, and from a hireling's hopeful desire, in which it is not so much goodness of the giver but rather the payment of a wage that is looked for, to adopted sonship, where there is no longer any fear or greed but rather that love which never fails and always abides."[49] The abba, having walked the itinerary to sonship, wants his children to discover the same beatitude in the divine *telos*.

Another monk, Abba Joseph, recognizes the marvelous virtue of friendship in John and Germanus, and proceeds to give a conference on true friendship in the Lord. He teaches that "only the ties of a friendship which is founded upon similarity of virtuousness are trustworthy and indissoluble, for 'the Lord makes those of one mind to dwell in the house.'"[50] John and Germanus certainly shared a powerful bond in their desire to see the Kingdom of God. Yet one could also say that they became true friends with all the fathers they met during their months of wandering. They discovered true Christian paternity in every amicable encounter and, as a result, became fathers themselves—especially John, who would lead his own spiritual children in Gaul. The fathers of the desert, with all their startling eccentricities,

---

47 John Cassian, *Conferences* XI, 5 (SC 54, 104; ACW 57, 411).
48 John Cassian, *Conferences* XI, 6, 1 (SC 54, 103; ACW 57, 411).
49 John Cassian, *Conferences* XI, 9, 1 (SC 54, 109; ACW 57, 415).
50 John Cassian, *Conferences* XVI, 3, 4 (SC 54, 225; ACW 57, 559).

laid down their lives for God and their children with fortitude and love. Could there be any greater friendship than that?

CONCLUSION

The mature Christian assumes the mantle of a teacher. Every moment becomes the fulfillment of Christ's mandate: "Go therefore and make disciples of all nations, baptizing them in the name of the Father and of the Son and of the Holy Spirit" (Matt 28:19). The form of teaching may depend on the vocation and the occasion. Parents, priests, monks, and even children, preach through words, deeds, and even presence. (Who has not been taught God's glory through the mere presence of an infant?) One does not truly become a Christian adult *until one gives away the gift*—a gift that does not diminish, but only expands the dimensions of the human heart.

CHAPTER 10

Servant

> *But Jesus called them to him and said, "You know that the rulers of the Gentiles lord it over them and their great men exercise authority over them. It shall not be so among you; but whoever would be great among you must be your servant, and whoever would be first among you must be your slave; even as the Son of man came not to be served but to serve, and to give his life as a ransom for many.*
>
> (Matt 20:25–28)

The previous chapter demonstrated that the mature Christian must become a teacher of truth and love. At the same time, however, maturity also demands service to those in physical need. Jesus shows the way. He displays deep love for the poor throughout the Gospels and makes alms a requirement for discipleship. He advises the rich young man (*neaniskos*), "If you would be mature [*teleios*], go, sell what you possess and give to the poor, and you will have treasure in heaven; and come, follow me" (Matt 19:21). Although one must put the emphasis on Jesus's invitation *to follow*, one must still acknowledge that discipleship demands attention to the least. If the young man wants to grow up, he needs to follow *and* serve.

In the Gospels, the incoming of the Kingdom of God regularly manifests itself through Jesus's healing of the sick, the infirmed, and the possessed.

He missions his followers to do the same: "And they cast out many demons, and anointed with oil many that were sick and healed them" (Matt 6:13). All the saints in the Church's history—from the apostles to recent heroes like Mother Teresa or Alberto Hurtado—dedicated themselves to many forms of service as part of their full appropriation of the Christ-form. They go beyond the ascetical practice of alms, and enter the lives of those who suffer.

The Fathers of the Church regularly practiced and preached service in the life of the Church. Among the greatest one finds the three Cappadocian Fathers—Basil of Caesarea, Gregory Nazianzus, and Gregory of Nyssa—and the renowned preacher, John Chrysostom. These men embraced Jesus's example and mandate in ways that came to model the Church's initiatives for centuries. Most of all, however, they reveal to Christians that service in Christ's name makes young Christians into mature saints.

AWAKENING THE CONSCIENCE

Human beings generally blind themselves to the plight of the poor. As the rich man neglected Lazarus at his gate, so even Christians stroll past their neighbors lying prone in the streets. Thus, the Fathers often apply their rhetorical gifts to awakening their flock to harsh realities. Their targets may be the rich, but their message redounds on their own heads as well: the pastors deliberately prick their own consciences as they stir the hearts of the faithful.

At times they draw attention to the shocking conditions of the poor. Gregory of Nazianzus notes the dehumanizing effects of poverty: "There lies before our eyes a dreadful and pathetic sight, one that no one would believe who has not seen it: human beings alive yet dead, disfigured in almost every part of their bodies, barely recognizable for who they once were or where they came from; or rather, the pitiful wreckage of what had once been human beings."[1] They desperately seek our attention, hoping to be seen: "Yet they throw themselves in our midst, miserable chattels, enough to make one weep."[2] One can imagine Gregory's flock exiting the church at the end of the liturgy, encountering a throng of the sick and the desperate, and seeing them anew through the lens of Gregory's preaching.

John Chrysostom, above all, forces the congregation to confront the wretched spectacle and their own sinful indifference:

---

1 Gregory of Nazianzus, *Oration 14*, 10 (PG 35, 869A; FC 107, 45).
2 Gregory of Nazianzus, *Oration 14*, 12 (PG 35, 873A; FC 107, 48).

> There are other poor men, of light and unsteady minds and not knowing how to bear hunger, but rather enduring everything than it. These having often tried to deal with us by piteous gestures and words and finding that they availed nothing, have left off those supplications and henceforward our very wonder-workers are surpassed by them, some chewing the skins of worn-out shoes, and some fixing sharp nails into their heads, others lying about in frozen pools with naked stomachs, and others enduring different things yet more horrid than these, that they may draw around them the ungodly spectators. And you, while these things are going on, stand laughing and wondering the while and making a fine show of other men's miseries, our common nature disgracing itself.[3]

In one of his sermons on the rich man and Lazarus, Chrysostom also notes that many poor, deprived of preaching and witness, do not even have the consolation of hope in Christ. Such was the case with Lazarus: "It is possible even to add another evil to these, namely that he could not console himself with any thought of resurrection, but he believed that the present situation was closed within the present life; for he was one of those who lived before the time of grace."[4] Material poverty, abandonment, ridicule, and even the eclipse of hope: how could any human being, never mind a follower of Christ, close his eyes to such a sight? Chrysostom moves hearts to respond with both material support and the preaching of Christ.

※ ※ ※ ※ ※

Basil the Great, during the great famine of 368/369, shone a light on the horrors of failed crops and parched earth:

> Abundant and reliable springs have failed us, and the flow of the great rivers has dried up; tiny children now play within their banks, while women carrying burdens cross them easily. Many have nothing to drink and are in danger of perishing from thirst... Thus, someone might now aptly invert the words of the Gospel and say, "the laborers are many, but the harvest is scant." Farmers sit in their fields and clasp their hands

---

[3] John Chrysostom, *Homily 21 on I Corinthians*, 5 (PG 61, 177; NPNF 1-12, 123).

[4] John Chrysostom, *Sermon on Lazarus and the Rich Man 1* (PG 48, 977; PPS 9, 32). For Chrysostom's rhetorical strategies in forging the identities and relations between rich and poor, see Silke Sitzler, "Identity: The Indigent and the Wealthy in the Homilies of John Chrysostom," *Vigiliae Christianae* 63 (2009): 468-79.

against their knees—this, of course, is the posture of those who mourn—weeping for their wasted efforts.⁵

Those who hoarded goods during such a plight had to open their barns! And, as if the plight of their fellow citizens were not enough, Basil calls the attention of the wealthy to the reality of their own situation during the crisis: "You have acquired all that you need except for one thing: the ability to feed yourself. With all your wealth, create even a single cloud! Contrive a means to produce a few raindrops; compel the earth to bear; loose with proud and arrogant wealth this catastrophe!"⁶ In the end, the destitute and the prosperous share the same precarious state in the world, and therefore the Christian of any class should remain attentive to the neighbor in times of both feast and famine.

JUSTIFYING SERVICE

The Fathers make their case for service in a variety of ways. When addressing the wealthy and educated, they often appeal to the common nature that humans share as a basis for *philanthropia*: love of humanity. Gregory of Nazianzus begins his oration on the poor by unveiling the unity that underlies the gross inequalities of the world: "My brothers and fellow paupers—for we are all poor and needy where divine grace is concerned, even though, measured by our paltry standards one man may seem to have more than another—give ear to my sermon on loving the poor."⁷ He goes on to state that the poor "have the same portion of the image of God just as we do and who keep it perhaps better, wasted though their bodies may be."⁸ If our common humanity has received the divine image as its form, how can one not serve the needs of his or her brothers and sisters?

John Chrysostom more than once likens the divisions between rich and poor as masks used by actors in a play: "In the same way even here, sitting in this world as if in a theater and looking at the players on the stage, when you see many rich people, do not think that they are truly rich, but that they are wearing the masks of rich people. Just as the man who acts the part of

---

5 Basil of Caesarea, *Oration 8*, 2 (PG 31, 305C; PPS 38, 74).
6 Basil of Caesarea, *Oration 8*, 4 (PG 31, 213D; PPS 38, 79).
7 Gregory of Nazianzus, *Oration 14*, 1 (PG 35, 857A and 860B; FC 107, 39).
8 Gregory of Nazianzus, *Oration 14*, 14 (PG 35, 875B; FC 107, 49).

king or general on the stage often turns out to be a household servant or somebody who sells figs or grapes in the market, so also the rich man often turns out to be the poorest of all."[9] Thus, one should not despise or extol persons by their outward appearances, but should look toward the inner life formed by grace: "I do not despise anyone; even if he is only one, he is a human being, the living creature for which God cares. Even if he is a slave, I may not despise him; I am not interested in his class, but his virtue; not his condition of master or slave, but his soul."[10] The distorted masks of the poor, the sick, and the mentally ill also disguise beautiful souls, beloved by God and called to sainthood. The Christian must receive them, not reject them.

Christian service most significantly has a Christological basis. God-Incarnate, Jesus Christ, has raised humanity beyond the confines of the created world and bestowed upon it a new dignity: participation in the life of the Trinity. Gregory of Nyssa teaches that, if we truly believe that the Son became man, we should now see the divine in every person: "Do not scorn those neglected ones as though they were worthy of nothing. Consider who they are and you will discover their worthiness: they wear the face of our Savior. For the Philanthropist [*philanthrōpos*] [Christ] gifted them with his own face that they might put to shame through it those without sympathy and those who hate the poor."[11] Jesus became one of us to heal us and bring us to the Father's house[12] and he asks us to assume the same liberating burden of love: "'Take,' he says, 'my yoke upon you.' He says the yoke is the doing of the commandments. Let us obey the One ordering this. Let us become those under Christ's yoke, let us dress ourselves in the yokes of love. Do not thrust

---

9 John Chrysostom, *Lazarus 2* (PG 48, 986; PPS 9, 46).

10 John Chrysostom, *Lazarus 6* (PG 48, 1029; PPS 9, 93). In fact, Chrysostom applies this principle even to the rich. To those complaining about his frequent rebukes toward the rich, he responded: "I do fasten upon the rich; or rather not the rich, but those who make a bad use of their riches. For I am continually saying that I do not attack the character of the rich man, but of the rapacious." See John Chrysostom, *Defense of Eutropius* II, 3 (PG 52, 399; NPFN I-9, 254).

11 Gregory of Nyssa, *De Beneficentia*, (GNO 9, 98, lines 23–25 and 99, lines 1–4).

12 "The Lord of the angels himself, the king of heavenly blessing, for your sake became man and put on this malodorous and stained flesh, along with a soul united to himself, in order that he might heal our passions through his own touch." See Gregory of Nyssa, *In illud quatenus uni ex his fecistis mihi fecistis* (GNO 9, 115, lines 15–19). See also John Chrysostom, *Lazarus 6* (PG 48, 1029; PPS 9, 93): "My Master was slain and poured out his blood for man. Shall I despise him? What pardon would I have?".

away so great a yoke. It is beneficial; it is light; it does not chafe the neck of the one bearing it, but it makes it smooth."[13]

One should also see material goods as gifts that God has bestowed for stewardship. Basil teaches that no one should make an absolute claim on any object of the world: "It befits those who possess sound judgment to recognize that they have received wealth as a stewardship, and not for their own enjoyment."[14] Those who hoard material goods and ignore the poor will one day face divine wrath. John Chrysostom holds nothing back in preaching this stark reality: "[The] rich man is a kind of steward of the money that is owed for distribution to the poor. He is directed to distribute it to his fellow servants who are in want. So if he spends more on himself than his need requires, he will pay the harshest penalty hereafter. For his own goods are not his own, but belong to his fellow servants."[15] In contrast, Basil directs the prosperous toward the communal rewards of philanthropy: "If it is the honor that derives from wealth that attracts you, just think how much more glory you will gain by having a multitude of children call you 'father' than by having a multitude of gold coins jingling in your purse."[16]

Refusing to serve one's neighbor, in the end, leads to spiritual infantilization. Basil, in his sermon on the great famine, describes the state of the rich who have been deprived of their normal abundance: "They pour out blasphemies, abandon prayer, and bitterly inveigh against God as against a debtor in arrears, instead of composing themselves like servants addressing a displeased master."[17] Instead of seeing the occasion of deprivation as a call to reform and action, the rich behave like spoiled infants: "Do not behave like foolish children, who smash their teacher's writing tablets when they are rebuked, or rip apart their father's garments when he sends them away from the table to teach them a lesson, or scratch their own mother's face with their fingernails."[18] One's immaturity becomes starkly evident in times of trial, especially since the selfish deprive themselves of God's maturing grace.

---

13 Gregory of Nyssa, *In illud* (GNO 9, 122, lines 7–13).
14 Basil of Caeserea, *Oration 7*, 3 (PG 31, 288B; PPS 38, 46).
15 John Chrysostom, *Lazarus 2* (PG 48, 988; Pollard, 48).
16 Basil of Caeserea, *Oration 6*, 3 (PG 31, 263D; PPS 38, 63).
17 Basil of Caeserea, *Oration 8*, 5 (PG 31, 316C; PPS 38, 80).
18 Basil of Caeserea, *Oration 8*, 5 (PG 31, 317C; PPS 38, 81).

All these justifications, both anthropological and theological, appeal to the revived conscience. Our common humanity made in the divine image, the Incarnation and the commandments of Jesus, the stewardship of divinely bestowed goods, and the real dangers of eternal punishment and demonic infantilization show the necessity of responding to the suffering around us. And yet, how may the Christian serve?

IMPLEMENTING SERVICE

"Others have had their cooks, and splendid tables, and the devices and dainties of confectioners, and exquisite carriages, and soft, flowing robes; Basil's care was for the sick, and the relief of their wounds, and the imitation of Christ, by cleansing leprosy, not by a word, but in deed."[19] Gregory of Nazianzus expressed this praise in the funeral oration for his great friend, Basil of Caesarea. While all the Cappadocians—including Macrina, Naucratius, and Peter—imitated Christ through service, Basil stands out for his remarkable organizational skills and intimate personal involvement with the suffering.[20] His rhetoric of Christian philanthropy awakened consciences and established Christian service on sound philosophical and theological grounds; his actions, however, gave the empire a glimpse of what a Christian society could become.

Basil came from a fabulously wealthy and well-connected family; as a result, he received an exceptional education in the home, in Constantinople, and in Athens, the center for the formation of orators. Yet the material abundance did not corrupt his parents, Basil the Elder and Emmelia, who demonstrated to him what it meant to serve as Christians: "The union of his parents, cemented as it was by a community of virtue, no less than by cohabitation, was notable for many reasons, especially for generosity to the poor, for hospitality, for purity of soul as the result of self-discipline."[21] Furthermore, as described in the previous chapter, his sister Macrina set him on a very different track than the one he undoubtedly envisioned during his student years in Athens. Through her witness he heard the injunction of Christ—"Go, sell

---

19 Gregory of Nazianzus, *Oration 43*, 63 (SC 384, 264, lines 40–45; NPNF II-7, 416).

20 On the Cappadocians' philanthropic endeavors, see Brian Daley, "The Cappadocian Fathers and the Rhetoric of Philanthropy," *Journal of Early Christian Studies* 7, no. 3 (1999): 431–61.

21 Gregory of Nazianzus, *Oration 43*, 9 (SC 384, 139, lines 1–4; NPNF II-7, 398).

all that you possess and give to the poor . . . and follow me"—and undertook a new path. Gregory describes the process that followed in his own words: "Accordingly, having read the Gospel and having seen clearly there that the greatest means for perfection is the selling of one's possessions, the sharing with needy brethren, the complete renouncing of solicitude for this life, and the refusing of the soul to be led astray by any affection for things of earth, I prayed to find some one of the brethren who had chosen this way of life, so as to pass with him over life's brief and troubled waters."[22] Thus Basil began the journey that would make him the great defender of the faith and the poor.

After visiting the renowned ascetics in Egypt and Palestine, he returned to the family estate and joined his siblings in order to establish a thriving monastic community on the property. Bishop Eusebius of Caesarea ordained him a priest in 365, and Basil succeeded him as bishop in 370. Until his death in 378, he poured himself out in inspired preaching, patient teaching, courageous debating, and humble service to his flock. His legacy endured not only in the triumph of Trinitarian orthodoxy at the Council of Constantinople in 381 but also in his enduring vision of a new city infused with visible Christian virtues.

Before he even became bishop, Basil leapt into action during the crisis of the great famine, which took place in either 368 or 369.[23] Starvation and despair led people to such desperate measures as the abandonment or the selling of children, while the rich hoarded what little remained to ride out the catastrophe. Gregory describes Basil's efforts as follows:

> For by his word and advice he opened the stores of those who possessed them, and so, according to the Scripture dealt food to the hungry, and satisfied the poor with bread, and fed them in the time of dearth, and filled the hungry souls with good things. And in what way? For this is no slight addition to his praise. He gathered together the victims of the famine with some who were but slightly recovering from it, men and women, infants, old men, every age which was in distress, and obtaining contributions of all sorts of food which can relieve famine, set before them basins of soup and such meat as was found preserved among us, on which the poor live. Then, imitating the ministry of Christ, who, girded with a towel, did not disdain to wash the disciples' feet, using for

22 Basil of Caesarea, *Letter 223*, 2 (PG 31, 824B; FC 28, 127–28).
23 On the great famine and drought, see Susan Holman, *The Hungry are Dying: Beggars and Bishops in Roman Cappadocia* (Oxford: Oxford University Press, 2001), 69–71.

this purpose the aid of his own servants, and also of his fellow servants, he attended to the bodies and souls of those who needed it, combining personal respect with the supply of their necessity, and so giving them a double relief.[24]

Basil himself joined in the efforts, serving food and bringing consolation to the frightened crowds. During the crisis, he never lost sight of the fact that, though providing material needs was essential, the real nourishment came from the hope of the Gospel message: "Further he provided the nourishment of the Word, and that more perfect bounty and distribution, which is really heavenly and from on high—if the word be that bread of angels, wherewith souls are fed and given to drink, who are a hungry for God, and seek for a food which does not pass away or fail, but abides forever."[25]

This service did not cease with the end of the crisis, but extended itself into Gregory's years in the episcopacy. In the countryside of Caesarea, he established a "new city" dedicated to Christian philanthropy. He called it a *ptōchotropheion*, from the Greek *ptōchos* ("poor") and *trephein* ("to nourish"); it also acquired the name *Basileias*—an obvious reference to its founder, though it also suggests a revelation of the Kingdom (*basileia*) of God.[26] It consisted of a network of hospices, soup kitchens, hospitals, and churches that served all who came seeking spiritual and physical sustenance.[27] Basil himself would at times serve in this colony of the poor, the beloved of Christ, and he inspired others to share in the citizenship of this new polity. His loyal friend describes the effects of this service to the destitute and the diseased:

> He [Basil] however it was, who took the lead in pressing upon those who were men, that they ought not to despise their fellowmen, nor to dishonor Christ, the one Head of all, by their inhuman treatment of them; but to use the misfortunes of others as an opportunity of firmly

---

24 Gregory of Nazianzus, *Oration 43*, 35 (SC 384, 202, lines 11–12 and 204, lines 13–27; NPNF II-7, 407).

25 Gregory of Nazianzus, *Oration 43*, 36 (SC 384, 204, line 9 and 206, lines 10–13; NPNF II-7, 407).

26 See Holman, *The Hungry are Dying*, 74–75.

27 Gregory of Nazianzus describes it as a new city: "A noble thing is philanthropy, and the support of the poor, and the assistance of human weakness. Go forth a little way from the city, and behold the new city, the storehouse of piety, the common treasury of the wealthy, in which the superfluities of their wealth, aye, and even their necessaries, are stored . . ." See Gregory of Nazianzus, *Oration 43*, 63 (SC 384, 260, lines 1–2 and 262, lines 3–5; NPNF II-7, 416).

establishing their own lot, and to lend to God that mercy of which they stand in need at His hands. He did not therefore disdain to honor with his lips this disease, noble and of noble ancestry and brilliant reputation though he was, but saluted them as brethren, not, as some might suppose, from vainglory, (for who was so far removed from this feeling?) but taking the lead in approaching to tend them, as a consequence of his philosophy, and so giving not only a speaking, but also a silent, instruction. The effect produced is to be seen not only in the city, but in the country and beyond, and even the leaders of society have vied with one another in their philanthropy and magnanimity towards them.[28]

Not all Christians have the character or means to accomplish what Basil achieved. Yet Basil shows all Christians the maturing effects of service in the name of Christ. Not every Christian can found a city; but any Christian can contribute to the building of the Kingdom, one brick at a time.

THE BENEFITS OF SERVICE

How does service mature us? First, giving of oneself to one's neighbor leads to greater freedom. If I cling to the goods of the world and ignore those around me, I imprison myself within the confines of my ego. Basil the Great exposes the harsh masters of wealth and security: "What neighbor, what confidant, what friend is not swept away? Nothing withstands the influence of wealth. Everything submits to its tyranny, everything cowers at its dominion."[29] Thus, poverty and service, as Gregory of Nazianzus teaches, restore the original freedom of Paradise: "He who created man from the beginning left him free and with free will, subject only to the law of his commandment and rich in the delights of Paradise. This was the gift he chose to bestow upon the subsequent generations of mankind also, through the one first seed. Freedom and wealth meant simply keeping the commandment; true poverty and slavery are its transgression."[30] Restoring the commandment of love, transgressed through humanity's radical turn to the self, therefore gives the Christian freedom to mature in the virtues and the reception of grace.

Second, Christian service directs us toward our *telos* in God. Jesus himself offers this teaching: "Do not lay up for yourselves treasures on earth,

---

28 Gregory of Nazianzus, *Oration 43*, 63 (SC 384, 264, lines 26–39; NPNF II-7, 416).
29 Basil the Caeserea, *Sermon 7*, 5 (PG 31, 293C; PPS 38, 51).
30 Gregory of Nazianzus, *Oration 14*, 25 (PG 35, 891B; FC 107, 58).

where moth and rust consume and where thieves break in and steal, but lay up for yourselves treasures in heaven, where neither moth nor rust consumes and where thieves do not break in and steal. For where your treasure is, there will your heart be also" (Matt 6:19–21). Alms and acts of charity turn Christians away from false pursuits and toward the *unum necessarium*. If one desires material goods and exploits the neighbor, one's treasure will be the instability of the world; if one gives the self away, one's *telos* will be in God.

Basil puts this idea in starker terms by calling service our preparation for death: "In anticipation, therefore, prepare yourself for your own burial. Works of piety are an excellent burial garment. Make your departure dressed in the full regalia of your good deeds; convert your wealth into a truly inseparable adornment; keep everything with you when you go! Be persuaded to this by Christ, the Good Counselor who loves you."[31] John Chrysostom notes that we want to be ready for the time when we do reach our end, when the separation of the sheep and the goats will take place (Matt 25:31–46): "What benefit is it, tell me, after walking on the easy road a little while, to come to a permanent destruction; after luxuriating in a dream, so to speak, to be punished in truth?"[32] Full maturity in God will therefore take its form from what one does in loving service: one leaves behind the illusions of the world to assume the reality of the Trinitarian life.

Finally, service reveals and forms the communion of the saints. Gregory of Nazianzus preaches the paradox of abandonment to God's love: "Indeed, to receive in the truest sense is to give oneself to God. No matter how much you offer, what remains is always more; and you will be giving nothing that is your own because all things come from God."[33] Something analogous takes place in our self-gift to the neighbor, since, when one loses the comforts and security of the world, one gains the riches of relationship. One even heals the shattering of the human community that took place in sin: "But sympathy corrects the difference and love makes all [men] even."[34] The Fathers understand service to give us a glimpse of the harmony of Paradise and the hope of human communion in God.[35]

---

31 Basil of Caeserea, *Oration 7*, 9 (PG 31, 304C; PPS 38, 57).
32 John Chrysostom, *Lazarus 7* (PG 48, 1047; PPS 9, 121).
33 Gregory of Nazianzus, *Oration 14*, 22 (PG 35, 885C; FC 107, 55).
34 John Chrysostom, *Lazarus 6* (PG 48, 1032; PPS 9, 98).
35 Brian Daley summarizes the overall philanthropic project of the Cappadocian Fathers: "[The] heart of their civic message was new: a vision of Christ as the true emperor and the

CONCLUSION

"In nothing does man's affinity with God lie so much as in his capacity to do good."[36] If human maturity is the divine likeness, then the mature Christian imitates the One who stooped to wash the feet of his disciples. These Fathers preached the Gospel, but they also embraced lives of simplicity and service to their flocks. Their prestige and authority did not blind them to the destitute and despairing. They heard Christ's commands and chose to follow him. If one wishes to be mature, one also must take on the yoke of Christ's love and join the Fathers on the way.

The image of the servant offers one other fundamental lesson for all Christians: *the mature person is ready to assume responsibility for the well-being of persons other than himself.* Thus, mature Christian parents, political and religious leaders, and others in positions of authority put their own desires aside to serve. Just as Basil neither claimed nor abused his status as an upper-class bishop, but instead sought to alleviate the suffering of his flock, so all Christians demonstrate their maturity through dedication to others.

---

full realization of godlike humanity; a trembling yet hopeful expectation that it was his law on which all Cappadocia's citizens would someday be judged, not simply the law of the Greeks; an awareness that the texts which now defined civility and reverence and virtue were not those of Homer and the tragedians, let alone those of the philosophers, but the books of Holy Scripture." See Brian Daley, "The Cappadocian Fathers," 459.

36 Gregory of Nazianzus, *Oration 14*, 27 (PG 35, 892D-893A; FC 107, 59).

CHAPTER 11

Fool

The mature Christian occupies a precarious place in the world. On the one hand, a person's manifestation of Baptismal grace, even in small ways, transforms society and offers it hope. The world sometimes reacts positively to such persons and even bestows honors on them. On the other hand, in an age infected with demonic infantilism, society will portray the mature as fools. Just as the youth of the West tore down the edifices of their elders in 1968, so the infants of every decade attack the wisdom of the ages on which their world stands. The mature Christian, inspired with divine Wisdom, therefore becomes the object of ridicule and scorn—an idiot in the eyes of the scolders.

Witness, Teacher, Servant . . . and Fool. This concluding chapter examines foolishness in the Scriptures and the later example of Symeon the *salos*. In light of such spiritual folly, this chapter draws some conclusions regarding the Christian maturity today and the hope it offers.

CHRIST THE FOOL

"And He went home. And the crowd came together again, such that they could not even eat bread. And those of his own, hearing [this], came out to lay hold of Him. They said that He was out of his mind [*exestē*]" (Mark 5:20–21). The Greek for "out of his mind" in fact means "to stand apart from" or "stand outside." It thus implies "standing outside of one's senses or wits."

Jesus's own family deems him non compos mentis, since he has abandoned his traditional pursuits in order to preach, teach, and perform wonders. It only gets worse, since those outside Jesus's personal circle soon accuse him of demonic activity: "He is possessed by Beelzebul, and by the prince of demons he casts out the demons" (Mark 3:22). They all see Jesus as being out of sync with their order of things; he is a madman and a demoniac.[1] John describes the reception of Jesus the fool in his prologue: "And he came to his own [*ta idia*: "the things particular to Him"], and his own [*hoi idioi*: "his own people"] did not receive Him" (John 1:11). Yet those who do receive him, despite the judgment of others, become children (*tekna*) of God, those who may grow to the full stature of Christ.

Saint Paul provides a theology of foolishness firmly grounded in Christology. In his *Letter to the Philippians,* Paul cites a magnificent hymn that extols Jesus's self-emptying. "[Christ Jesus], who, though he was in the form [*morphē*] of God, did not count equality with God a thing to be grasped [*harpagmon*], but emptied himself [*ekenōsen*], taking the form [*morphēn*] of a servant, being born in the likeness [*homoiōmati*] of men" (Phil 2:6–7). Scholars debate whether the first lines refer to the preexistence of Christ in his equality with the Father, or to Jesus, as human, refusing to yield to the temptation of Adam to become "like God." Dennis Hamm, in supporting the former interpretation, states that the form (*morphē*)—the outward manifestation of one's nature—refers first to the qualities of Christ's divinity, which he "empties" in taking on the form of man: "By becoming man, the Son emptied himself of the glory, majesty, and privilege that belong to him as divine."[2] This self-emptying extends to the ignominious death of the Cross: "And being found in human form he humbled himself and became obedient unto death, even death on a Cross" (Phil 2:8). Thus, the truth of the Son remains masked to the eyes of the world, which only sees a man "out of his mind" and condemned to a shameful death. Only in the Resurrection and the Ascension does the Son become "highly exalted," receiving "the name" before which all bow.[3]

---

1 On the connection between the versions, see Mary Healy, *The Gospel of Mark* (Grand Rapids, MI: Baker Academic, 2008), 75–78.

2 Dennis Hamm, SJ., *Philippians, Colossians, Philemon* (Grand Rapids, MI: Baker Academic, 2013), 99.

3 On the identity of the name with the tetragrammaton (YHWH), see Hamm, *Philippians, Colossians, Philemon,* 102.

The wisdom of the world could not perceive the identity of the One before them, and so the world sees the Cross and Christians as fools. Saint Paul develops this theme in his *First Letter to the Corinthians*. He first considers the world's judgment of the Cross: "For the word of the Cross is folly [*mōria*] to those who are perishing, but to us who are being saved, it is the power of God . . . For the foolishness [*to mōron*] of God is wiser than men, and the weakness of God is stronger than men" (1 Cor 18: 25). In this context, the wisdom of the world applies to the dominant and admired Greek culture apart from the revelation of Christ.[4] The Cross, however, expresses the self-emptying love of God that opens to the new life of the Resurrection—a life that transcends the limited vision of time and history held by the Greeks and even many of Paul's fellow Jews.[5] The folly of a self-emptying God, mad with love, who assumes death for the sake of fallen humanity—such a teaching clashes with the closed wisdom of the world.

Paul commits himself to this divine foolishness: "For I think that God has exhibited us apostles as last of all, like men sentenced to death; because we have become a spectacle [*theatron*] to the world, to angels and to men. We are fools [*mōroi*] for Christ's sake, but you are wise [*phronimoi*] in Christ. We are weak, but you are strong. You are held in honor, but we in disrepute" (1 Cor 4:9–10). Like the low-life mimes in Greek theater (*theatron*), who were often executed within the storylines of plays, Paul and other apostles find themselves following the footsteps of Christ the fool, who perished on the Cross: their denouement will also find its place on the Cross, the divine Wisdom that confounds all men.[6]

---

4 "Those who embraced Hellenism, whether the Greek nationality or not, participated in a learned culture through philosophy, rhetoric and art, as represented in the gymnasium, the assembly, and the theater. Thus the concept of 'foolishness' that Paul applies to his preaching is not derived from the Gentile inhabitants of the Roman Empire in general, but, more specifically, from those whose identity as Hellenes centered on the possession of wisdom." See Laurence Welborn, "*Mōros genesthō*: Paul's Appropriation of the Role of the Fool in 1 Corinthians 1–4," *Biblical Interpretation* 10, no. 4 (2002): 423.

5 On the contrast between Paul's apocalyptic vision, the Greek "circular" understanding of time, and the rejection of resurrection by many Jews, see George Montague, SM, *First Corinthians*, (Grand Rapids, MI: Baker Academic, 2011), 47. Montague asks why Paul extols the Cross before the world's wisdom, and not the more hopeful teaching of the Resurrection. He answers, "But resurrection is a phenomenon that goes beyond our normal human experience. Suffering does not: it is the lot of every human being. That is why we understand the cross better than we understand the resurrection. It is love, sacrificial love to the extreme" (*First Corinthians*, 44).

6 See Welborn, "*Mōros genesthō*," 428–30. See also Montague, *First Corinthians*, 87.

One should note that the foolishness of Paul in no way condones the rejection of reason or the goodness of the world. John Saward stresses that "Folly is a relative concept. It only has meaning in distinction from some kind of wisdom. This is an obvious but far from trivial truth, for the New Testament never beatifies wisdom or folly *in general*, but only wisdom or folly under a certain description."[7] Christians do not pride themselves on being stupid or naïve; they recognize, alongside such special luminaries as Augustine or Basil, that the Greeks and the Romans have much to offer the faithful. Yet Paul rejects the elitist stance of the Corinthians who exalt themselves on the basis of their cultural patrimony and scorn those who fail to share it. What they count as foolish, however, only reveals their closed-mindedness. Following Christ will, in the end, open one's mind to the Truth and the Hope for new life without end.

SYMEON THE HOLY FOOL

The Holy Fool continues to confound and scandalize Christians to this day. One may discover the disruptive power of the fool in the Scriptures, especially in the actions of the prophets. Isaiah walked about naked and barefoot for three years as a sign against Egypt and Ethiopia (Isa. 20:1–6). God tells Ezekiel to eat food cooked on human dung in order to awaken the people to impending suffering (Ezek. 4:12). The prophet also simulates an escape from the city through a hole in the wall to illustrate the encroaching conquest of Judah (Ezek. 12:1–7). These bizarre acts disturb and enlighten; their "madness" rocks the complacency of those who no longer listen to God.

The saints known as the *saloi* dot the landscape of Christianity's early centuries, adding striking colors to an already variegated field of blessed eccentrics. *Salos*, generally translated as "fool," was a colloquial word that came to designate a type of ascetic who adopted bizarre and scandalous behaviors that made even the most radical monks appear to be mainstream.[8] John Saward summarizes the *salos*'s vocation as follows: "The fool for Christ's sake . . . is one who is recognized not only by the world but also by his fellow Christians as foolish—a foolishness which conceals his spirituality, or rather

---

[7] John Saward, *Perfect Fools: Folly for Christ's Sake in Catholic and Orthodox Spirituality* (Oxford: Oxford University Press, 1980), 3.

[8] On the term *salos*, see Derek Krueger, *Symeon the Holy Fool: Leontius's Life and the Late Antique City* (Berkeley: University of California Press, 1996), 63; Irina Goraïnoff, *Les fols in Christ dans la tradition orthodoxe* (Paris: Desclée de Brouwer, 1983), 15–16.

which is a medium for the foolishness of God, wiser than men."⁹ Thus, as we shall see, the public behavior of a *salos* outwardly challenged the customs stemming from worldly wisdom, inspired "mainstream" ascetics to reinvigorate their call, and provided a medium for divine wisdom to shake Christians from their complacency. Abba Ammonas, Mark the Mad, Theophilus and Maria—a betrothed couple who chose a life of prayer, celibacy, and feigned madness—the great Symeon, and many others have acquired lasting fame for their unusual form of asceticism.

Leontius of Neapolis, a seventh-century bishop in Cyprus, composed *The Life of Symeon the Holy Fool* between 641 and 648.¹⁰ Leontius states that he wrote the work in order to provide Christians with a model to follow— though to what extent one should embrace Symeon's folly remains unclear. He desires "through his [the reader's] hearing, and through the stories which are told to him, a divine yearning be aroused in him [the reader] to shake his soul from its sleep, that he may travel through the straight and narrow path and begin eternal life now."¹¹

One may divide the work into two parts. The first part offers an account of Symeon's more "conventional" monastic period. Initially, Symeon and his friend John leave their families—John left his young wife—to enter a monastery in Palestine. They do not, however, stay for long. Discerning a call to live as solitaries in the desert, they exit the community with the blessing of the monk who briefly acted as their formator:

> May their [Symeon's and John's] body, and their soul, and their spirit be enlightened with the light of your knowledge, so that, arriving at the unity of the faith and the full knowledge of the holy and venerable Trinity, attaining mature manhood, and the measure of the stature (Eph 4:13), they will extol forever and ever, together, with the angels and all those well pleasing to you, O God, since eternity, your all-honorable and protecting name of the Father, the Son, and the Holy Spirit. Amen.¹²

---

9 Saward, *Perfect Fools*, 14.

10 For the dating of the text, see Alexander Y. Syrkin, "On the Behavior of the 'Fool for Christ's Sake,'" *History of Religions* 22, no. 2 (1982): 150–52. For the translation, see the appendix in Krueger, *Symeon: The Holy Fool*, 131–71.

11 Leontius of Neapolis, *The Life of Symeon the Fool* 122 (Rydén 56, lines 8–10 [1672A]; Krueger, 132).

12 Leontius, *Symeon* 135 (Rydén, 69, lines 18–23 [1693A]; Krueger, 143).

The two friends then set out to wrestle with the Devil and immerse themselves in a life of prayer.

In the second part, Symeon returns to the inhabited regions for a new stage in his vocation. After twenty-nine years of dedication to the ascetic life, Symeon tries to convince his friend John to join him in this daring new enterprise: "What more benefit do we derive, brother, from passing time in this desert? But if you hear me, get up, let us depart; let us save others. For as we are, we do not benefit anyone except ourselves, and have not brought anyone else to salvation."[13] The city now calls Symeon to enter its walls and live as a spiritual provocateur among the people. Although John chooses to stay, the two remain steadfast friends in the spirit for their remaining days.

After returning to public life, Symeon never abandons his rigorous disciplines and regimen of prayer. However, in order to maintain his humility, he elects to feign madness. His grand entrance into the city of Emesa involves tying a dead dog to his leg and enduring the jeers of the local children, who call him a "fool." In the years that follow, his actions amuse, annoy, and scandalize the residents. He blows out candles and throws nuts at worshippers in the church. Sometimes "he pretended to have a limp, sometimes he jumped around, sometimes he dragged himself along on his buttocks, sometimes he stuck out his foot for someone running and tripped him. Other times when there was a new moon, he looked at the sky and fell down and thrashed about."[14] He entered the women's bathhouse, punched a possessed man in the face, and ate food like a ravenous beast. If anyone began to discern his hidden wisdom and holiness, he would perform yet another bizarre act to suppress any recognition and praise.

Was there a method to his madness? Leontius writes, "[The] all-wise Symeon's whole goal was this: first, to save souls, whether through afflictions which he sent them in ludicrous and methodical ways, or through miracles which he performed while seeming not to understand, or through maxims which he said to them while playing the fool; and second, that his virtue not be known, and he receive neither approval nor honor from men."[15] Indeed, under the cover of insanity, Symeon healed bodies and spirits. When the deacon John was framed for murder, Symeon went to a hidden place to pray

---

13 Leontius, *Symeon* 142 (Rydén, 76, lines 13–16 [1704A]; Krueger, 148).
14 Leontius, *Symeon* 155 (Rydén, 89, lines 20–24 [1725A]; Krueger, 159).
15 Leontius, *Symeon* 157 (Rydén, 91, lines 12–16 [1728C]; Krueger, 161).

and, just before the deacon's execution, men arrived to announce that the real murderer had been found.[16] In another tale, he makes a man who stole a goat go blind, but then restores the man's sight with the advice never to steal again. And in another bizarre story, when a man becomes possessed owing to his acts of adultery, Symeon heals and converts him through a punch on the jaw.

Leontius notes that exorcisms were Symeon's most important ministry:

> Symeon had extraordinary compassion for those possessed by demons, so that from time to time he went off to make himself like one of them, and passed his time with them, healing many of them through his own prayer, and therefore some daimoniacs cried out and said, "O violence, Fool, you jeer at the whole world. Have you also come by us to give us trouble? Retreat from here; you are not one of us. Why do you torture us all night long and burn us?"[17]

In short, the mask of madness conceals an unrecognized ministry of healing grounded in a hidden asceticism. In addition, when his holiness becomes manifest after his death, his example inspires greater compassion toward those who genuinely suffer from mental and physical illnesses. Leontius concludes his history with a call to spiritual awakening: "How can the wisdom of the tongue praise the one who obliterated all wisdom and prudence in the folly according to God? Truly human in face, but God in heart. Truly God will not see thus as a human sees. Truly no one knows a person's deeds without knowing the person's spirit. Truly we must not judge someone before the time, O friends of Christ, before the Lord comes and illuminates everything."[18]

In many ways, Symeon's life radically follows the pattern set by Jesus himself. Jesus spent most of his life in obscurity, culminating in a complete separation from the world during his forty days of trial in the desert. In the same way, Symeon spends years away from the eyes of the world practicing *askēsis* and battling temptations. Thus, Jesus's example of prayer, fasting, and struggle with the Devil provides the model for the *salos*'s own preparatory period.

After defeating the Devil "for a time," Jesus initiates his public life. His teaching, preaching, and healing attract disciples, call sinners to conversion,

---

16 Leontius, *Symeon* 160 (Rydén, 94, lines 5–24 [1732D–1733A]; Krueger, 163).
17 Leontius, *Symeon* 163 (Rydén, 96, lines 12–17 [1736B–C]; Krueger, 165).
18 Leontius, *Symeon* 169 (Rydén, 103, lines 10–16 [1745C]; Krueger, 170).

and give hope for the coming of the Kingdom of God. In the same way, the call to "save souls" draws Symeon out of his retreat and leads him back into the bustle of the city. He receives the grace to heal both bodies and souls, while also inspiring sinners to reform their lives. Jesus's public life therefore gives shape to Symeon's radical ministry.

As we have already seen, many people thought Jesus was either insane or possessed. His teachings and actions, such as his healings on the sabbath or associations with sinners, broke societal conventions, and his challenging of authorities led to his condemnation and death. Here, one can certainly note that Symeon's life does not exactly imitate Jesus's life. Symeon *feigns* madness, and many of his actions would rightly offend most Christians. This is not the Pauline folly that emerges from the world's reaction to the Cross as authentic wisdom. And yet, nevertheless, Symeon sought to imitate Christ's life while at the same time *humbling himself*.[19] Just as Saint Peter did not deem himself worthy to be crucified in the same way as Christ—he turns the manner of Jesus's death on its head—so Symeon embraces folly in a topsy-turvy manner that only highlights the authentic innocence and power of Jesus. Symeon's miracles in no way come from himself, the fool, but from God's power; his feigned madness speaks to his own unworthiness to be counted as a "fool for Christ." Still, the world judges him insane unto death, and only in the aftermath does the truth come to light.

CONCLUSION

The world very often portrays the mature Christian as a fool. This should come as no surprise. Given the Pauline folly of the Cross—a death to all the false promises of the world and an act of self-abandonment to the Father through Christ—even the disciple's "own people" may diagnose him as "outside himself." Such judgments should not embitter the disciple, but serve as part of his joyful ministry: his folly stems from the gift of divine Wisdom, which, in the end, will overcome the wisdom of the world.

What of the feigned madness of Symeon? Flannery O'Connor once wrote about her use of the grotesque in fiction: "When you can assume that your audience holds the same beliefs you do, you can relax and use more normal means of talking to it; when you have to assume that it does

---

19 On the rejection of *kenodoxia*, or "vainglory," through feigned madness, see Gilbert Dagron, "L'homme sans honneur ou le saint scandaleux," *Annales Histoire, Sciences Sociales* 45, no. 4 (1990): 931–34.

not, then you have to make your vision apparent by shock—to the hard of hearing you shout, and for the almost-blind you draw large and startling figures."[20] Symeon's methods did indeed awaken a lethargic Christian population to a greater practice of their faith. His spectacle drew people away from the mundane and forced them to confront forgotten truths regarding the power of hidden sanctity. He was a large and startling figure in a realm of complacent Christians.

One need not assume Symeon's path, since any mature Christian's adherence to the Way of Christ will shake the world to its core; nonetheless, Symeon still has lessons to teach us. First, the wisdom of the Christian stems not from the display before the world but from the hidden life of prayer, asceticism, and the Mysteries. It takes place in secret, within the intimate relationship with God and the power of silence. Second, most Christians must bring the fruits of their interior lives into the world for the salvation of souls. As servants and teachers, they share the gifts: "For nothing is hidden that shall not be made manifest, nor anything secret that shall not be known and come to light" (Luke 8:17). Finally, the Christian grows in the virtue of humility through the inevitable condemnations of the world. Vainglory corrupts the good works of Christians; humility allows the witness to point away from the self and toward the Lord: "Behold the Lamb of God, who takes away the sin of the World" (John 1:29). Folly is a friend who brings one back to earth—"humility" comes from the Latin *humus*, or earth—so that God might raise him to heaven, to the eternal communion of blessed fools for Christ.

The Holy Fool has an incredible power in the world. At times societies may designate mature Christians—witnesses, teachers, and servants—as fools, but that folly inevitably overturns the dominant order of things. The Holy Fool, so united with Christ, unmasks the deleterious effects of worldly wisdom, shakes up the oppressive status quo, and directs all eyes toward the love of Christ, Wisdom Incarnate.

---

20 Flannery O'Connor, "The Fiction Writer and His Country," in *Mystery and Manners*, ed. Sally and Robert Fitzgerald (New York: Farrar, Straus & Giroux, 1969), 33–34.

CONCLUSION
Time to Grow Up

It is time to consider in full what the Fathers offer us regarding Christian maturity. However, before considering the fruits of their insights, let us revisit the problem of elected immaturity in the modern age.

DEMONIC INFANTILISM AND ITS DISCONTENTS

Our age vaunts its immaturity as a badge of honor. Sadly, this boast has even infected many Christians and has led to the loss of an essential sobering influence in the world. The following traits reveal that demonic infantilism thrives in our nations, communities, and our pews:

The Rejection of the *Telos* and the Rise of Elasticity

C. S. Lewis anticipated the assault against human nature in his novel *That Hideous Strength*. Mark Studdock, an atheist sociologist, comes to work for a think tank that, unknown to him, strives to bridge the gap between demonic spiritualism and scientific materialism. Mark's colleagues aspire to be new men who embrace "elasticity," the complete liberation from physical or moral norms. Only such radical freedom, achieved through technological advances and sociological manipulation, will promote the infinitely malleable man. No constraints will limit his redefining of the self or the human race as a whole. In the new age, men can become as amorphous as demons:

> What should they regard as too obscene, since they held that all morality was a mere subjective by-product of the physical and economic situations of men? The time was ripe. From the point of view which is accepted in Hell, the whole history of our Earth had led up to this moment. There was now at last a real chance for fallen Man to shake off that limitation of his powers which mercy had imposed upon him as a

protection from the full results of his fall. If this succeeded, Hell would be at last incarnate.[1]

Lewis's fears have at last come to pass. The sexual revolution in all its deleterious forms, the denunciation of "the normal," and the many scientific promises to remake humanity in body and mind define our practices and aspirations. We have the power to make hell on earth.

Christians have not been immune to this infection. In the analysis of Joseph Ratzinger, the future Pope Benedict XVI, many Christians have abandoned the *factum*, the givenness of nature and tradition, and ceded all to the *faciendum*, what can be made of ourselves and the world. They reduce their own beliefs to mere instruments for societal and personal reconstruction.[2] While Christianity *does* positively change persons and societies, the extreme shift to the side of the *faciendum* and the rejection of many or all governing norms have rendered Christians susceptible to the culture's celebration of absolute malleability. Such a "reformed" Christianity then becomes an ally to forces that threaten to dissolve humanity as a whole.

The rejection of the *telos*—the *telos* of the human person in the Christ-form—creates a society of spoiled children. Not a day passes without witnessing a new tantrum from ideological infants. To propose a moral norm or a beautiful form provokes many to whine and protest, if not to perform acts of violence. These children, however, often inhabit adult bodies and, as a result, they have the power to exercise their rage in dangerous ways that literal infants do not. They have elected immaturity and shudder before a future that has no hope.

Virtues Gone Mad

Nearly a century ago, G. K. Chesterton noted this peculiar fact of our times: "The modern world is full of the old Christian virtues gone mad. The virtues have gone mad because they have been isolated from each other and are wandering alone. Thus, some scientists care for truth; and their truth is

---

[1] C.S. Lewis, *That Hideous Strength* (New York: Scribner, 2003), 200–201. Lewis perhaps did not entirely anticipate the radical individualism that now facilitates elasticity and the abolition of man. For a review of the intellectual and social influences on the contemporary situation, see Carl Trueman, *The Rise and Triumph of the Modern Self* (Wheaton, IL: Crossway, 2020).

[2] See Joseph Ratzinger, *Introduction to Christianity* (San Francisco: Ignatius Press, 2004), 66–69.

pitiless. Thus, some humanitarians only care for pity; and their pity (I am sorry to say) is often untruthful."³

Christianity promotes the totality of the virtues in Christ. The unity of the virtues, a theme one may discover in the writings of the ancient Platonists, finds its authentic grounding in Christian teachings. As we saw, the virtues both perfect human nature—a gift created in the divine likeness—and reflect divine qualities. To grow in *all* the virtues therefore leads to maturation and an assimilation to the Christ-form. The rejection of any or all of the virtues, however, allies the self with the tendencies of the demonic: vices wound our nature and detract from the form of Christ.

With postmodernity's rejection of human nature and the Christian *telos*, we find ourselves in an age of confusion. The culture promotes virtues such as tolerance, kindness, self-care, and mercy, but denies a nature to which these virtues adhere. Furthermore, having rejected such virtues as chastity, fidelity, goodness, truthfulness, and justice, other authentic virtues become vices: self-care leads to self-indulgence and narcissism; tolerance becomes indifference and irresponsibility; and mercy ignores genuine justice. Once again, we find ourselves among children who elect to remain in lives of gnawing vices and enfeebled virtues—the demonic triumph on a large scale.

The Consumers and the Consumed

Abandoning any conception of nature and swimming in a sea of incoherent pseudo-virtues, people lead lives of consuming and being consumed. Contemporary market consumerism thrives in a culture that eschews asceticism and has no other goal than to indulge personal desires. Thus, the protean person flits from one product to the other, from one fad to the next. He constructs the self from pieces sliced from the slick offerings of the ever-growing marketplace of entertainment, dresses in the newest celebrity identity, and grasps at the latest medications formulated to produce happiness. Like a child in a candy store, he rushes from one offering to the next and, without any restraints, will indulge until he is sick to his stomach.

Such a culture also turns all persons into the consumed. In C. S. Lewis's *Screwtape Letters*, the devil Screwtape describes the demonic vision of creation:

---

3 G. K. Chesterton, *Orthodoxy*, in *Complete Works*, vol. 1 (San Francisco: Ignatius Press, 1986), 233.

> The whole philosophy of Hell rests on recognition of the axiom that one thing is not another thing, and, specially, that one self is not another self. My good is my good, and your good is yours. What one gains another loses. Even an inanimate object is what it is by excluding all other objects from the space it occupies; if it expands, it does so by thrusting other objects aside or by absorbing them. A self does the same. With beasts the absorption takes the form of eating; for us, it means the sucking of will and freedom out of a weaker self into a stronger. "To be" *means* "to be in competition."[4]

Unbridled self-indulgence can only lead to the competition that marks modern consumerism. Some people are the prime consumers or devourers, growing ever richer at the expense of others and often supporting the instruments of infantilization. In the name of population control, sexual liberation, and other utopian schemes, they rob people of their self-defenses—family, faith, and authentic hope—to keep them perpetually laboring and spending in the expanding marketplace. They exercise a pedagogy of corruption such that persons, especially the weak, become their food, "the consumed." (Yet even such elites do not remain safe for long: there is always a bigger fish in the pond.)[5]

Rejection of Commitment

Undefined freedom in a consumer society cancels authentic maturity. The collapse of marriage, family, religious vocations, and fidelity to Baptismal promises in the Western world stems from a false fear of constraints: "How can I be free if I am committed to a particular way of life? Since the self is completely malleable, I need the space to perpetually reinvent my life. No form should enclose me in a prison." Such a view results in shallow personalities who avoid the adventure of going deep. If I have a pitcher of water, and pour it into a wide bowl, it will have breadth, but little depth; yet if I pour it

---

[4] C. S. Lewis, *The Screwtape Letters* (New York: Bantam Books, 1982), 52–53.

[5] A recent article in *Business Ethics Quarterly* critiques the rise of "organized immaturity," which they define as "the erosion of individuals' and collectives' capacities for public use of reason, facilitated by recent sociotechnological developments that simultaneously collect, analyze, and manipulate data on social exchange and have the capacity to normatively influence the behavior of individuals and social groups instantaneously." Thus, collective immaturity is enhanced by a consumer society that wrests control through technological manipulation. See Andreas Georg Scherer et al., "New Challenges to the Enlightenment," 411.

into a cylinder, it may not spread out far, but it acquires profundity. Vocation and commitment do not cancel freedom, but give it the essential boundaries to acquire depth. Thus, the flight from a commitment to one's Baptismal mission, marriage, and religious life renders people anxious adolescents who never know where they stand in the world. And ideologies, politics, and celebrity cults, owing to their unstable nature, cannot substitute for genuine vocations. It is no wonder that the demonic inspires people to abandon their true commitments: the demon desires to hear a chorus of "Non serviam" that echoes its own primordial defiance.

THE MATURE CHRISTIAN

The Fathers of the Church have reminded us of what it means to be Christian adults. The paradox of Christian maturity remains that of the adult child: the Christian is childlike in his reception of the Christ-form, since deification is gift; yet he is also an adult in his receptivity of the Christ-form through growth in virtue and the affirmative response to vocation. He avails himself of the means that God offers in the Scriptures, in the Mysteries with the community that shares in them, and in asceticism. When Christians of all ages grow in the divine likeness, the world benefits from the presence of witnesses, teachers, and servants. Although Christians will make use of their talents to assume the responsibilities of serving others, many in the world will still see them as fools. Yet, without mature Christians, the world will continue to transform itself into a vicious playground for wounded souls.

There is always hope for an awakening to maturation. I return to the character of Mark Studdock in C. S. Lewis's *That Hideous Strength*. In order to initiate Mark into the "objective" view of elasticity, the superiors of the Institute lock him in a room full of subtle, but grotesque, distortions meant to kill all healthy human reactions and accustom him to the formless world they desire. But Mark has a very different reaction to his enervating surroundings:

> As the desert first teaches men to love water, or as absence first reveals affection, there rose up against this background of the sour and the crooked some kind of vision of the sweet and the straight. Something else—something he vaguely called the "Normal"—apparently existed. He had never thought about it before. But there it was—solid, massive, with a shape of its own, almost like something you could touch, or eat, or fall in love with . . . He was not thinking in moral terms at all; or else (what is much the same thing) he was having his first deeply moral

experience. He was choosing a side: the Normal. "All that," as he called it, was what he chose . . ."[6]

Now that our society has become a room of not so subtle distortions, we see souls like Mark Studdock's beginning to appear. The inherent desire for form, purpose, responsibility, meaning, and commitment—the hope to grow into *something and someone*—will lead to both a rebellion and a search. The "normal" that Christianity offers to such souls is neither an abstract vision of man nor an artificial imposition of sterile laws, but a person, Jesus Christ, who gives form through a relationship of love. These restless hearts will, we hope, discover their fulfillment in the *Alpha* and the *Omega*, the Word who sweetly articulates all things.

I have called this book an *introduction* to Christian maturity. To advance in this important journey, I recommend consulting the Fathers of the Church who both taught and modeled the Way. They have much, much more to offer. Most of all, however, I pray that we all respond to Jesus's invitation to become perfect or mature. With his grace, we have no excuse for choosing infantilism; we have been created in the image that God wills to become the likeness. "See what love the Father has given us, that we should be called children of God; and so we are" (1 John 3:1). May we live out the gift of this divine adoption to the fullest.

---

6 Lewis, *That Hideous Strength*, 296–97.

APPENDIX
Brief Portraits of the Fathers

Ambrose of Milan (ca. 339–97): Ambrose was born into a noble Christian family in Trier, though the family moved to Rome after his father's death around 353. He received superb training in rhetoric and the law, leading to his appointment to an imperial post in Milan in 368. After the death of the Milanese Arian bishop, a crisis erupted among the Catholic and Arian Christians that Ambrose, as the city's consul, sought to quell. But, in a surprising twist, Ambrose, still a catechumen, was elected bishop. He was consecrated to the episcopacy one week after his Baptism. Ambrose led his flock during turbulent years in the fragmented empire. His preaching, teaching, and public witness formed many in the Christian faith, including his most famous spiritual son, Augustine of Hippo. He died on April 4, 397.

Athanasius of Alexandria (ca. 295–373): Athanasius received a superb education in his native city, Alexandria, one of the economic and intellectual hubs of the Roman Empire. He was ordained a deacon by Bishop Alexander in 319, served his bishop in the Council of Nicaea in 325, and became Bishop of Alexandria in 328. His years as bishop were tumultuous, marked by sharp debates regarding the Meletian schism and Trinitarian doctrine, multiple exiles, and daring escapes from imperial authorities. He spent the six years of his third exile among the Egyptian desert monks, where he came to know the great Antony of the Desert. His works include theological and dogmatic works that contributed to the defense of the full divinity of the Son and Spirit, as well as letters and ascetical treatises.

Augustine of Hippo (354–430): Augustine remains a giant in the history of Latin Christianity and culture. His remarkable and moving conversion story, recounted in *The Confessions*, traces his life from his birth in the Roman province of Numidia, through his tumultuous youth, to his reversion to Christian orthodoxy. His long life truly entered the public stage with his ascendency to the episcopacy of Hippo, in North Africa, in 395. Over a period of nearly four decades, he engaged in controversy, taught and guided his flock, and composed masterworks in theology, scriptural commentary, and spirituality.

Basil of Caesarea (ca. 330–79): Born in Caesarea in Cappadocia—in central Anatolia in modern-day Turkey—Basil received his earliest formation from a saintly and noble family. One of ten children, his siblings included Saint Gregory of Nyssa, Saint Peter of Sebaste, Saint Naucratius, and Saint Macrina the Younger. He went on to study rhetoric in Caesarea—where he met his friend, Gregory of Nazianzus—Constantinople, and Athens. After initiating a career as a rhetorician, his sister Macrina convinced him to change course and dedicate his life to God. He and his friend Gregory spent time in the desert regions learning from the great ascetics. Basil then drew from these experiences to found his own monastic communities. In 370, he became Bishop of Caesarea, dedicating himself to works for the poor and the defense of the full divinity of Father, Son, and Spirit. He was beloved for his leadership, compassion, and courageous articulation of the faith.

Clement of Alexandria (ca. 150–215): Clement was born and educated in Athens. He converted to Christianity and spent some time studying with Christian teachers in various regions. He eventually arrived in Alexandria, where he became a student of the Christian teacher Pantaenus. He later succeeded his teacher as the head of the Alexandrian catechetical school. He fled Alexandria during a persecution at the beginning of the third century and died in exile. His teachings present a remarkable vision of Christian culture that would influence Origen of Alexandria and many others.

Evagrius Ponticus (345–99): Evagrius grew up in a Christian family in what is now Turkey. He later became a lector under Basil the Great and a deacon under Gregory of Nazianzus. He accompanied Gregory to Constantinople when the latter became, for a brief period, the capital's patriarch. After Gregory's departure, Evagrius remained to enjoy the extravagances that the city offered. Eventually awakened to the dangers of his sensuous lifestyle, he departed first for Jerusalem and then for the Egyptian desert in order to live in the manner of the renowned ascetics in the region. His masterful treatises on monastic spirituality became widespread and influential.

Gregory of Nazianzus (ca. 330-90): Gregory was born to a noble family in Arianzum in Cappadocia. He studied rhetoric in Caesarea, Alexandria, and Athens, during which time he came to know his friend Basil. After completing his studies, he spent time as a monk with Basil, until he was recalled by his father, a bishop, to be ordained a priest in 362. Basil later consecrated a reluctant Gregory to be bishop of the small town of Sasima—a position that Gregory neglected, choosing instead to remain in Nazianzus. In 379, the Nicene party successfully brought Gregory to Constantinople to serve as bishop on the eve of the great council of 381. However, not long after the council began, Gregory was forced to leave when his opposition noted that the Council of Nicaea forbade a bishop to change his see. He spent his final days in a monastic retreat on the family estate. His writings include powerful sermons, dogmatic works, and even poetry.

Gregory of Nyssa (335-95): Gregory of Nyssa was the true mystic among the great Cappadocian Fathers, whose number includes Basil the Great and Gregory of Nazianzus. He received a superb education from his sister, Macrina, and spent a short period as a professional rhetorician. Through the influence of his brother, Basil the Great, he became Bishop of Nyssa in 372. He was active in the doctrinal debates of his day, especially those regarding the Trinity, and he was a participant in the Council of Constantinople in 381.

Irenaeus of Lyons (second century): We have little information about the life of this towering theological genius and saint. He was born in Asia Minor, perhaps in the city of Smyrna. He went to Gaul around the year 177 and was ordained as a priest. He acted as a delegate to Rome and was later consecrated as a bishop in Gaul. Some traditions state that he died a martyr. His reputation for theological acumen stems from his masterful refutation of the gnostics, *Against the Heresies,* which survives in a Latin translation, though extensive Greek passages have been recovered.

John Cassian (360-435): The birthplace of John Cassian remains unknown, though some scholars point toward the region of modern Romania. As a young man he spent time in a monastery in Bethlehem and later came to know the monks of Egypt. His time with the legendary ascetics gave him a rich supply of wisdom regarding the Christian pursuit of holiness. After some years of controversy and travel, he accepted an invitation to found a monastery in Marseilles. He successfully imported many of the practices and structures he had encountered in Egypt, along with his own modifications for Western Christian living. His *Conferences,* which consist of a series of conversations with famed Egyptian ascetics on a variety of topics, and his *Institutes* influenced many Western monks, including Benedict of Nursia.

John Chrysostom (349–407): John "the Golden-mouth" was born in the Syrian city of Antioch and received rhetorical training from the renowned pagan teacher, Libanius. He spent two years as a hermit and dedicated himself intensely to the study of the Scriptures. He was then ordained a deacon in 381 and a priest in 386. In the subsequent years his reputation as a preacher and defender of the poor spread far and wide. In 397, he became the Patriarch of Constantinople. Though bishop of the capital, he lived an ascetic lifestyle and openly defended the poor and downtrodden, thereby often provoking the ire of the elite class. Jealousies and political machinations motivated powerful figures to form a conspiracy against the saintly preacher and a synod of his enemies exiled John from his see in 403. He died in exile in 407. His published homilies, treatises, and reputation for sanctity established him as one of the most beloved Christian figures of antiquity.

John Moschos (died ca. 619): We know little about this author, a wandering monk who died in Rome around 619. In his travels he encountered many practitioners of *anachōrēsis*—that is, people who withdrew from society to dedicate themselves to the ascetic life—and he compiled their stories for the wider Christian community. One may categorize this work as a collection of "beneficial tales" (*diēgēseis psykōpheleis*), anecdotes meant to inspire a more devout and faithful Christian life through wonder and delight.

Leontius of Neapolis (seventh century): Leontius was a bishop in Cyprus during the seventh century. He composed lives of Saint John the Merciful and Symeon the Fool, as well as an important defense of icons.

Mark the Monk (fifth century): We know little about the spiritual master and theologian known as Mark the Monk. Scholars generally date his active years to the second half of the fifth century, but they locate his monastic and hermetic life to such settings as Palestine or Egypt. Nearly all, however, affirm the remarkable depth and influence of his surviving works that treat such topics as Baptism, repentance, Christology, prayer, and asceticism. Not all his positions remain acceptable to Christians, especially when confronted with

Augustinian teachings on the state of postlapsarian humanity. However, the modest surviving corpus of his ascetical works provides a treasure trove of wisdom from the experience of desert solitaries.

Maximus the Confessor (580–662): Extant lives of Maximus conflict with one another regarding the origins of this great ascetic, theologian, and martyr. One account maintains that Maximus was an official in the court of Emperor Heraclius and that he gave up his prestigious career to become a monk. He was forced to flee his monastery on the Bosporus when the Persians invaded and he spent time in the North African monastery of Sophronius, the future Patriarch of Jerusalem. His prodigious learning made him a powerful defender of orthodoxy during the monothelite controversy (the debate regarding the number of Christ's wills) and he traveled to Rome in 649 to participate in the Lateran Council. He and Pope Martin I rejected the emperor's demands to affirm monothelitism and they defended the two wills of Christ at the cost of their lives: Pope Martin died after torture and imprisonment; Maximus died in exile after having his tongue cut out and his right hand cut off. His dense and complicated writings are some of the most sublime contributions to Christian theology and spirituality from the late ancient world.

Origen of Alexandria (184–253): Origen remains one of the most influential and controversial theologians of Christianity. The son of a martyr, Leonides, Origen received an exceptional formation in the commercial and intellectual hub of Alexandria. His later work as a teacher and Christian philosopher brought him both renown and, at times, condemnation from bishops and laity alike. His writings include scripture commentaries, apologetics such as *Against Celsus,* the great work of speculative and systematic theology called *On First Principles*, and other writings of tremendous spiritual value. He spent his later life in Caesarea and died after being released from a brutal two-year imprisonment during a persecution under Emperor Decius.

Tertullian (155–240): Tertullian has received the title of "The Father of Latin Christianity." Born in Carthage, he was a trained rhetor and bilingual scholar (Latin and Greek) who converted to Christianity in his early forties. His extant writings traverse such subjects as apologetics (*The Apologeticus, On Idolatry, Against Praxeas,* etc.), theology (*On the Flesh of Christ, On the Resurrection of Christ,* etc.), and Christian living (*An Exhortation to Chastity,*

On Monogamy, On Fasting, etc.). Although his later association with the Christian sect known as Montanism has made him suspect for many, his writings nonetheless influenced generations of Christians.

BIBLIOGRAPHY

Ancient Christian Sources

Ambrose of Milan

Concerning Repentance. Translated by Eide Romestin and H. T. F. Duckworth. NPNF II-10, 327–60. New York: Christian Literature, 1896.

De paenitentia. Edited by Roger Gryson. SC 179. Paris: Éditions du Cerf, 1971.

De mysteriis. Edited by Bernard Botte. SC 25, 156–93. Paris: Éditions du Cerf, 1994.

On the Mysteries. Translated by Roy Defarrari. *Theological and Dogmatic Works.* FC 44, 1–28. Washington, DC: Catholic University of America Press, 1963.

De sacramentis. Edited by Bernard Botte. SC 25, 60–155. Paris: Éditions du Cerf, 1994.

On the Sacraments. Translated by Roy Defarrari. *Theological and Dogmatic Works.* FC 44, 265–328. Washington, DC: Catholic University of America Press, 1963.

Arethas of Caesarea

Commentary on Apocalypse. PG 106: 486–786.

Athanasius of Alexandria

The Life of Antony and The Letter to Marcellinus. Translated by Robert Gregg. New York: Paulist Press, 1980.

Vita Antonii. Edited by G. J. M. Bartelink. SC 400. Paris: Éditions du Cerf, 1994.

Augustine of Hippo

Confessiones. Edited by James O'Donnell. *Confessiones I–III.* Oxford: Oxford University Press, 2012.

Confessions. Translated by Maria Boulding, OSB. WSA I-11. Hyde Park, New York: New City Press, 1997.

De catechizandis rudibus. Edited by I. B. Bauer. CCSL 46, 121–78. Turnhout: Brepols, 1959.

Instructing Beginners in the Faith. Translated by Raymond Canning. WSA 5. Hyde Park, NY: New City Press, 2006.

De civitate Dei. Edited by E. Dombart and A. Kalb. CCSL 47–48. Turnhout: Brepols, 1955.

The City of God. Translated by William Babcock. WSA I-6 and I-7. Hyde Park, NY: New City Press, 2013.

De doctrina christiana. Edited by Joseph Martin. CCSL 32, 1–167. Turnhout: Brepols, 1962.

Teaching Christianity. Translated by Edmund Hill, OP. WSA I-11. Hyde Park, NY: New City Press, 1996.

De Genesi ad litteram. Edited by Joseph Zycha. CSEL 28.1. Vienna: Tempsky, 1888.

The Literal Meaning of Genesis. In *On Genesis: A Refutation of the Manichees, Unfinished Literal Commentary on Genesis,* translated by Edmund Hill, OP, 155–406. WSA I-13. Hyde Park, NY: New City Press, 2002.

De Genesi contra Manichaeos. Edited by Dorothea Weber. CSEL 91. Vienna: Verlag der Österreichischen Akademie Wissenschaften, 1998.

On Genesis against the Manichees. In *On Genesis,* translated by Edmund Hill, OP, 25–102. WSA I-13. Hyde Park, NY: New City Press, 2006.

De magistro. Edited by W. M. Green. CCSL 29, 157–203. Turnhout: Brepols, 1970.

On the Teacher. In *The Teacher; The Free Choice of the Will; Grace and Free Will,* translated by Robert Russell, 1–62. FC 59. Washington, DC: Catholic University of America Press, 1968.

De Trinitate. Edited by W. J. Mountain. CCSL 50/50A. Turnholt: Brepols, 1968.

On the Trinity. Translated by Edmund Hill, OP. WSA I-5. Hyde Park, NY: New City Press, 1991.

Basil of Caesarea

Letter 223. PG 32: 819–34. In *Letters,* translated by Agnes Clare Way, 125–34. FC 28. Vol. 2. Washington, DC: Catholic University of America Press, 1955.

On the Human Condition. Translated by Nonna Verna Harrison. PPS 30. Crestwood, NY: St. Vladimir's Seminary Press, 2005.

On the Origin of Humanity 1–2. Edited by Alexi Smets, SJ and Michel van Esbroeck, SJ SC 160. Paris: Éditions du Cerf, 1970.

Oration 6. PG 31: 261–78. In *On Social Justice,* translated by C. Paul Schroeder, 59–72. PPS 38. Crestwood, NY: St. Vladimir's Seminary Press, 2009.

Oration 7. PG 31: 277-304. In *On Social Justice,* translated by C. Paul Schroeder, 41–58 . PPS 38. Crestwood, NY: St. Vladimir's Seminary Press, 2009.

Oration 8. PG 31: 303–28. In *On Social Justice,* translated by C. Paul Schroeder, 73–88. PPS 38. Crestwood, NY: St. Vladimir's Seminary Press, 2009.

Why God is Not the Cause of Evil. PG 31: 329–54. In *On the Human Condition,* translated by Nonna Verna Harrison, 65–80. PPS 30. Crestwood, NY: St. Vladimir's Seminary Press, 2005.

Benedict of Nursia

The Rule of St. Benedict in English (Regula). Translated by Timothy Fry, OSB. Collegeville, MN: Liturgical Press, 1982.

Clement of Alexandria

Stromateis IV. Edited by Annewies van den Hoek. SC 463. Paris: Éditions du Cerf, 2001. Translated by William Wilson. ANF 2, 409–41. New York: Charles Scribner and Sons, 1913.

Dionysius the Areopagite

The Celestial Hierarchy (De caelesti hierarchia). Edited by G. Heil and A. M. Ritter. PTS 36, 7–59. Berlin: De Gruyter, 1981.

De divinis nominibus. Edited by B. R. Suchla. PTS 33. Berlin: De Gruyter, 1990.

The Divine Names. In *Pseudo-Dionysius: The Complete Works,* translated by Colm Luibheid, 47–131. New York: Paulist Press, 1987.

Epistula (Letter 8). Edited by G. Heil and A. M. Ritter. PTS 36, 171–92. Berlin: De Gruyter, 1981.

Evagrius Ponticus

The Antirhētikos. In *Talking Back: A Monastic Handbook for Combating Demons,* translated by David Brakke. Collegeville, MN: Liturgical Press, 2009.

Sur les Pensées [*On Thoughts*]. Edited by Paul Géhin, Clarie Guillaumont, and Antoine Guillaumont. SC 438. Paris: Les Éditions du Cerf, 1998. Translation by Robert Sinkewicz in *Evagrius of Pontus: The Greek Ascetic Corpus*, 136–82. Oxford: Oxford University Press, 2003.

Traité Pratique ou Le Moine [*The Praktikos*]. Edited by Antoine Guillaumont and Claire Guillaumont. SC 171. Paris: Les Éditions du Cerf, 1971.

To Eulogios: On Confession of Thoughts and Counsel. In *Evagrius of Pontus: The Greek Ascetic Corpus*, translated by Robert E. Sinkewicz, 12–59. Oxford: Oxford University Press, 2003.

Gregory of Nazianzus

Oration 1. Edited by Jean Bernardi. SC 247, 72–82. Paris: Éditions du Cerf, 1978. Translated by Charles Gordon Browne and James Edward Swallow. NPNF II-7, 203–4. New York: Christian Literature, 1894.

Oration 2. Edited by Jean Bernardi. SC 247, 84–240. Paris: Éditions du Cerf, 1978. Translated by Charles Gordon Browne and James Edward Swallow. NPNF II-7, 203–27.

Oration 14. PG 35: 857–910. In *Select Orations of Gregory of Nazianzus*, translated by Vinson Martha Pollard, 39–71. FC 107. Washington, DC: Catholic University of America Press, 2004.

Oration 40. PG 36: 359–426. Translated by Charles Gordon Browne and James Edward Swallow. NPNF II-7, 360–77.

Oration 43. Edited by Jean Bernardi. SC 384, 116–306. Paris: Éditions du Cerf, 1992. Translated by Charles Gordon Browne and James Edward Swallow. NPNF II-7, 395–421.

Gregory of Nyssa

De anima et resurrectione. Edited by Andreas Spira. GNO 3.3. Leiden: Brill, 2014.
On the Soul and the Resurrection. In *Ascetical Works*, translated by Virginia Woods Callahan, 195–272. FC 58. Washington, DC: Catholic University of America Press, 1999.

De beatitudinibus. Edited by J. Callahan. GNO 7.2, 75–170. Leiden: Brill, 1992.
Sermons on the Beatitudes. In *The Lord's Prayer: The Beatitudes*, translated by Hilda Graef, 85–175. ACW 18. New York: Paulist Press, 1954.

De beneficentia. Edited by Adrian van Heck. GNO 9, 93–108. Leiden: Brill, 1967.

De instituto Christiano. Edited by W. Jaeger. GNO 8.1, 1–89. Leiden: Brill, 1963.

On the Christian Mode of Life. In *Ascetical Works*, translated by Virginia Woods Callahan, 125–60. FC 58.

De perfectione. Edited by W. Jaeger. GNO 8.1, 173–214. Leiden: Brill, 1963.

On Perfection. In *Ascetical Works*, translated by Virginia Woods Callahan, 93–124. FC 58.

De vita Moysis. Edited by Herbertus Musurillo. GNO 7.1. Leiden: Brill, 1964.

The Life of Moses. Translated by Abraham Malherbe and Everett Ferguson. New York: Paulist Press, 1978.

In illud quatenus uni ex his fecistis mihi fecistis. Edited by Adrian van Heck and Gunter Heil. GNO 9, 111–27. Leiden: Brill, 1967.

The Life of St. Macrina. In *Ascetical Works*, translated by Virgina Woods Callahan, 161–94. FC 58.

Vita Sanctae Macrinae. Edited by Pierre Maraval. SC 178. Paris: Les Éditions du Cerf, 1971.

Irenaeus of Lyons

Against the Heresies II *(Contra haereses).* Edited by Adelin Rousseau and Louis Doutreleau, SJ SC 294.2. Paris: Éditions du Cerf, 1982. English translation by Dominic J. Unger, OFM. ACW 65. New York: Newman Press, 2012.

Against the Heresies III *(Contra haereses).* Edited Adelin Rousseau and Louis Datreleau, SJ SC 211.2. Paris: Editions du Cerf, 1974. English translation by Dominic J. Unger, OFM. Cap. ACW 64..

Against the Heresies IV *(Contra haereses).* Edited by Adelin Rousseau. SC 100.2. Paris: Éditions du Cerf, 1965. English translation by Alexander Roberts and James Donaldson. ANF 1, 462–525. New York: Charles Scribner and Sons, 1885.

Against the Heresies V *(Contra haereses).* Edited by Adelin Rousseau, et al. SC 153. Paris: Éditions du Cerf, 1969. English translation by Alexander Roberts and James Donaldson. ANF 1, 526–67.

On the Apostolic Preaching. Translated by John Behr. Crestwood, NY: St. Vladimir's Seminary Press, 1997.

John Cassian

Collationes. Edited by Étienne Pichery. SC 42 (I–VII), SC 54 (VIII–XVII), SC 64 (XVIII–XXIV). Paris: Éditions du Cerf, 1955, 1958, 1959.

The Conferences. Translated by Boniface Ramsey. ACW 57. New York: Newman Press, 1997.

John Chrysostom

Defense of Eutropius II. Translated by W. R. W. Stephens. NPFN I-09, 252–65. New York: Christian Literature, 1889.

In Eutropium. PG 52: 395–414.

Homily 19 on I Corinthians. PG 61: 151–60. In *On Marriage and Family Life*, translated by Catherine Roth and David Anderson, 25–42. PPS 7. Crestwood, NY: St. Vladimir's Seminary Press, 1986.

Homily 21 on I Corinthians. PG 61: 169–80. Translated by W. R. W. Stephens. NPNF I-12, 118–25. New York: Christian Literature, 1889.

Homily 20 on Ephesians. PG 62: 135–50. In *On Marriage and Family Life*, translated by Catherine Roth and David Anderson, 43–64. PPS 7.

Homily 21 on Ephesians. PG 62: 149–56. In *On Marriage and Family Life*, translated by Catherine Roth and David Anderson, 65–72. PPS 7.

Baptismal Instructions. Translated by Paul W. Harkins. ACW 31. London: Newman Press, 1963.

On Baptism 1–8. Edited by Antoine Wenger. SC 50. Paris: Éditions du Cerf, 1970.

On the Holy Martyrs. PG 50, 705–12. In *The Cult of the Saints*, translated by Wendy Mayer, 217–26. PPS 31. Crestwood, NY: St. Vladimir's Seminary Press, 2006.

On Maccabees 1. PG 50: 617–24. In *The Cult of the Saints*, translated by Wendy Mayer, 135–46. PPS 31. Crestwood, NY: St. Vladimir's Seminary Press, 2006.

On St. Romanus 3. PG 50: 605–12. In *The Cult of the Saints*, translated by Wendy Mayer, 227–38. PPS 31. Crestwood, NY: St. Vladimir's Seminary Press, 2006.

Sermon on Lazarus and the Rich Man 1. PG 48: 963–82. In *On Wealth and Poverty*, translated by Catherine Roth, 21–38. PPS 9. Yonkers, NY: St. Vladimir's Seminary Press, 2020.

Sermon on Lazarus and the Rich Man 6. PG 48: 1027–44. In *On Wealth and Poverty,* translated by Catherine Roth, 91–115. PPS 9.

Sermon on Lazarus and the Rich Man 7. PG 48:1043–51. In *On Wealth and Poverty,* translated by Catherine Roth, 117–30. PPS 9.

John Moschos

The Spiritual Meadow (Pratum spirituale). PG 87.3:2851–3116. Translated by John Wortley. Collegeville, MN: Cistercian, 1992.

John of Scythopolis

Scholia in epistulas S. Dionysii Areopagitae. PG 4: 527A–558C. In *John of Schythopolis and the Dionysian Corpus: Annotating the Areopagite,* translated by Paul Rorem and John Mamoreaux, 250–63. Oxford: Clarendon Press, 1988.

Leontius of Neapolis

Vie de Syméon le Fou et Vie de Jean de Chypre [*The Life of Symeon the Fool*]. Edited by Lennart Rydén. Paris: Librairie Orientaliste Paul Geuthner, 1974. In *Symeon the Holy Fool: Leontius's Life and the Late Antique City,* translated by Derek Krueger, 130–71. Berkeley: University of California Press, 1996.

Mark the Monk

De baptismo. Edited by George-Matthieu de Ourand, OP. SC 445, 246–97. Paris: Les Éditions du Cerf, 1999.

On Baptism. In *Counsels on the Spiritual Life,* translated by Tim Vivian and Augustine Casiday, 287–327. PPS 37. Crestwood, NY: St. Vladimir's Seminary Press, 2009.

De paenitentia. Edited by George-Matthieu de Durand, OP. SC 445, 214–59. Paris: Les Éditions du Cerf, 1999.

On Repentance. In *Counsels on the Spiritual Life,* translated by Tim Vivian and Augustine Casiday, 141–64. PPS 37.

Maximus the Confessor

The Ascetic Life. In *The Ascetic Life: Four Centuries on Charity,* translated by Polycarp Sherwood, 103–35. ACW 21. Westminster, MD: Newman Press, 1955.
Liber asceticus. Edited Peter van Duen. CCSG 40. Turnhout: Brepols, 2000.

Capita de caritate. Edited by Aldo Ceresa-Gastaldo. Rome: Editrice Studium, 1963.

Centuries on Charity. In *Maximus the Confessor: Selected Writings*, translated by George Berthold, 33–98. New York: Paulist Press, 1985.

Chapters on Knowledge (Capita theologia et oeconomica). PG 90: 1083–176. In *Maximus the Confessor: Selected Writings*, translated by George Berthold, 127–80.

Commentary on the Our Father. In *Maximus the Confessor: Selected Writings*, translated by George Berthold, 99–126.

Expositio orationis dominicae. Edited by P. van Deun. CCSG 23. Turnhout: Brepols, 1991.

Letter 2 (Epistula 2). PG 91: 392D–408C. In *Maximus the Confessor*, translated by Andrew Louth, 84–93. New York: Routledge, 1996.

Mystagogia. In *On the Ecclesistical Mystagogy: The Theological Vision of the Liturgy*, edited and translated by Jonathan Armstrong. PPS 59. Yonkers, NY: St. Vladimir's Seminary Press, 2019.

On the Difficulties (Ambigua ad Ioannem et ad Thomam). In *On the Difficulties of the Church Fathers: The Ambigua*, edited and translated by Nicholas Constas. Vols. 1–2. Cambridge, MA: Harvard University Press, 2014.

Questiones ad Thalassium. Edited by Jean-Claude Larchet. SC 529 (1–40), SC 554 (41–55), SC 569 (56–65). Paris: Les Éditions du Cerf, 2010, 2012, 2015.

Responses to Thalassius. In *On Difficulties in Sacred Scripture: The Responses to Thalassios*, translated by Maximos Constas. FC 136. Washington, DC: Catholic University of America Press, 2018.

"Record of the Trial." In *Maximus the Confessor and his Companions: Documents from the Exile*, edited and translated by Pauline Allen and Bronwen Neil, 47–84. Oxford: Oxford University Press, 1999.

Origen of Alexandria

Homiliae in Exodum. Edited by Marcel Borret, SJ SC 321. Paris: Éditions du Cerf, 1985.

Homilies on Exodus. Translated by Ronald Heine. FC 71, 227–387. Washington, DC: Catholic University of America Press, 1982.

Homiliae in Lucam. Edited by Henri Crouzel. SC 87. Paris: Éditions du Cerf, 1962.

On First Principles Volumes 1–2 (De principiis). Latin, Greek, and English edited and translated by John Behr. Oxford: Oxford University Press, 2017.

The Passion of Perpetua and Felicity

The Passion of Perpetua and Felicity (Passio Sanctorum Perpetuae et Felicitatis). Edited and translated by T. J. Heffernan. Oxford: Oxford University Press, 2012.

Tertullian

Apology (Apologia). In *Tertullian: Apology and De Spectaculis; Minucius Felix: Octavius*, translated by Gerald Rendall, 2–229. LCL 250. New York: Putnam and Sons, 1931.

Ancient Non-Christian Sources

Aristotle. *Metaphysics*. In *The Complete Works of Aristotle*, edited by Jonathan Barnes and translated by W. D. Ross, 1552–728. Vol. 2. Princeton, NJ: Princeton University Press, 1995.

Aristotle. *Nicomachean Ethics*. In *The Complete Works of Aristotle*, edited by Jonathan Barnes and translated by W. D. Ross, 1729–867. Vol. 2. Princeton, NJ: Princeton University Press, 1984.

Cicero, Marcus Tullius. *On Old Age*. In *On Friendship, On Old Age, On Divination*, edited and translated W. A. Falconer, 2–102. LCL 154. Cambridge, MA: Harvard University Press, 1923.

1 Enoch. Translated by George W. E. Nickelsburg and James C. VanderKam. Minneapolis: Fortress Press, 2012.

The Gospel of Truth. In *The Gnostic Scriptures*, translated by Bentley Layton, 250–64. Garden City, NY: Doubleday, 1987.

Hesychius of Alexandria. *Hesychii Alexandrini Lexicon*. Edited by Moriz Schmidt. Jeone, Sumptibustormam Duffti: Libreria Maukiana, 1867.

Philo of Alexandria. *De mutatione nominum*. In *The Works of Philo*, translated by C. D. Yonge, 341–264. Peabody, MA: Hendrickson, 1993.

Plato. *The Meno*. In *Plato: Complete Works*, edited by John Cooper and translated by G. M. A. Grube, 870–97. Indianapolis: Hackett, 1997.

———. *Theaetetus*. In *Plato: Complete Works*, edited by John Cooper and translated by M. J. Levett and Myles Buryeat, 157–234. Indianapolis: Hackett, 1997.

Plotinus. *Ennead I*. In *Porphyry on Plotinus and Ennead I*. LCL 440, 92–325. Translated by A. H. Armstrong. Cambridge, MA: Harvard University Press, 1966.

———. *Ennead II*. LCL 441. Translated by A. J. Armstrong. Cambridge, MA: Harvard University Press, 1966.

Proclus. *The Elements of Theology*. Edited and translated by E. R. Dodds. Oxford: Clarendon Press, 1963.

Secondary Sources

Allen, Pauline. "Life and Times of Maximus the Confessor." In *The Oxford Handbook of Maximus the Confessor*, edited by Pauline Allen and Bronwen Neil, 3–18. Oxford: Oxford University Press, 2015.

Ambrose, Z. Philip. "The Homeric Telos." *Glotta* 43 (1965): 38–62.

Baker, Aelred. "Messalianism: The Monastic Heresy." *Monastic Studies* 10 (1974): 135–41.

Baldovin, John. "Relics, Martyrs, and the Eucharist." *Liturgical Ministry* 12 (2003): 9–19.

Balthasar, Hans Urs von. "Christ: Alpha and Omega." *Communio* 23, no. 3 (1996): 465–71.

———. *Who is a Christian?* Translated by John Cumming. New York: Newman Press, 1968.

Behr, John. *Irenaeus of Lyons: Identifying Christianity*. Oxford: Oxford University Press, 2013.

Benedict XVI. *Jesus of Nazareth*. Vol. 3, *The Infancy Narratives*. Translated by Philip Whitmore. New York: Image, 2012.

Betschart, Christof. *L'humain image filiale de Dieu. Une anthropologie théologique en dialogue avec l'exégèse*. Paris: Les Éditions du Cerf, 2021.

Blowers, Paul. "The Dialectics and Therapeutics of Desire in Maximus the Confessor." *Vigiliae Christianae* 65 (2011): 425–51.

———. *Maximus the Confessor: Jesus Christ and the Transfiguration of the World.* Oxford: Oxford University Press, 2016.

Bly, Robert. *Iron John: A Book about Men.* Boston: Da Capo Press, 2015.

Boersma, Hans. *Embodiment and Virtue in Gregory of Nyssa: An Anagogical Approach.* Oxford: Oxford University Press, 2013.

Bolkestein, Hendryk. *Telos ho gamos.* Amsterdam: Noordhollandsche uitgevers-maatschappij, 1933.

Bowersock, G. W. *Martyrdom and Rome.* Cambridge: Cambridge University Press, 1995.

Brakke, David. *The Gnostics: Myth, Ritual, and Diversity in Early Christianity.* Cambridge, MA: Harvard University Press, 2010.

Brown, Peter. "The Rise and Function of the Holy Man in Antiquity." *Journal of Roman Studies* 61 (1971): 353–76.

Burns, J. Patout. *Cyprian the Bishop.* New York: Routledge, 2002.

Byassee, Jason. *Praise Seeking Understanding: Reading the Psalms with St. Augustine.* New York: Eerdmans, 2007.

Cavadini, John. "The Sweetness of the Word: Salvation and Rhetoric in Augustine's *De Doctrina Christiana*." In *De Doctrina Christiana. A Classic of Western Culture,* edited by Duane W. H. Arnold and Pamela Bright, 164–81. Notre Dame, IN: University of Notre Dame Press, 1995.

Chadwick, Henry. "John Moschus and his Friend Sophronius the Sophist." *Journal of Theological Studies* 25, no. 1 (1984): 41–74.

Chadwick, Owen. "The Identity and Date of Mark the Monk." In *History and Thought of the Early Church,* 125–30, London: Variorum Reprints, 1982.

Chapman, John. "Papias on the Age of Our Lord." *Journal of Theological Studies* 9, no. 33 (1907): 42–61.

Chesterton, G. K. *Orthodoxy.* In *Complete Works,* 211–368. Vol. 1. San Francisco: Ignatius Press, 1986,.

Chin, Catherine. "Time, Narrative, and Pedagogy in *De Catechizandis Rudibus.*" *Augustinian Studies* 37, no. 1 (2006): 43–62.

Chlup, Radek. *Proclus: An Introduction*. Cambridge: Cambridge University Press, 2016.

Cross, Gary. *Men to Boys: The Making of Modern Immaturity*. New York: Columbia University Press, 2008.

Dagron, Gilbert. "L'homme sans honneur ou le saint scandaleux." *Annales Histoire, Sciences Sociales* 45, no. 4 (1990): 929–39.

Daley, SJ, Brian. "The Cappadocian Fathers and the Rhetoric of Philanthropy." *Journal of Early Christian Studies* 7, no. 3 (1999): 431–61.

———. *God Visible. Patristic Christology Reconsidered*. Oxford: Oxford University Press, 2018.

———. "'Is Patristic Exegesis Still Usable?' Reflections on Early Christian Interpretation of the Psalms." *Communio* 29 (2022): 181–216.

Daryl, Charles. "The Angels Under Reserve in 2 Peter and Jude." *Bulletin for Biblical Research* 15, no. 1 (2005): 39–48.

de Guibert, SJ, Joseph. *The Theology of the Spiritual Life*. New York: Sheed and Ward, 1953.

DiVito, Robert. "Old Testament Anthropology and the Construction of Personal Identity." *Catholic Biblical Quarterly* 61, no.2 (1991): 217–38.

Du Plessis, Paul Johannes. *Teleios: The Idea of Perfection in the New Testament*. Kampen: J. H. Kok, 1959.

Dupont, V. L. "Le dynamisme de l'action liturgique: une etude de la Mystagogie de Saint Maxime le Confesseur." *Revue des Sciences Religieuses* 65 (1991): 363–98.

Fergerson, Everett. *Baptism in the Early Church*. Grand Rapids, MI: Eerdmans, 2009.

Fleishman, Joseph. "The Age of Legal Maturity in Biblical Law." *Journal of the Ancient Near Eastern Society* 21, no. 1 (1992): 35–48.

Fraade, Steven D. "Ascetical Aspects of Ancient Judaism." In *Jewish Spirituality I: From the Bible through the Middle Ages,* edited by Arthur Green, 253–88. New York: Crossroad, 1986.

Galenianos, Michail. "The Value of Martyrdom in Times of Persecution According to St. John Chrysostom." *International Journal of Orthodox Theology* 6, no. 1 (2015): 51–62.

Gavin, SJ, John. "Souls and Bodies, History and Eternity: John Scottus Eriugena and the Intermediate State." *Annales Theologici* 29 (2015): 139–54.

Goraïnoff, Irina. *Les fols in Christ dans la tradition orthodoxe*. Paris: Desclée de Brouwer, 1983.

Greenspahn, Frederick. *When Brothers Dwell Together: The Preeminence of Younger Siblings in the Hebrew Bible*. Oxford: Oxford University Press, 1994.

Hamm, SJ, Dennis. *Philippians, Colossians, Philemon*. Grand Rapids, MI: Baker Academic, 2013.

Harrington, OP, Wilfrid. *Revelation*. Collegeville, MN: Liturgical Press, 2008.

Healy, Mary. *The Gospel of Mark*. Grand Rapids, MI: Baker Academic, 2008.

Holman, Susan. *The Hungry are Dying: Beggars and Bishops in Roman Cappadocia*. Oxford: Oxford University Press, 2001.

Hütter, Reinhard. "Experience and its Claim to Universality." *Communio* 37 (2010): 186–208.

Ihssen, Brenda Llewellyn. *John Moschos' Spiritual Meadow: Authority and Autonomy at the End of the Antique World*. Burlington, VT: Ashgate, 2014.

John Paul II. *Love and Responsibility*. Translated by H. T. Willetts. New York: Farrar, Straus, and Giroux, 1981.

Johnson, Luke Timothy. "Persecuting the Persecuted." *Commonweal* (August 2013): 28–30.

Klein, Elizabeth. *Augustine's Theology of Angels*. Cambridge: Cambridge University Press, 2018.

Klein, Elizabeth. "Perpetua, Cheese, and Martyrdom as Public Liturgy in the *Passion of Perpetua and Felicity*." *Journal of Early Christian Studies*. 28, no. 2 (2020): 175–202.

Koester, Craig. *Revelation: A New Translation with Introduction and Commentary*. New Haven, CT: Yale University Press, 2015.

Krueger, Derek. *Symeon the Holy Fool: Leontius's Life and the Late Antique City.* Berkeley: University of California Press, 1996.

Layton, Bentley. "Prolegomena to the Study of Ancient Gnosticism." In *The Social World of the First Christians: Essays in Honor of Wayne A. Meeks,* edited by Michael White and Larry Yarborough, 334–50. Minneapolis: Fortress Press, 1995.

Levko, SJ, John. "The Relationship of Prayer to Discretion and Spiritual Direction for John Cassian." *St. Vladimir's Theological Quarterly* 40, no. 3 (1996): 155–71.

Lewis, C. S. *Mere Christianity.* New York: Macmillan Publishing, 1996.

———. *The Screwtape Letters.* New York: Bantam Books, 1982.

———. *That Hideous Strength.* New York: Scribner, 2003.

Louth, Andrew. "St. Makrina: The Fourth Cappadocian?" *International Journal of Orthodox Theology* 9, no. 2 (2018): 9–31.

Luneau. A. *L'histoire du salut chez les Pères de l'Eglise: La doctrine des ages du monde.* Paris: Beauchesene, 1964.

Markus, R. A. *Saeculum: History and Society in the Theology of St. Augustine.* Cambridge: Cambridge University Press, 1970.

McCann, Christine. "Spiritual Mentoring in John Cassian's *Conferences.*" *American Benedictine Review* 48, no. 2 (1997): 212–23.

McConville, J. Gordon. *Being Human in God's World: An Old Testament Theology of Humanity.* Grand Rapids, MI: Baker Academic, 2016.

Meconi, SJ, David. *The One Christ.* Washington, DC: Catholic University of America Press, 2013.

Montague, SM, George. *First Corinthians.* Grand Rapids, MI: Baker Academic, 2011.

Montgomery, James. "Ascetic Strains in Early Judaism." *Journal of Biblical Literature* 51, no. 3 (1932): 183–213.

Moss, Candida. *The Myth of Persecution: How Early Christians Invented a Story of Martyrdom.* New York: HarperOne, 2013.

Muehlberger, Ellen. *Angels in Late Ancient Christianity*. Oxford: Oxford University Press, 2013.

Mueller, SJ, Joseph. "Why Did Ancient Christians Call Their Ministers Priests?" In *New Narratives for Old: The Historical Method of Reading Early Christian Theology*, edited by Anthony Bridgman and Ellen Scully, 273–92. Washington, DC: Catholic University of America Press, 2022.

Nicholson, Oliver. "Preparation for Martyrdom in the Early Church." In *The Great Persecution. Proceedings of the Fifth Patristic Conference*, edited by Vincent Twomey and Mark Humphries, 61–90. Dublin: Four Courts Press, 2009.

O'Connor, Flannery. "The Fiction Writer and His Country." In *Mystery and Manners*, edited by Sally and Robert Fitzgerald, 25–35. New York: Farrar, Straus & Giroux, 1969.

Paiaoannou, Kim. "The Sin of the Angels in 2 Peter 2:4 and Jude 6." *Journal of Biblical Literature* 140, no. 2 (2021): 391–408.

Percy, Walker. *Lost in the Cosmos: The Last Self-Help Book*. New York: Farrar, Straus & Giroux, 1983.

Perl, Eric. *Theophany. The Neoplatonic Philosophy of Dionysius the Areopagite*. Albany: State University of New York Press, 2007.

Perrone, Lorenzo. "Confessio e Narratio. Introduzione al *De catechizandis rudibus* di sant'Agostino." *Salesianum* 65 (2003): 161–72.

Peterson, Jordan. *12 Rules for Life: An Antidote to Chaos*. New York: Penguin, 2019.

Phillips, Suzette. "Fit or Unfit for Priesthood? Priestly Ministry According to the Writings of Gregory of Nazianzus." *Logos: A Journal of Eastern Christian Studies* 41/42 (2001): 333–62.

Plested, Marcus. "The Ascetic Tradition." In *The Oxford Handbook of Maximus the Confessor*, edited by Pauline Allen and Bronwen Neil, 164–76. Oxford: Oxford University Press, 2015.

———. *The Macarian Legacy: The Place of Macarius-Symeon in the Eastern Christian Tradition*. Oxford: Oxford University Press, 2004.

Polyzozogopoulos, Theodoritus. "The Anthropology of Diadochus of Photice." *Theologiai Athinai* 55, no. 4 (1984): 1072–101.

Quay, Paul. *The Mystery Hidden for Ages in God*. New York: Peter Lang, 1995.

Radner, Ephraim. "Unmythical Martyrs." *First Things* (May, 2013): 53–55.

Ratzinger, Joseph. *Introduction to Christianity.* San Francisco: Ignatius Press, 2004.

Rensberger, David. "Asceticism and the Gospel of John." In *Asceticism in the New Testament,* edited by Leif Vaage and Vincent Wimbush, 29–48. New York: Taylor and Francis, 1999.

Rist, John. *Plato's Moral Realism.* Washington, DC: Catholic University of America Press, 2012.

Rorem, Paul, and John C. Lamoreaux. *John of Scythopolis and the Dionysian Corpus. Annotating the Areopagite.* Oxford: Clarendon Press, 1998.

Rylaarsdam, David. *John Chrysostom on Divine Pedagogy: The Coherence of His Theology and Preaching.* Oxford: Oxford University Press, 2014.

Saldarini, Anthony. "Asceticism in the Gospel of Matthew." In *Asceticism in the New Testament,* edited by Leif Vaage and Vincent Wimbush, 11–28. New York: Taylor and Francis, 1999.

Saward, John. *Perfect Fools: Folly for Christ's Sake in Catholic and Orthodox Spirituality.* Oxford: Oxford University Press, 1980.

Scherer, Andreas Georg, Cristina Neesham, Dennis Schoeborn, and Markus Scholz. "New Challenges to the Enlightenment: How Twenty-First Century Sociotechnological Systems Facilitate Organized Immaturity and How to Counteract It." *Business Ethics Quarterly* 33, no. 3 (July 2023): 409–39.

Sitzler, Silke. "Identity: The Indigent and the Wealthy in the Homilies of John Chrysostom." *Vigiliae Christianae* 63 (2009): 468–79.

Smith, J. Warren. *Christian Grace and Pagan Virtue.* Oxford: Oxford University Press, 2011.

Staniloae, Dumitru. *The Experience of God.* Vol. 5, *The Sanctifying Mysteries.* Translated by Ioan Ionita and Robert Barringer. Brookline, MA: Holy Orthodox Press, 2012.

Steenberg, Matthew. "Children in Paradise: Adam and Eve as 'Infants' in Irenaeus of Lyons." *Journal of Early Christian Studies* 12, no. 1 (2004): 1–22.

Steenberg, Matthew. *Irenaeus on Creation: The Cosmic Christ and the Saga of Redemption.* Leiden: Brill, 2008.

Stewart, OSB, Columba. *Cassian the Monk*. Oxford: Oxford University Press, 1998.

Stewart, OSB, Columba. *"Working the Earth of the Heart": The Messalian Controversy in History, Texts, and Language to AD 431*. Oxford: Oxford University Press, 1991.

Summerson, Andrew. *Divine Scripture and Human Emotion in Maximus the Confessor. Exegesis of the Human Heart*. Leiden: Brill, 2021.

Syrkin, Alexander. "On the Behavior of the 'Fool for Christ's Sake.'" *History of Religions* 22, no. 2 (1982): 150–71.

Taggart, Andrew. "Secular Monks." *First Things*. March 2020. https://www.firstthings.com/article/2020/03/secular-monks.

Teresa Benedicta of the Cross (Edith Stein). *The Mystery of Christmas: Incarnation and Humanity*. Translated by Josephine Rucker, SSJ. Darlington: Darlington Carmel, 1985.

Thunberg, Lars. *Microcosm and Mediator*. Chicago: Open Court, 1995.

Torrance, Alexis. "Repentance as the Context of Sainthood in Mark the Monk." In *Studies in Church History*, edited by Charolette Methuen and Andrew Spicer, 80–89. Vol. 47, *Saints and Society*. Cambridge: Cambridge University Press, 2011.

Trueman, Carl. *The Rise and Triumph of the Modern Self*. Wheaton, IL: Crossway, 2020.

Vatican Council II. *Dei Verbum*. November 18, 1965.

———. *Gaudium et spes*. December 7, 1965.

———. *Lumen gentium*. November 21, 1964.

Ware, Kallistos. "The Imitation of Christ According to Saint Maximus the Confessor." In *A Saint for East and West*, edited by Daniel Haynes, 69–84. Eugene, OR: Cascade, 2019.

Ware, Timothy (Kallistos). "The Sacrament of Baptism and the Ascetic Life in the Teaching of Mark the Monk." In *Studia Patristica* 10, edited by F. L Cross, 441–52. Berlin: Akademie-Verlag, 1970.

———. "The Way of the Ascetics: Positive or Affirmative?" In *Asceticism,* edited by Vincent Wimbush and Richard Valantasis, 3–15. Oxford: Oxford University Press. 2002.

Weinandy, Thomas. "St. Irenaeus and the Imago Dei: The Importance of Being Human." *Logos: A Journal of Catholic Thought and Culture* 6, no. 4 (2003): 35–50.

Welborn, Laurence. "*Mōros* genesthō: Paul's Appropriation of the Role of the Fool in 1 Corinthians 1–4." *Biblical Interpretation* 10, no. 4 (2002): 420–35.

White, Devin. "Jesus at Fifty: Irenaeus on John 8:57 and the Age of Jesus." *Theological Studies* 40, no. 1 (2020): 158–63.

Wolff, Hans Walter. *Anthropology of the Old Testament.* Translated by Margaret Kohl. Philadelphia: Fortress Press, 1974.

GENERAL INDEX

Abraham, 12, 25, 75, 79–80
Adam, 12, 15, 18–19, 21, 26, 73–75, 80, 90–91, 93, 97, 105, 112, 160
adoption, 3, 25, 44, 76, 86, 144, 174
adulthood, 3–5, 10, 19, 22–23, 31, 42–43, 46, 48, 79, 120, 122, 145, 170, 173
allegory, 78–79, 81, 84, 94,
almsgiving, x, 45, 109, 111, 114, 129, 148–49, 157,
Ambrose of Milan, Saint, 78, 86–88, 92–93, 96–98, 132, 175
anachōrēsis, 102, 127, 178
angel, 51, 56–59, 64–65, 67, 74, 93, 95, 122, 142, 155, 161, 163
Antony of the Desert, Saint, 60, 62
apatheia, 108,
Apostle, 32, 47, 64, 88, 110, 161
Arethas of Caesaria, 47
Aristotle, 11, 28, 50,
asceticism, 5, 42, 71, 88–90, 101–14, 141, 143, 163, 165, 167, 171, 173
Athanasius of Alexandria, Saint, 60, 175
Augustine of Hippo, Saint, 5, 55, 58–59, 77–79, 81–82, 84, 98, 118, 132–39, 162, 175

Balthasar, Hans Urs von, 1, 14
baptism, 16, 42–45, 53, 85–92, 94, 96–99, 107, 121–23, 132–33, 140, 159, 172–73, 175
Basil of Caeserea, Saint, 5, 26–27, 30–31, 140–41, 148–50, 152–58, 162, 176
beauty, 10, 18, 33, 38, 78,
Behr, John, 76
Benedict XVI, Pope: *See* Ratzinger, Joseph
Benedict of Nursia, Saint, 142–143
birth, 15–17, 31, 39, 44, 79–80, 86–87, 89–90, 92, 123, 142
Blowers, Paul, 17
body, 15, 17, 20, 23, 25, 30, 33, 46, 66, 81, 92–93, 99, 101, 105, 110, 114, 119, 128, 163
Byassee, Jason, 78

catechesis, 43
Catherine of Siena, Saint, 3
Cato the Elder, 10
Cavidini, John, 136
Chesterton, G.K., 170
child, 3–4, 10, 19, 23–24, 38–40, 44, 46, 72–74, 78–80, 83–84, 94, 97, 106, 120, 122, 132, 143, 152, 160, 170
choice: 16, 27, 30, 31, 39. *See also* freedom

Christ, ix, 9, 19–23, 42–45, 56, 60, 65–67, 79–81, 84–86, 88, 92–95, 98–99, 103, 107–109, 117–18, 121–26, 128–31, 133–35, 137, 141, 145, 148–49, 154–58, 165–67, 171, 173; and the Church, 47–49; as fool, 159–163; and humanity, 3–5, 15; and martyrdom, 119–120; and mercy, 96–97; and the priesthood, 51–53; and recapitulation, 24–26, 71–78; and service, 151–53; as *telos*, 12–17, 20–21; and the virtues, 31–35. See also Jesus.

Church, ix, 1, 3, 5–6, 10, 15, 17, 28, 33, 37, 43–45, 47–48, 53, 56, 65, 71–72, 77, 79, 82, 84, 86, 87, 92–99, 101, 118, 124, 126–27, 132, 137–38, 140, 148, 173–74

Cicero, Marcus Tullius, 9

Clement of Alexandria, 117–18, 176

contemplation, 5, 84, 113

Cornelius, Saint, 45

Creed, 123, 125–26

Cross, 9, 15, 17, 42, 47–48, 56, 64, 98, 108, 119, 161, 166

Crucifixion, 76–77, 97, 166. See also Cross.

Daley, S.J., Brian, 72, 124

David, King, 29, 39, 75, 77, 79–80, 125–26

death, 14, 23, 25, 39, 49, 75, 86, 90, 92, 98, 105–6, 108, 118–19, 121, 140, 157, 160–61, 165–66

de Guibert, Joseph, 2

deification, x, 4, 10, 17, 20, 22, 29–30, 57, 59–60, 81, 85, 104, 107, 114, 173

Dei Verbum, 71

demon, 56–67, 128–29, 148, 160, 165, 170. See also Devil. See also Satan

Devil, 61, 65–67, 97, 98, 105–6, 165. See also demon. See also Satan

Devito, Robert, 38

Diocletian, Emperor, 127

Dionysius the Areopagite, 46, 60–61, 94

Erikson, Erik, 2

Esau, 39

Eucharist, 47–48, 85, 92, 94–96, 98–99, 121–22, 130

Evagrius Ponticus, 62–64, 66, 109, 113, 176

Eve, 18–19, 26, 74, 75,

evil, 4, 38, 55–56, 61–63, 67, 89, 105, 107, 109–10, 149

family, 1, 39–40, 46, 48–50, 53, 66, 104, 140–41, 160, 172

fasting, x, 62, 66, 101–3, 110, 114, 165

Father (God), x, 2–3, 5, 9, 12, 14, 16, 20–22, 26, 39–42, 64, 71–72, 74–75, 86, 88, 104–6, 113, 123, 125–26, 132, 137, 145, 151, 160, 163, 166

fatherhood, 38, 132, 139, 143

Felicity, Saint, 121

fool, 159–67

form, 1, 3, 5, 9–10, 15, 20, 28, 34–35, 38, 56–61, 63–64, 76, 79, 84, 87, 89, 91, 94–95, 104, 148, 150, 160, 170, 173; and Christ, 22, 33, 71–72, 79, 86, 98, 106, 109, 148, 171

Francis of Assisi, Saint, 3

freedom, ix, 3–4, 10, 16–17, 23, 26–27, 30–31, 33, 38, 40–42, 45, 62, 66, 71, 81, 89, 90–93, 97, 103, 105–8, 114, 156, 169, 172–73. See also choice.

gnosticism, 11–12, 72, 166, 177
grace, ix–x, 2, 4, 14, 16–17, 22–23, 26, 29–31, 33, 37, 41–42, 50, 57–58, 60, 66, 71, 76–77, 81, 84–85, 91–93, 95, 96–97, 103, 105–9, 112, 114, 119–20, 130, 140–52, 156, 159, 166, 174; and sacraments, x, 86, 89–90
Gregory of Nazianzus, Saint, 5, 15, 50–53, 140, 148, 150, 153, 155–57, 176
Gregory of Nyssa, Saint, 5, 28–32, 34, 140–42, 151–52, 176

Hamm, Dennis, 160
Heraclius, Emperor, 124
Hesychius of Alexandria, 46
hierarchy, 60, 64,
holiness, 4, 42–45, 48, 53, 72, 140, 164–65
Holy Spirit, x, 1, 4–5, 14, 16, 20–22, 29, 30, 33, 42, 44, 51–52, 77, 82, 84, 86–88, 91–92, 95, 103, 109, 113, 121, 123, 126, 137, 145, 163, 175
hope, 2, 35, 43, 57, 59, 67, 76, 79, 84, 86, 112–13, 122–23, 134, 139–40, 142, 149, 155, 157, 159, 162, 166, 170, 172–74
Hurtado, Alberto, Saint, 148
Hütter, Reinhard, 133

image: of God, 5, 14–18, 20–21, 24, 26–27, 48–49, 51, 73, 75, 83, 90, 94, 104, 135, 150, 153, 174
imitation: of Christ, 20, 26, 32, 48, 53, 98, 107–8, 153–54, 158, 166; of God, 26–27, 29, 74
Incarnation, 14, 17, 19, 22, 75, 77, 95, 106, 153

infancy, 3–4, 18–19, 22–24, 26, 31, 38, 43–44, 73–75, 77, 79–81, 83–84, 95–96, 120, 122, 139
infantilism, 5, 55–67, 152–54, 159, 169–73
Irenaeus of Lyons, Saint, ix, 5, 17–21, 24–26, 72–77, 177

Jacob, 39
Jesus, 2–3, 10, 12, 18, 20, 23, 31–32, 48, 51, 64, 67, 75, 77, 84–86, 97, 106, 121–24, 129, 142, 147–48, 151, 153, 156, 160, 165–66, 174; and asceticism, 103–4; and the Eucharist, 93; as fool, 159–62; and mission, 39–42; and recapitulation, 24–26; and the Resurrection, 16; as *telos*, 17, 21. *See also* Christ.
John the Baptist, Saint, 130
John Cassian, 5, 60, 65, 132, 142–44, 177
John Chrysostom, Saint, 43–45, 48–50, 119, 121, 148–50, 152, 157, 178
John the Curcularius, 104
John Moschus, 127–30
John Paul II, Pope, 37
John of Scythopolis, 46
justice, 28, 44, 83, 171

kingdom, 3–4, 50, 76, 86, 143–44, 147, 155–56, 166
Klein, Elizabeth, 122

Lazarus, 90, 148–49
Leontius of Neapolis, 163–65, 178
Lewis, Clive Staples, 13, 22, 169–70, 172, 174

likeness: of God, 5, 17–18, 20–21, 24, 26–29, 32, 43, 45, 48, 52–53, 56, 58, 73–75, 83, 85, 87, 89, 94–95, 106, 114, 135, 158, 160, 171, 173–74

logismos, 62. *See also* vice.

Logos, 14, 17, 19, 57–58, 65, 95, 104–5, 109–10, 112, 127. *See also* Word.

love, 4, 22, 33, 37, 44, 71, 78, 84, 98, 108, 110, 117, 119, 121, 125, 135–140, 143–45, 147, 150–51, 156–58, 161, 167, 174; and asceticism, 103–106; God's love, 12–13, 30, 49, 52, 76, 113–14, 129, 132, 134, 138; and marriage, 46–50. *See also philanthropia*.

Macarius, Saint, 88

Macrina the Younger, Saint, 140–42, 153

Marcion of Sinope, 77

Mark the Monk, 5, 86, 88–92, 96–98, 178

marriage, 1, 42, 46–50, 53, 172–73

Martin, Pope, 124–125

martyrdom, 61, 108, 117–130, 137

Mary, Mother of Jesus, 4, 15–16, 40, 129–130

maturation, ix–x, 1–5, 9, 62, 67, 71–72, 76–78, 81, 90–92, 97, 99, 103, 114, 118, 121, 123, 125, 127, 130, 136, 141, 143–44, 147, 157–59, 169, 172–74; and finality, 9–22; and virtue, 23–33; and vocation, 37–53

Maximus the Confessor, Saint, 5, 15–17, 20, 46–47, 55–58, 60, 86, 94–96, 98, 101, 104–14, 124–27, 179

McConville, J. Gordon, 17–18

mercy, 29, 87, 96–97, 105, 129, 142, 156, 169, 171

Messalianism, 88–89, 91,

monk, 5, 60, 62, 66–67, 86, 88, 96–97, 101–2, 118, 127–30, 142–43, 145, 162–63

Monoenergism, 124

Monothelitism, 124, 179

Moses, 13, 26, 29, 32, 39, 75, 77, 92, 143

motherhood, 38, 132, 139

Mystery: Sacrament, 46–47, 50, 52, 85–99

nature, 2, 12–13, 23, 27, 31, 41–42, 55, 57–59, 62, 64, 73, 92, 104, 109, 130, 133, 150, 170, 173; human nature, 1, 9, 11, 15–17, 20–22, 24, 30, 72, 103, 107–8, 112, 124, 150, 160, 169, 171

Neoplatonism, 11, 28, 55, 134

Nicholson, Oliver, 118

Novatianism, 96

obedience, 24, 40, 42, 52, 91–92, 96, 104–6, 124

O'Connor, Flannery, 166

Origen of Alexandria, 5, 18, 26–27, 42, 72, 113, 176

Original Sin, 90–91

Paradise, 1, 18–19, 74, 122, 156–57

Paschal Mystery, 14, 22, 75, 77, 95

Paul, Saint, 3–4, 31, 47, 49, 160–62

penance, 98, 103

Percy, Walker, 2

perfection, 2–4, 10–12, 26–27, 29–32, 42, 47, 72–73, 75, 91, 98, 117, 142, 154

Perpetua, Saint, 121–23

person, 10, 14–15, 17, 21–23, 25–26, 29, 32–33, 37, 40, 42, 45–46, 76–77, 79, 81, 84, 87, 89, 91, 94–95, 102, 104–9, 111, 114, 120, 130, 135–36, 151, 158–59, 170–72, 174

philanthropia, 150–53, 155–56

Philo of Alexandria, 12

Piaget, Jean, 2

Plato, 28

Platonism, 28, 134, 171. *See also* Neoplatonism.

Plotinus: 28, 29,

poverty, 102, 104, 141, 148–49, 156

prayer, x, 45–46, 61–62, 83, 88–89, 97, 109, 112–14, 142, 152, 163–65, 167. *See also* contemplation.

preaching, 78, 135, 148–49, 152, 154, 165,

priesthood, 1, 32, 35, 42, 50–53, 98, 126, 127

Proclus, 11,

Quay, Paul, 77

Ratzinger, Joseph, 13, 41, 170

reason, 83, 104, 109–12, 114, 162

recapitulation, 21, 24–26, 41–42, 72, 75–77, 82, 84

reconciliation, 86, 96–97, 99

redemption, 31, 35, 93, 103

repentance, 85, 88, 96, 99

responsibility, 1, 3–4, 38, 49, 96, 107, 109, 158, 171, 174

resurrection, 2, 16, 75, 81, 84, 95, 99, 140, 142, 149, 160, 161

Romanus, Saint, 120

Sacrament: *See* Mystery

Saldarini, Anthony, 102

salos, 159, 162–63, 165,

salvation, 17, 21, 50, 74–77, 79, 82, 84, 96, 138, 142, 164, 167

Satan, 55–56, 64. *See also* Demon. *See also* Devil.

Saward, John, 162

Scriptures, 3, 5–6, 24, 31–32, 37, 38–42, 56, 71–84, 103, 131, 136, 141, 159, 162, 173, 178

self-love (*philautia*), 105–6, 112,

servant, 147–58

Servius, Patriarch, 124

sin, 15, 21, 25, 30, 44, 73–75, 79, 82–83, 89–91, 94, 96–98, 103, 105, 112, 122, 133, 138, 142, 157, 167. *See also* Original Sin.

Smith, J. Warren, 96

Solomon, 39

soul, 15, 17, 20, 23, 25, 29–31, 35, 42, 51–52, 62, 66, 71, 80, 83, 86–87, 89–90, 104, 108–13, 117, 125, 128–29, 131, 133, 140, 142, 151, 153–55, 163–64, 166–67, 173

Staniloae, Dumitru, 86, 91

Steenberg, Matthew, 19, 25, 74

Stein, Edith (Saint Teresa Benedicta of the Cross), 9

Stewart, Columba, 88

Symeon the Holy Fool, 5, 88, 159, 162–167, 178

synergia, 23, 103, 114,

teacher, 5, 24, 26, 40, 53, 131–14

teleios, 2, 10–12, 46–47, 90, 147

telos, 10–14, 19, 20–23, 45–47, 55, 60, 65, 73, 76, 81–82, 84, 99, 108, 142–44, 156–57, 169–71 temptation, 19, 62, 83, 105, 120, 138, 160, 165

Teresa, Mother, 148

Tertullian, 118, 179

therapeutae, 103

Torrance, Alexis, 98

Trinity, ix–x, 4, 5, 23, 86, 88, 103, 106–107, 113–14, 123, 131, 135, 151, 163, 177

truth, 1, 4, 12, 14, 24, 26, 33, 39, 42, 51, 56, 59, 64–65, 78, 82–83, 118, 126–27, 130, 132, 139, 147, 160, 162, 166–67, 170

typology, 72, 75, 78, 87

Vatican, Second Council, 12, 42–43, 71

vice, 31, 33, 61–63, 66, 102, 105, 109, 171

virtue, ix, 5, 10, 12, 21, 23–27, 33, 44–45, 49–50, 52–53, 67, 71, 83, 87, 102, 105–6, 109, 112, 114, 141, 144, 151, 153–54, 156, 167, 170–71, 173; and Christ, 34–35; and the likeness of God, 28–32; rejection of virtue, 60–64. *See also* vice.

vocation, 5, 22, 33, 37–53, 64–67, 71, 91, 127–28, 139, 141–43, 145, 162, 164, 172–73

Ware, Kallistos, 89, 101

Weinandy, Thomas, 21

wisdom, x, 10, 12, 24, 28, 29, 31, 34, 38, 40–41, 45, 57, 113, 131–32, 140, 142, 144, 161, 162–67

Word: Divine, 5, 12, 14–15, 17, 19–21, 23, 25, 29, 32, 57, 67, 71–72, 74–76, 78, 84, 124, 131, 135, 155, 174. *See also Logos.*

youth, 1, 10, 24, 38–40, 80, 83–84, 92, 123, 159

SCRIPTURE INDEX

Old Testament

Genesis
1:26, 17
3:15, 122
27:1–40, 39

Exodus
19:14–15, 103
27–28, 103

Leviticus
27:1–8, 38

Numbers
6, 103

Deuteronomy
6:4–5, 103
34:7, 39

Judges
8:20, 38
13:4–5, 103

1 Samuel
2:26, 41
7:6, 103
16:1–13, 39
31:13, 103

1 Chronicles
22:6–10, 39

Job
12:12, 38

Psalms
8:2–3, 120
42:4, 92
48:10, 66

Proverbs
20:29, 38
26:22, 67

Ecclesiastes
12:1, 38

Song of Solomon
4:1, 87

Isaiah
6:1, 123
6:1–3, 39
11:1–2, 41
20:1–6, 162
38:19, 39
40:31, 39

Jeremiah
16:1–2, 103

Ezekiel
2–3:1–3, 39
4:12, 162
12:1–7, 162

Daniel
9:1, 103

Zechariah
3:3, 87

New Testament

Matthew
1:17, 79
2:13, 40
2:20–21, 40
3:8–10, 4
4:1–12, 104
5:48, 2, 9
6:19–21, 157
7:13, 122
8:20, 104
10:19–20, 137
12:46–50, 104
13:1–23, 4
18:2–3, 3
19:21, 147
20:1–16, 22
20:25–28, 147
25:31–46, 157
28:19, 145

Mark
3:22, 160
5:20–21, 159

Luke
2:7, 39
2:41–52, 40
2:52, 41
2:49, 40
2:52, 24
3:23, 24, 25

7:33–34, 104
8:17, 167
9:1–6, 104
13:6–9, 4
22:42, 104

John
1:4, 14
1:11, 160
1:29, 130, 167
1:31, 174
2:23, 24
3:3, 86
3:5–6, 86
5:19, 104
6:4, 24
8:57, 25
10:11–18, 122
11:55, 24
12:21, 24
13:34–35, 104
15:5, 4
19:30, 15

Acts of the Apostles
10:1–33, 45

Romans
5:14, 12
6:4, 86

1 Corinthians
1:24, 31
1:30, 31
4:9–10, 161
3:6, 78
13:11, 3
14:20, 4
18:25, 161

2 Corinthians
11:2, 47
12:9, 119

Galatians
4:1–5, 3

Ephesians
1:7, 14
2:7, 76
2:14, 31
2:23–28, 14
3:9, 15
4:13, 15, 92, 163
4:14–15, 4
5:31–42, 47

Philippians
2:6–7, 160
2:8, 160

Colossians
1:20, 14

1 Timothy
6:16, 31

2 Timothy
2:4–5, 67

Titus
3:5, 87

Hebrews
1:3, 14
4:14, 31

Jude
6–7, 56

Revelation
1:8, 13
1:17–18, 14
6:2, 123
12:3, 122
19:7, 47
19:11–13, 14
19:11–14, 123
21:5–6, 13
22:12–14, 14

www.ingramcontent.com/pod-product-compliance
Lightning Source LLC
Chambersburg PA
CBHW072000290426
44109CB00018B/2080